NEW DIRECTIONS IN COGNITIVE THERAPY

NEW DIRECTIONS IN COGNITIVE THERAPY
A CASEBOOK

Edited by

GARY EMERY
University of Southern California Medical School

STEVEN D. HOLLON
University of Minnesota

RICHARD C. BEDROSIAN
Leominster Mental Health Clinic

THE GUILFORD PRESS

New York, London

Printed in the United States of America

Third printing, March 1983

Library of Congress Cataloging in Publication Data
Main entry under title:
New directions in cognitive therapy.

Includes bibliographical references and indexes.
1. Cognitive therapy.   I. Emery, Gary.   II. Hollon, Steven D.
III. Bedrosian, Richard C.
RC489.C63N48   616.89'14   81-1264
ISBN 0-89862-606-4   AACR2

TO TIM BECK, MARIKA KOVACS,
and all the many people who have made
the Center for Cognitive Therapy (formerly the Mood Clinic)
such an exciting place in which to learn.

CONTRIBUTORS

Janis Lieff Abrahms, PhD, Private practice, Bloomfield, Connecticut

Diane B. Arnkoff, PhD, Department of Psychology, The Catholic University of America, Washington, D.C.

Richard C. Bedrosian, PhD, Leominster Mental Health Clinic, Leominster, Massachusetts

Ronald E. Coleman, PhD, Department of Psychology, Friends Hospital and University of Pennsylvania, Philadelphia, Pennsylvania

Raymond A. Di Giuseppe, PhD, Hofstra University, Hempstead, New York, and Institute for Rational–Emotive Therapy, New York, New York

Gary Emery, PhD, Department of Psychiatry, University of Southern California Medical School, Los Angeles, California

Sonja Fox, Center for Cognitive Therapy, University of Pennsylvania, Philadelphia, Pennsylvania

Arthur Freeman, EdD, Center for Cognitive Therapy, University of Pennsylvania, Philadelphia, Pennsylvania

Steven D. Hollon, PhD, Department of Psychology, University of Minnesota, Minneapolis, Minnesota

A. John Rush, MD, Department of Psychiatry, University of Texas Health Sciences Center, Dallas, Texas

William P. Sacco, PhD, Department of Psychology, University of South Florida, Tampa, Florida

Brian F. Shaw, PhD, Department of Psychiatry, The University of Western Ontario, and Department of Psychological Services, University Hospital, London, Ontario, Canada

John T. Watkins, PhD, Department of Psychiatry and Behavioral Sciences, University of Oklahoma Health Science Center, Oklahoma City, Oklahoma

Jeffrey E. Young, PhD, Department of Psychiatry, University of Pennsylvania, Philadelphia, Pennsylvania

PREFACE

The idea for this book took shape over drinks at a hotel bar. We were taking time out from convention meetings to talk over issues and cases we were treating. Rich Bedrosian talked about how he was incorporating his training in family therapy with cognitive therapy. This led to a general discussion on new directions that cognitive therapy was taking.

One of us made the observation that we were plugged into a network of cognitive therapists—a network that we all rely on. If we wanted to know how cognitive therapy was working with children, we would give Ray Di Giuseppe in New York a call; if we wanted to know how cognitive therapy could be applied to agoraphobia, we would contact Ron Coleman in Philadelphia. We decided it would be helpful to others to put the expertise of this network into print, in the form of a series of edited chapters.

We decided to use two guidelines in choosing chapters. First, we wanted the contributors to write about what they were turned on by—we asked potential contributors if there was any topic dear to their hearts that they were eager to write about. Second, we wanted to choose material that a large number of clinicians would find useful. To determine this, we compiled a list of the questions we were asked most often at workshops and talks.

These two guidelines generated a range of topics. To our delight, we found that the topics fell neatly into three areas: special demographic populations, specific clinical problems, and special therapeutic techniques. We discovered that each section could stand on its own: the chapters in each section complemented one another.

We told the contributors we wanted chapters that would be practical and useful. The book was to be for clinicians. We wanted a minimum amount of discussion on theoretical constructs and empirical findings—there are several books that already cover this material (Foreyt & Rathjen, 1978; Kendall & Hollon, 1979; Mahoney, 1974).

Rather, we told the contributors we wanted material those in the trenches could use.

Now that the book is finished, we're content that we have done what we set out to do that afternoon over drinks—compiled a clinical guide to new directions in cognitive therapy.

GARY EMERY
STEVEN D. HOLLON
RICHARD C. BEDROSIAN

REFERENCES

Foreyt, J. P., & Rathjen, D. P. (Eds.). *Cognitive behavior therapy: Research and application.* New York: Plenum, 1978.

Kendall, P. C., & Hollon, S. D. (Eds.). *Cognitive-behavioral intervention: Theory, research, and procedures.* New York: Academic Press, 1979.

Mahoney, M. J. *Cognition and behavior modification.* Cambridge, Mass.: Ballinger, 1974.

CONTENTS

NEW DIRECTIONS IN COGNITIVE THERAPY

SPECIAL POPULATIONS

Therapists often prefer clients with the most resources—middle-class, educated, and employed adults. The writers in this section focus on clients with fewer resources—the hospitalized, the poor, the young, and the old. Why do so many therapists shy away from less powerful clients? The diminished status and lowered financial benefits derived from working with them certainly are factors. But many more therapists avoid these clients because they believe they can't be helped; therapists often lack the confidence and skills for helping people in more difficult situations.

The chapters here provide useful guidelines for working with these special populations. The writers describe how cognitive therapy can be adapted and used with these groups. The chapters provide practical treatment strategies and outline how common pitfalls can be avoided.

The groups covered here have much in common. One of the most salient is their perceived and real sense of powerlessness. They often have less control over their environment. Outside agents of social control (parents, teachers, social workers, doctors, etc.) have larger degrees of control over their lives than for the rest of society. Their decreased sense of power is often accentuated by social stereotypes. Stereotypes may have a real influence on how others treat them and may lead to the adoption of these beliefs by the client in the form of self-fulfilling prophecies.

Because of the similarities, this section can be read as a whole; much of what applies to one group applies to the others. Many of the therapeutic challenges cut across the groups. Common challenges involve socializing clients for treatment, correcting misconceptions about therapy, establishing a working relationship, working within the limits of clients' real problems, and overcoming the therapist's own pessimism and concept of stereotypes.

The writers in this section outline practical ways these challenges can be met. A. John Rush and John T. Watkins (Chapter 1) discuss the importance of adequately socializing the lower-SES (socioeconomic strata) client into treatment. Therapists must be aware of the distor-

1

tions psychologically naive clients often have about therapy—that is, "only crazy people go for therapy." Similar distortions are also present in the other groups described in subsequent chapters. Therapists must address these beliefs in order to keep clients in treatment and to insure follow-through on homework assignments. Rush and Watkins in their chapter describe direct and indirect ways the therapist can correct these distortions.

A frequent criticism of cognitive therapy is that while it might work with college students or with those with mild problems, it won't help the severely disturbed. Brian F. Shaw (Chapter 2) shows how cognitive therapy can be effectively used with one of the most difficult groups, nonfunctional hospitalized patients. He describes how those in the patient's immediate environment (nurses, aides, occupational therapists, etc.) can become part of the team in applying cognitive therapy. His concept of continuation of care should be kept in mind no matter whether the therapist is working with teachers, physicians, social workers, or family members. As Shaw points out, the ultimate goal is the maintenance and generalization of the person's treatment gains.

Another criticism of cognitive therapy is that it is too intellectual for all but the brightest. For this reason it isn't seen as being applicable for children, poor, old, hospitalized, or less bright clients. Raymond A. Di Giuseppe (Chapter 3) describes how cognitive therapy *can* be applied to children. He shows why it's a mistake to underestimate children's reasoning powers. This is a mistake that's often made with the other groups mentioned as well.

Many therapists have difficulty in communicating with clients from different reference groups. Although frustrating, this block can be overcome. In Chapter 4, Richard C. Bedrosian describes methods for communicating with a group that can be particularly frustrating, adolescents. Many of the procedures he outlines can be adapted to the other groups. He underlines the importance of being extremely honest with the adolescent. This is good advice for working with other groups in this section. Clients with fewer resources often are keenly aware of hypocrisy.

Stereotypes and myths about groups of people abound in our society. Frequently the client's emotional and behavioral problems are attributed (by the client and others) to a social myth: "What can you expect from someone that's on welfare, a teenager, an old woman?" In Chapter 5, Gary Emery discusses "age-ism" attitudes. These attitudes, whether held by the client or others, are often interwoven with the client's presenting problem. He spells out ways therapists can work with these self-defeating attitudes. Therapists not only have to help free clients from these myths but must avoid adopting them as well.

Cognitive therapy may turn out to be the treatment of choice for the groups described here. Many of the problems of doing therapy with those with fewer resources revolve around lack of trust. The emphasis in cognitive therapy on collaborative empiricism and on making each step of therapy explicit does much to create trust. The strategy of running experiments and testing out ideas appears to be more acceptable than a reliance on the authority or prestige of the therapist.

Rather than dwelling in the past or bogging down in abstractions, cognitive therapy shows clients how they can go about getting over their problems. The focus on common sense and solving current concerns appeals to clients.

COGNITIVE THERAPY WITH PSYCHOLOGICALLY NAIVE DEPRESSED OUTPATIENTS

A. John Rush
John T. Watkins

INTRODUCTION

Cognitive therapy has been applied to a variety of disorders. Although depressive disorders have been most carefully studied (Rush & Beck, 1978a, 1978b), the populations treated have generally been middle- and upper-middle-socioeconomic-strata (SES) patients or college students. This chapter summarizes our experience in applying cognitive therapy to depressed lower-SES or psychologically naive patients. We have adapted previous strategies and developed new methods to deal with this population. These changes in cognitive therapy may also be of value in cognitive therapy of other types of problems such as drug dependency.

We have chosen to deal with the issue of psychological naiveté because the majority of our patients, regardless of SES, have no previous dealings with any mental-health professional (psychiatrist, psychologist, or social worker). Often they have no acquaintances who have had such a contact, and they have not read any of the psychological or self-help publications sold in paperback stores. In general, their attitudes toward mental health professionals and mental illness seem to reflect family and/or cultural mythology, gossip, rumor, and television or film portrayals. Such attitudes are not the exclusive attribute of

A. John Rush. Department of Psychiatry, University of Texas Health Sciences Center, Dallas, Texas.
John T. Watkins. Department of Psychiatry and Behavioral Sciences, University of Oklahoma Health Science Center, Oklahoma City, Oklahoma.

a specific socioeconomic level. Although poverty adds special real problems in addition to psychological naiveté, the latter factor constitutes a powerful influence on adherence to treatment or efficacy.

The contention that psychological naiveté is a critical factor is supported by several authors. Strupp and Bloxom (1973) reported that the effects of role induction procedures were inversely proportional to sophistication of the patient audience; that is, procedures designed to outline, demonstrate, and familiarize patients with what to expect in the course of psychotherapy produced an improved outcome, particularly with psychologically naive patients. Garfield (1971) argued that subjects from all social strata initially knew little about how the techniques of therapy worked, the appropriate topics for discussion, or even the usual duration of treatment. In his review of studies of relating SES and patients' expectations, he concluded that "differences among SES groups were generally ones of degree rather than of kind"; that is, lower-SES patients do not qualitatively differ from upper-SES patients in the nature of their expectations. Thus, psychological naiveté rather than SES per se significantly influences response to and participation in therapy.

ADHERENCE TO TREATMENT

Most studies indicate that psychotherapists working with these patients are confronted with two major problems: a consistently *high rate of premature defection (or dropout)* from treatment and *a poor rate of response to conventional psychotherapies, which is less well documented* (Lorion, 1975). Perhaps both of these problems reflect a single basic problem, namely, *poor adherence*, either to the appointment schedule and/or to the procedures of treatment.

The available literature does not answer the question of whether low-SES patients adhere less well to specific treatment procedures than higher-SES persons. For example, are low-SES patients less likely to carry out homework assignments than patients from higher SES? This is an important question since cognitive therapy utilizes written homework with each session, and diligence with homework performance has been associated with progress in psychotherapy in a statistically significant manner (Shelton & Ackerman, 1974).

Studies of compliance to other therapeutic regimens (e.g., taking medication, doing exercises, and other health-maintenance activities) might provide data from which to infer whether low SES or naiveness to treatment would influence compliance with homework assignments and other procedures involved in cognitive psychotherapy. Sackett and Haynes (1976) found that demographic features (e.g., sex, race, social class, and intelligence quotient) for patients who continue in medical treatment for a variety of nonpsychiatric illnesses are *not associated* with compliance patterns. Their review indicates that *complex* medical regimens and treatments that continue over time are associated with poorer compliance.

Other sociobehavioral factors pertinent to psychotherapy with psychologically naive patients overshadow the foregoing variables. Patients who perceived their illnesses as more serious and who perceived the treatments as more efficacious (regardless of both their factual knowledge and the truth of these matters) had higher compliance with treatment. Furthermore, compliance is generally higher among patients with "supportive" intact families and lower among those from unstable families. If one can generalize from these studies of compliance with medical regimens, then a time-limited, structured psychotherapy in which each step in treatment is defined should lead to greater adherence than time-unlimited therapies that are perceived as more complex by the patient. Obviously, cognitive therapy satisfies these general requirements.

ATTITUDINAL FACTORS

For lower-SES patients both practical and attitudinal factors may contribute to early defection and/or poor adherence to treatment procedures. Transportation and occupational and child-care problems are the most frequently encountered practical issues. Public transportation may be poor or the patient from a rural area may not have access to an automobile or the money for gasoline to come to therapy once or twice a week. The lower-class mother is often a single parent who has no reliable child-care resources that allow her to attend therapy. The working lower-class patient is likely to lose two or three hours in wages while attending an hour of therapy, or the patient might not be able to gain permission to be away from the job on a recurrent basis.

The attitudinal problems are as follows: Psychologically naive patients do not see psychotherapy as a treatment of choice; they are uncertain about the appropriateness or efficacy of psychotherapy; they are frightened by and ashamed of needing treatment; they are affronted by intimations that difficulties have an emotional basis; they may be defensive and threatened by the prospect of self-evaluation; and they may come wanting advice and guidance with problems (Lorion, 1975).

Therapists' attitudes implicated in early defection and/or poor adherence include (1) difficulty developing empathy; (2) frustration at being unable to practice "appropriate therapeutic roles"; and (3) negative feelings toward and indeed disapproval of the patient's behavior.

Patients' behaviors are determined by the roles they expect themselves and the therapist to play. Discrepancies between what the patient expects (e.g., directness and advice) and what actually occurs in psychotherapy (e.g., listening and reflection) may also relate to early defection or poor results.

Theoretically, the problem of discrepancy of expectations can be overcome by better aligning the client's feelings, attitudes, and expectation about psychotherapy with what he or she actually is about to experience in the course of treatment. This formulation has spawned a number of practical attempts to reduce early defection and/or improve response to treatment. Improved treatment duration and outcome were found when psychotherapy candidates were given an explanation of the nature of therapy and the role of participants. "Role-induction interviews" have been used to socialize persons for psychotherapy. Role-induction interviews to develop accurate therapy expectations significantly increase the effectiveness of individual therapy. Participation in treatment by someone from the client's environment also increases the effect of therapy (Rush, Shaw, & Khatami, 1980).

Heilbrun (1972) reported that briefing clients who were rated low in readiness for counseling resulted in a significant reduction in the incidence of early defection or dropout. In advance of their first interview, therapy candidates were given information about therapist directive–nondirective behavior. High-counseling-ready clients demonstrated similar incidences of continuation regardless of whether or not they were briefed. On the other hand, 66.7% of the low-counseling-ready clients who were briefed continued beyond the first interview, whereas only 30.8% of those who did not receive a briefing continued beyond the first interview.

In an important study, Heitler (1973) found that lower-class clients who were prepared for group therapy more readily and adequately immersed themselves in the tasks of the psychotherapeutic situation. Each of the lower-class clients received an "anticipatory socialization interview," geared to foster realistic expectations about group therapy; the control group received an equivalent amount of extra time, warmth, and accurate information about other aspects of hospital life. These "prepared" clients had lower latencies for voluntary participation; communicated more frequently, spent more time communicating; communicated more frequently on a self-initiated basis; and engaged in self-exploratory efforts more frequently. *Thus, socialization positively changed the patient's actual behavior in the therapy session.*

Strupp and Bloxom (1973) developed a role-induction film (*Turning Point*) as a more economical and widely available procedure to socialize these patients. The results of the role-induction film were compared against a role-induction interview and a no-presentation control. Both role-induction procedures improved the degree of improvement with group psychotherapy with their patients. The interview was superior in conveying a detailed knowledge of the process of group therapy, whereas the film was superior over a wider range of measures. These studies indicate that the primary contributions of role-induction procedures are (1) to provide accurate information concerning the process of therapy; (2) to dispel misconceptions and prejudice common among unsophisticated persons; (3) to enhance the prospective client's motivation for psychotherapeutic change; and (4) to pave the way for a more realistic view concerning emotional problems in living and their resolutions.

Cognitive therapy also involves enlisting the patient in carrying out specific assignments or homework tasks. Although techniques to increase adherence to these assignments have been suggested (Beck, Rush, Shaw, & Emery, 1979), there is little research available that has assessed the efficacy of these techniques. Again, the literature on compliance with medical therapeutic regimens may offer some relevant suggestions (Sackett & Haynes, 1976). Behavioral strategies have been more effective than educational strategies to increase compliance with medical regimens.[1] Specifically, simplifying schedules, role modeling

1. "Educational" refers to the transmission of information about a disease and its treatment to patients. "Behavioral" refers to attempts to (1) reduce barriers to compliance (e.g., expense or inconvenience); (2) use reinforcers; and (3) reward or reinforce compliance.

with selective reinforcement, token rewards, "contracts," compliance monitoring and feedback, and home visits have been shown to increase compliance. Interestingly, most interventions to increase attendance and adherence with psychotherapy treatments have been based on educational methods (e.g., role-induction films or interviews). Greater reliance on behavior paradigms may hold some promise for improving adherence with specific procedures in cognitive therapy.

A COGNITIVE FORMULATION

Let us assume that two important goals of working with psychologically naive patients are to decrease attrition and to increase adherence to the procedures within the therapy session and to assignments between sessions. We have developed a cognitive formulation of the problems of attrition and adherence. This formulation provides a basis for developing specific techniques to improve adherence with psychologically naive patients.

These patients bring to treatment a set of notions, ideas, and expectations about mental illness, medical treatment, and psychotherapy. These ideas (cognitions) are unrecognized and poorly thought out by most patients. In fact, these ideas only come to mind as patients discover they are having distresses (e.g., a depression), as they approach the psychiatric clinic, as they interact with the staff and other patients in the waiting room, and as they hear the responses of friends and family members to their beginning psychotherapy. These reactions and interactions are particularly important during the first several (one to four) visits, where attrition is highest.

As a consequence of specific beliefs (schemas) patients attend to selected aspects of these initial visits and the response of persons in their social system, specifically, those aspects that confirm previously held notions about therapy. These notions are based on family and cultural mythology and are often erroneous. We hypothesize that the actual content of cognitions elicited in association with seeking psychiatric help in psychologically naive patients is determined by the patient's illness (e.g., depression) and by his or her sociocultural background, particularly the family and social system.

Depression is associated with negative views of oneself, the future, and day-to-day experiences (Beck, 1976). These negative ideas are likely to be reinforced by specific aspects of the patient's interactions with the mental health delivery system. For example, depressed patients construe having to wait an hour or two in a clinic as evidence that "no one cares." Alternatively, when the therapist comments that the patient's record is lost or unavailable, the depressed patient may think, "I do not count even as a number." The depressed patient may think an unlimited treatment contract is evidence that he or she is hopelessly ill, or that it will take forever to get well.

In addition to cognitions related to specific psychopathology, we have observed another set of cognitions that surround the treatment process with psychologically naive patients; we believe these contribute to premature termination and to poor adherence to treatment procedures (e.g., doing homework). These cognitions contain themes such as (1) comparing themselves with others and concluding they are stupid, sinful, or crazy; (2) seeing the therapist as powerful and potentially dangerous—more like a policeman; (3) thinking in terms of an unjust, unresponsive, and inhuman world; (4) assuming they are more at the mercy of others in authority; (5) perceiving their unhappiness as more directly attributable to external circumstances; and (6) assuming that the therapist's competence and personal interest are questionable until proven otherwise. These themes seem particularly apparent in psychologically naive patients.

BELIEFS THAT CONTRIBUTE TO POOR ADHERENCE

Perhaps the most common notion is that only crazy people see a psychiatrist. Believing this, our patients refrain from reporting problems for fear of being judged crazy or they pay close attention to the therapist's behavior to determine whether he or she believes the patient is crazy.

In addition, "being crazy" often means "thinking crazy things." Recall that the cognitive therapist asks patients to write down their thoughts. As patients consider complying they may think, "If I write down what I think the therapist will think I am crazy. I might get committed." In fact, several psychologically naive patients have specifically told us that they thought we would commit them for thinking about suicide, since suicide is illegal. Thus, for the first one to two interviews the patient's attention is focused on the questions of being committed or judged crazy while the therapist may be completely oblivious to these thoughts (since most patients do not spontaneously report such ideas).

Another important theme reported by these patients involves the therapist's competency and concern. While depressed patients may construe silence or lack of activity as rejection, psychologically naive persons may infer from such pauses that the therapist is confused or incompetent. Rather than silence, these patients expect more direction and information. As one patient said, "If I knew what to do, I wouldn't be here, would I?" The therapist's apparent half-hearted response to a current crisis (e.g., getting a form signed for welfare) will trigger thoughts such as "He doesn't care or understand."

Another major theme in cognitions reported by these patients concerns evidence for an unjust world. As mentioned earlier, their thinking often portrays the world as uncaring, cold, ungiving, inflexible, and inhuman. Individual people are identified as parts of systems rather than as empathic indidivuals (e.g., "the welfare lady" was used in reference to a woman whom the patient saw weekly for two years.)

A particularly predominant theme consists of recurrent thoughts that patients were being disloyal to their spouses by coming to treatment and talking about marital problems. These ideas are often part of a larger set of themes, of seeing oneself in a helpless position and of externalizing causes. For example, one patient on unemployment compensation was about to drop out of treatment because she had to return to work. Only later did she disclose her thoughts: "I have to go back to work." "I can't continue treatment." "I'll never get out of being depressed." Without disclosing this problem, she asked the therapist, "Do you see people after hours?" The therapist answered, "No." Only four sessions later when the patient needed insurance forms signed did the therapist learn that she was planning to discontinue therapy. She had dismissed the possibility of requesting time off for therapy from her supervisor, thinking, "They'll never give me time off." Thus, she had not pursued this option.

Psychologically naive patients seem to have a number of other distinguishing themes in their thinking. While the depressed psychologically sophisticated patient might drop out of treatment thinking, "I'm incurably ill," the psychologically naive patient may discontinue treatment thinking, "The therapist is incompetent since he didn't do 'X.' " Alternatively, the psychologically naive patient almost always regards himself as weak or crazy for being depressed and seeing a psychiatrist, while the psychologically sophisticated patient appears to feel less shame and guilt about seeking treatment. The psychologically naive patient often seems more preoccupied with thoughts of being laughed at, derided, or made fun of by others. Because of more profound misconceptions, these patients require more time to develop trust in the therapist than more sophisticated patients.

Early defection and / or poor adherence may increase if these and other ideas are inadvertently reinforced by interactions between the patients, the clinic staff, and the therapist. The patient concludes that he or she should quit treatment or participate with caution. Thus, poor adherence and / or attendance will ensue. If techniques to correct these misconceptions are applied early in treatment, they improve the efficacy of treatment.

This formulation allows us to (1) elicit and correct specific notions that predispose patients to early defection; (2) change these notions within a cognitive paradigm, thereby preparing the patient for subsequent cognitive change procedures designed to relieve depression; and (3) circumvent negative therapist attitudes that often surround work with lower-SES or psychologically naive patients.

By conceptualizing attrition and adherence problems in terms of cognitions, the therapists can directly elicit and respond to maladaptive and / or distorted thoughts with methods to overtly counter cognitions. Alternatively, the therapist might respond to or counter some cognitions *without* actually asking the patient to directly state these thoughts. We will call these covert or indirect methods to change cognitions. We contend that many cognitions are normally covertly or indirectly countered, without either the therapist or the patient attending to such cognitive correction strategies. The following section will describe some of the methods derived from both this model and our clinical experience with these patients.

TECHNIQUES TO COUNTER POOR ATTENDANCE AND ADHERENCE

PREPARING PATIENTS FOR THERAPY

We prepare or socialize patients for cognitive therapy in hopes of reducing premature defections, which usually occur within the first three to four appointments. This preparation includes an explanation for the rationale of treatment (e.g., introduction of the notion that thoughts play a critical part in emotional states and behavior) *and* the elicitation and correction of cognitions that may lead to early defection.

Once the evaluation is completed, the clinician may choose from various alternatives to help the patient start treatment. Some therapists illustrate the ABC paradigm by using material provided by the patient during the first interview. The patient learns how his or her negative thoughts mediate between an event at point A and feeling(s) at point C.

Another method to introduce this cognitive model relies on patients reporting any changes in mood that occurred just prior to coming to the appointment or while waiting just before the appointment began. Most patients will have felt either less depressed or more depressed prior to their appointment. The therapist asks what thoughts went through the patient's mind at that time. With psychologically naive patients, the therapist may suggest possible thoughts to see if they "fit." Thoughts such as "The doctor seems to know what he's doing; maybe I am going to get some help" may lead to less sadness and pessimism. On the other hand, the patient's thinking "He may have helped others, but I doubt he can help me; I'm too far gone" can result in a deepening of depressed mood. In either case, such examples illustrate how thoughts relate to mood and how a shift in mood may be useful as a way to search for associated thoughts. Such examples also serve to demystify therapy itself as patients can readily see how thoughts and feelings relate. The concept that thoughts and feelings are related is also more readily grasped than abstract ideas, such as unconscious determinants, repressed anger, etc.

Another way to prepare patients for cognitive therapy is to ask patients to read a brief written introduction prior to the first treatment session. The authors typically use Beck and Greenberg's (1976) pamphlet, *Coping with Depression.* The patient is given a copy to keep, is asked to read it several times, to mark passages that seem to describe his or her experiences, and to bring the pamphlet to the initial treatment session. This written information gives the patient a basis for conceptualizing depression and the treatment process. Most psychologically naive patients can read and comprehend the pamphlet in its present form.

Secondly, the therapist should try to convey a realistically positive attitude about the potential value of therapy. In general, depressed persons attend to selected aspects of situations that are then construed in negative ways; in addition, we have found that lower-SES patients are more responsive to therapists who convey an action-oriented, yet understanding attitude. It is important to convey a sense of confidence without promising magic. For instance, during the socialization phase, we often tell patients something like the following: "Depression is a serious illness. We believe your depression will respond to cognitive psychotherapy in which we meet twice a week for ten weeks. Most depressed persons who are selected for this treatment begin to feel better in six to twelve visits. If we find the treatment we have chosen is not working, we will reevaluate the situation and consider alternative methods of treatment."

After this positive introduction to therapy the therapist elicits, considers carefully, and helps make more realistic, those specific thoughts that come to the patient about therapy; that is, the therapist asks for the patient's responses to this introductory information to determine what the patient actually heard and understood. For instance, in the case of D. S., the therapist had carefully explained the therapeutic plan and how the approach would help her cope with depression. He presented an accurately optimistic expectation about therapeutic outcome. D. S. smiled, having apparently taken it all in. When asked if she had any thoughts about the proposed therapy, D. S. replied, "I don't see how looking at my thoughts is going to make me feel any better. I'll never be happy. I can't satisfy my husband. What's the use in going on? Besides, without a car or any transportation, I wouldn't be able to get down here twice per week." This kind of hopeless response is not unusual in depressed persons. However, by detecting this type of thinking before the first therapy session and by correcting these ideas *before therapy begins,* the therapist increases the likelihood of continued adherence. In this case, the therapist might either enjoin the patient to test out the negative notion that nothing good will come of therapy by attending a few sessions or pointing out the role of these negative thoughts in spoiling her very chances of getting help.

D. S. also illustrates a second feature of many depressives, helplessness. She says that she has no automobile or transportation. Negative thoughts aside, lower-SES patients do have a number of reality-based problems that make regular attendance more difficult. For example, not having an automobile, not having access to good public transportation, the loss of wages for hourly employees, the absence of cheap or accessible child care to the single parent, inconvenient treatment hours, and lengthy clinic waits or time away from home or work are all likely to decrease attendance and/or adherence (Sackett & Haynes, 1976).

In the face of the hopelessness and helplessness presented by the lower-SES patient, it is useful for the therapist to collaborate with the prospective patient to problem-solve specific reality-based issues. The therapist asked D. S. if there were any other ways to arrange transportation so she could keep her first appointment. She offered to ask a relative for that one appointment, but she could not rely on the relative regularly. The therapist replied that this sounded like a useful plan worth carrying out. He asked her to bring at least one additional idea about transportation to future appointments to the first session, and he promised to provide her with two other possibilities during the session. When D. S. made the first appointment the therapist gave her telephone numbers of two programs (Red Cross and Neighbor to Neighbor) that provided transportation for patients attending medical appointments. We believe that eliciting and correcting negatively based-thinking about therapy and a willingness to collaborate in problem-solving real difficulties *before* treatment commences raises the probability that lower-SES patients will see therapy as less mysterious and the therapist as more genuine. In this way the probability of adherence is increased.

During this pretherapy socialization, psychologically naive patients have also expressed the following:

1. "I want advice on what to do and haven't gotten it, he can't help me."
2. "It's not my thinking, I just need some medicine so I can get some sleep."
3. "Coming here twice a week for ten weeks is crazy; why don't they just give me some pills?"
4. "I shouldn't need someone else to help me with my problems."

We advise therapists to elicit, reality test, and correct these and other thoughts *before* therapy.

CORRECTING COGNITIONS DURING THERAPY

Preparation for therapy alone is not sufficient to hold patients in treatment. Socialization is only the beginning. As patients begin treatment, their often unexpressed expectations about what will or should happen are being compared with what is really happening. Thus, a part of *each* treatment session should be devoted to further elicitation and correction of cognitions that may predispose to erratic attendance or premature defection.

The therapist actively elicits and explores thoughts that come to patients about *therapy* or the *therapist*. Psychologically naive patients are particularly reluctant to disclose these sorts of negative thoughts. Sometimes telling patients of cognitions reported by other patients frees them to divulge their own automatic thoughts. Some of the thoughts our psychologically naive patients reported include:

1. "I don't see how talking is going to help."
2. "I don't see how looking at my thoughts and writing them down is going to help."
3. "Writing my thoughts down makes me more depressed."
4. "I am too depressed for this kind of therapy."
5. "He doesn't really understand how I feel, that I'm too depressed to do the homework assigned."
6. "I'm not cured (after the first visit, third visit, etc.)."
7. "I don't see how changing my thinking will change any of the problems I have. They will still be here."
8. "I am weak (or sinful) if I need help. Everyone gets depressed but only I can't handle things."

These notions may lead to defection unless they are explored and corrected in therapy.

After three visits, M. O. was still quite depressed. At first she was unresponsive when the therapist asked about any thoughts she was having about therapy. After some coaxing, she admitted that her current thoughts were "I'm not any better. Writing my automatic thoughts down is not helping; it makes me feel worse. This type of therapy is not going to work for me." The therapist used the patient's observation that she felt more depressed while writing down her negative thoughts as a *cause célèbre*. He invited her to observe the relationship once again between her thoughts and mood change. He suggested that since she was doing something that deepened her depression, it was also possible for her to change her thinking to reduce her depression. The therapist further illustrated the relationship of thoughts to affect by recalling a previous event reported by the patient in which pleasure and positive thoughts had been associated. Thus, negative thoughts about therapy itself provide valuable opportunities to further the treatment process and to increase adherence.

VIDEOTAPES TO COUNTER COGNITIVE DISTORTIONS

We have also used audiovisual materials prepared for patients to combat cognitive distortions that lead to poor adherence. We have produced several videotapes to demonstrate specific techniques and stages in cognitive therapy to depressed persons. Each tape shows a psychotherapist working with a simulated patient. A moderator introduces each scene to direct the viewer's attention to specific features of the interaction and at the conclusion of each scene the moderator reviews what has been accomplished in the session. The moderator states and then corrects specific cognitions that depressed, psychologically naive viewers are likely to have. For example, following the first session the moderator remarks:

> Some patients who are depressed are afraid of doing their homework. They're afraid of failing or not doing it well enough. It's important to try the assignment. There's no grade so there's no way to fail.

Following another scene, the moderator states and then refutes cognitions that might contribute to low adherence:

> What you have just viewed is a demonstration of how to answer automatic thoughts. Initially, you might wonder if you can learn this task. Getting it down absolutely right is not important; trying to answer your negative thoughts is what counts. If you have a feeling that this might be difficult or impossible for you, it is important to talk with your therapist who might provide alternative ways to accomplish the task of answering your negative thoughts.

Here the moderator anticipates that the viewer may assume he or she will be unable to imitate what was demonstrated on the tape. The moderator anticipates "absolutistic" thinking and corrects possible perfectionistic cognitions by stating that trying is what counts. The moderator assures the viewer that there are "alternative" ways to accomplish this task since the scene on the tape demonstrates writing down thoughts, and many lower-SES patients are uncomfortable with writing.

Other events in the course of therapy may also contribute to defection with psychologically naive patients. Patients often construe both exacerbations and improvements in symptoms as evidence that therapy should stop. Specific videotape sequences confront both alternatives.

In the simulated seventh session, the patient reports a relapse into depression. The moderator anticipates the viewer's possible negative reaction to this event and comments:

> Often, some relief from depression is obtained for some hours or even days initially, and then the negative, unrealistic thinking returns. It is important not to misconstrue fluctuating feelings of sadness as a setback or as an indication that the therapy is not working. Rather, this is a reflection of what might be expected when a new skill is being learned, namely, the skill of attending to and answering one's automatic, negative thinking. It's essential to continue the homework assignment even if things begin to feel worse for a while so that the negative thoughts associated with feeling worse can be used during the next therapy session. In fact, this offers a further opportunity to identify negative thinking and to correct it.

In the 11th session, the moderator anticipates possible defection as the patient's symptoms subside. The moderator says:

> What you have just seen is an advanced stage of cognitive therapy. The patient is answering her automatic thinking. It is common for patients ment to feel a substantial reduction in depression. This may be misinterpreted as a sign that therapy should be terminated. In fact, this is the time to rework the silent assumptions or themes to make them more realistic and practical.

The videotapes demonstrate specific techniques and provide patients with a map of how the client and therapist will interact. Although the tapes are intended to increase adherence, depressed psychologically naive patients may have mixed reactions to them. When asked for her responses to one of the videotapes, K. C. stated, "It's helpful in showing me how to answer automatic thoughts, and to work out bad feelings." K. C. went on to remark upon the simulated client who had become very depressed and guilty over the misbehavior of her two-year-old child. Gaining some distance from herself, K. C. stated, "I can see that it is ridiculous what she [simulated client] was doing with her two-year-old . . . [yet] I'm doing the same thing with my children."

Responses are not always so positive. At the next session K. C. was asked if she had thought about the videotape in the past few days since viewing it. She responded that she had thought about it on at least two occasions. "I thought about how to answer my automatic thoughts, how she [simulated client] did it. Didn't do much good. I can't seem to answer some of them.'' The videotapes seems to have been fruitful in providing a cognitive model for the patient, even though she was not able to match her own behavior to the behavior observed on the tape. However, the positive development here is that K. C. had been working between sessions on answering her negative thoughts, at least partially as a result of the material viewed in the last session. The therapist was able then to work with her on the particular difficulties she was experiencing.

Patients have reported other negative thoughts after watching these tapes:

1. "I feel like she [simulated patient] is making fun of me, mocking me.''
2. "If she were a real patient, I would feel better.''
3. "I can't stand someone who feels sorry for herself.''
4. "The patient [simulated] does not look as depressed as I am; I am too sick for this to work.''

It is important to elicit and correct these negative cognitions since they too may lead to poor adherence or early defection.

HOMEWORK ASSIGNMENTS: THE OPPORTUNITY TO CORRECT DISTORTED COGNITIONS

Homework assignments are an integral part of cognitive therapy. However, patients vary greatly in carrying out these tasks. For example, homework assignments might consist of recording automatic negative thoughts in association with events and feelings of depression (the triple-column technique), and later answering these cognitive distortions (the four-column technique). Patients who are reluctant to carry out these tasks may return to the next session without having made an attempt, or they may even miss the session entirely. A homework assignment may elicit negative cognitions at several points: when it is explained; when the patient tries to undertake the task; when the patient evaluates how well he or she did the task; or when the patient assesses what effect the task had on the depression. For instance, after the presentation of the homework assignment, one patient reported thinking, "Oh, God, I can see that this is going to be a long drawn-out business. I need help now! I can't do this.'' These negative thoughts must be elicited and corrected before the patient undertakes the assignment.

It is critical to elicit the patient's perception of the task and what it means both *before* and *after* trying it as homework. At times the therapist should even encourage the patient to call between sessions if there is any difficulty with the task itself. Some patients will predict that they are unable to carry out the assignment. Others will see the assignment as so simple as to constitute an insult. Other thoughts about the homework will reflect psychological naiveté or social class. Some of the cognitions reported by our psychologically naive patients included:

1. "No single thing depressed me; I'm depressed all the time, so I didn't write anything."
2. "It sounds simple, but I know I won't be able to do it right."
3. "My situations are so unimportant, they are not worth mentioning."
4. "Nothing upsetting has happened since I last saw you."
5. "I can't spell; I'm too embarrassed to show my writing."

L. R. initially presented herself as depressed all the time, exclaiming, "No single thing depressed me, I'm always depressed." Homework assignments were particularly important if the therapist was to get a handle on the cognitions that presumably kept her depressed. The therapist explained the goals of homework (e.g., assignments would speed up therapy, help her focus on what was depressing her between that could contribute to depression.) He assigned L. R. to the three-column technique of recording fluctuations in mood in the third column and what was happening at the time in the first column. Anticipating that she believed "My situations are so unimportant, they're not worth mentioning," the therapist told her that no mood fluctuations or events were too minor to record. The therapist also wrote in her notebook to illustrate how to perform the task. Finally, she practiced the assignment in the office. The therapist felt that to ask this patient to record cognitions was premature (judging she would fail) because she had so little awareness of her thinking.

After assigning homework, the therapist should ask the patient about the homework. In the case of L. R., she replied, "It sounds simple, but I won't be able to do it right." This response provided the therapist another opportunity for cognitive correction. The therapist emphasized the importance of trying the task rather than completing it perfectly. The therapist tried to inoculate L. R. against possible perceived failure should she not complete the task to her own satisfaction, or to what she perceived as the therapist's expectations. He told her, "Even if you feel that you've not recorded things just so, bring your homework with you. That way I can assist you with questions you may have." In concluding, the therapist provided additional structure by asking L. R. to "put at least two things down in your notebook each day over the next three days until our next appointment." Specific assignments such as this increase patient follow-through.

The therapist should highlight any approximations of assignments carried out. For instance, when L. R. had not recorded her automatic thoughts but had noted events and feelings, the therapist complimented her for these recordings. Then, he used the session to uncover what thoughts might have been associated with the feelings recorded in her notebook. As she became aware of her negative thoughts and began recording them as part of the three-column technique, the therapist further acknowledged the benefits of homework assignments carried out: "Very good, you are uncovering how you depress yourself." And later on as she began to use the four-column technique (answering automatic thoughts), he again highlighted this advance: "It's really paying off for you, isn't it?"

Both patient and therapist can become frustrated with homework assignments. We suggest the following guidelines to increase adherence to these assignments:

1. Explain goals of homework.
2. Explain rationale of specific assignment.
3. Illustrate or model for patient.
4. Have patient practice in office.
5. Avoid assignment of premature task or multiple tasks.
6. Emphasize importance of attempting assignment rather than the quality or completion of the task.
7. Provide clear structure as to specifics of task.
8. Undercut "resistance" by eliciting and correcting negative cognitions.
9. Inoculate against preceived failure should patient have difficulty with assignment.
10. Praise for having attempted homework, highlighting any approximations of assignments.

11. Acknowledge any benefits of homework assignment carried out.
12. Review assignment at beginning of therapy session so as to:

    a. reflect therapist's genuine valuing of homework;
    b. influence completion of future assignments;
    c. establish a "task orientation" set to offset client's hopelessness and helplessness; and
    d. collect cognitions surrounding difficulty in attempting the task.

INDIRECT METHODS TO CORRECT COGNITIONS

Cognitive therapy is based on the premise that correction and reality testing of depressogenic cognitions should occur well within the patient's awareness (Beck, 1976). On the other hand, we believe that some cognitions that contribute to early defection with psychologically naive patients can be corrected *without* directly eliciting these thoughts. The "indirect" methods must be used with caution. For example, patients are concerned about the therapist's expertise in treating their depression. Lower-SES patients often seem to expect action, not just talk, on the part of the doctor. The patient's belief in the therapist's authority may be increased by outlining the treatment program in a stepwise, "preprogrammed" way, by distributing a clinic brochure, by playing professionally produced videotapes, and by being active and directive as needed in the therapy sessions. If the therapist conducts each session with an established agenda that facilitates a confident and active style, some hesitations about "talking therapy" may be overcome. An agenda for each session is particularly of value. An example of such an agenda might be to:

1. obtain responses to previous sessions;
2. obtain responses to homework assigned;
3. review homework completed;
4. reinforce tasks carried out or attempted;
5. model next steps in therapy;
6. ask for practice of these steps by the patient in the session;
7. ask for other concerns the client may have; and
8. assign next homework, etc.

Both the therapist *and* patient must collaborate to develop an agenda.

Furthermore, an agenda is not a substitution for active, empathic listening and attending to the current concerns of the patient.

Often the therapist can answer the unspoken thought, "Tell me what to do," by providing models on videotape, demonstrations, and role-playing in the sessions. The therapist can covertly refute the doubt, "The therapist doesn't care," by a variety of behaviors, including asking about real-life problems first in each session, seeing patients promptly rather than having them wait, assisting in meeting specific real-life needs when appropriate (e.g., transportation, notebooks, reading material, social service referrals).

Written material about depression will often counter patients' feelings of weakness or shame. Several of these brochures name prominent people (e.g., Abraham Lincoln) as having suffered from depressions, thereby belying the notion that being depressed is equivalent to being weak. Again, the therapist should discuss this material with the patient. These patients also have unspoken concerns about various physical symptoms, which commonly accompany depression. A careful medical evaluation, physical examination, and clear explanations provide relief from unexpressed concerns about heart disease, cancer, etc. Furthermore, various medical disorders do cause depression (Rush & Beck, 1978a); therefore, a careful evaluation is essential.

Another valuable tool to correct beliefs that lead to defection consists of the direct and immediate involvement of an important other person, both at evaluation and in the treatment process (Rush *et al.*, 1980). This other person can often influence both attendance and adherence. The therapist should interview this person to elicit and correct common misconceptions at the outset of treatment. For example, the spouse might be told, "It is very common to feel angry at a person who is depressed. At first you try to do everything to cheer him or her up, but when all your efforts fail, either you will tend to get depressed or angry yourself or just give up." The therapist can ask the spouse to read materials relevant to depression and cognitive therapy. The therapist may also directly involve this person in observing and participating in treatment. Alternatively, videotapes that increase understanding of depression and the treatment process will facilitate adherence.

The therapist can directly and covertly correct misconceptions about medication. Often psychologically naive patients believe that only medication will help them because they believe there is no treatment alternative. An explanation (during evaluation or through an introductory brochure) about different types of depression and accordingly different treatments (both medication and talking therapies) is often helpful, particularly when cognitive therapy is prescribed. Even if medication is not prescribed, there may be an advantage in keeping an open dialogue around the issue (i.e., that it would be made available should there develop a specific indication for medication and/or should therapy not succeed).

DESIGNING PROCEDURES UNIQUE TO LOWER-SES CLIENTS

F. T. had become a recluse during the depths of her depression, seldom leaving her house. She found it especially difficult to keep her twice per week cognitive therapy appointments because she had to spend over two hours on the city bus to attend each appointment. After a dozen visits, F. T. had reduced her automatic negative thoughts and her mood had improved. She dropped from the range of severe depression to mild depression, as measured by the Beck Depression Inventory. However, F. T. continued to stay close to home except for therapy appointments.

The client seemed to be ready for some greater involvement in the world as her depression was lifting. The therapist discussed her willingness to try something outside her home as a homework assignment. (She had been working productively with her homework and was accustomed to task assignments.) After learning that her bus stopped at a major shopping center midway between her home and the clinic, the therapist outlined the following strategy. He told her to continue having two therapy sessions per week. One session would be in the office, while the other weekly session would be at the shopping center. He asked her to take her regular bus, get off halfway to the office, and spend an hour or more browsing around the shopping center.

Money is a critical problem for most lower-SES clients. F. T. was paying a nominal fee of $7.50 per hour. As an additional feature of this assignment, the therapist asked her to spend the $7.50 (her therapy fee) on shopping or lunch. She smiled and said she thought this was a funny idea, but she was willing to try it.

This assignment was tailor-made for this patient. The therapist carefully anticipated with her any possible negative cognitions about either visiting the shopping center or spending the money. She could have very well become guilty and depressed over "wasting" money or spending it on herself. This innovative assignment seemed safe enough in that F. T. had postponed many purchases and had a backlog of items attributable to her having not been out of the house for some time. She carried out this assignment over several consecutive weeks and found it pleasurable. She subsequently organized a weekend shopping trip on her own.

The therapist is advised to be flexible and willing to depart from his or her usual routine in working with lower-SES clients. For instance, attending twice per week treatment sessions may be particularly difficult for some patients who struggle with transportation or child-care difficulties. A willingness to employ a 30-minute session (instead of the traditional 50-minute hour) at a time when the person has transportation is preferable to rigidly requiring the client to adhere to the designated appointment schedule. Also, rather than passively accepting a cancellation caused by last-minute transportation difficulties on the part of the client, the therapist might offer to "meet" with the client over the telephone at the regular time. Some of our most productive cognitive therapy has occurred on days when we resorted to telephone interviews. Flexibility in regard to money is also to be advised. Working with lower-SES clients, the therapist must be willing to see clients for a nominal fee, on a "partially deferred payment plan," or even to forego the fee in the interest of generating cognitive–behavioral changes, such as in the above case of F. T.

CONCLUSION

We have provided a cognitive conceptualization of therapy with psychologically naive patients. This conceptualization has allowed us to develop some specific techniques to reduce attrition and increase adherence. However, little empirical research is available to isolate those techniques that are of value. Furthermore, a variety of additional methods can readily be developed from this model. We need additional research and clinical experience upon which to design methods to deal with this too often neglected population of patients.

SUMMARY

We have identified two problems, high defection and low adherence to treatment procedures, in our psychologically naive depressed outpatients. We believe that both these problems can be reduced by identifying cognitions and underlying schemas that induce patients to quit therapy. Once identified, these notions can be directly refuted or indirectly corrected without asking the patient to specifically state his or her false beliefs.

A number of changes in cognitive therapy methods have been described that appear to be valuable in increasing adherence to treatment procedures and decreasing attrition. This chapter presents a clinical report of our experience with these innovations in cognitive therapy.

REFERENCES

Beck, A. T., & Greenberg, R. *Coping with depression*. Philadelphia: Center for Cognitive Therapy, 1976.

Beck, A. T., Rush, A. J., Shaw, B. F., & Emery, G. *Cognitive therapy of depression*. New York: Guilford Press, 1979.

Garfield, S. L. Research on client variables in psychotherapy. In A. E. Bergin & S. L. Garfield (Eds.), *Handbook of psychotherapy and behavior change: An empirical analysis*. New York: Wiley, 1971.

Heilbrun, A. B. Effects of briefing upon client satisfaction with the initial counseling contact. *Journal of Consulting and Clinical Psychology*, 1972, *38*, 50–56.

Heitler, J. B. Preparation of lower-class patients for expressive group psychotherapy. *Journal of Consulting and Clinical Psychology*, 1973, *41*, 251–260.

Hollingshead, A. B., & Redlich, F. C. *Social class and mental illness*. New York: Wiley, 1958.

Lorion, R. P. Mental health treatment of the low-income groups. *Contemporary Issues of Mental Health*, 1975, *1*, 1–53.

Redlich, F. C., Hollingshead, A. B., & Bellis, E. Social class differences in attitudes toward psychiatry. *American Journal of Orthopsychiatry*, 1955, *25*, 60–70.

Rush, A. J., & Beck, A. T. Behavior therapy in adults with affective disorders. In M. Hersen & A. S. Bellack (Eds.), *Behavior therapy in the psychiatry setting*. Baltimore: Williams & Wilkins, 1978. (a)

Rush, A. J., & Beck, A. T. Cognitive therapy of depression and suicide. *American Journal of Psychotherapy*, 1978, *32*, 201–219. (b)

Rush, A. J., Shaw, B. F., & Khatami, M. Cognitive therapy of depression:

Utilizing the couples system. *Cognitive Research and Therapy*, 1980, *4*, 103–113.

Sackett, D. L., & Haynes, R. B. *Compliance with therapeutic regimens.* Baltimore: John Hopkins Press, 1976.

Shelton, J. L., & Ackerman, J. M. *Homework in counseling and psychotherapy*, Springfield, Ill.: Charles C. Thomas, 1974.

Strupp, H. H., & Bloxom, A. L. Preparing lower-class patients for group psychotherapy: Development and evaluation of a role-induction film. *Journal of Consulting and Clinical Psychology*, 1973, *41*, 373–384.

COGNITIVE THERAPY WITH AN INPATIENT POPULATION

Brian F. Shaw

INTRODUCTION

A significant number of people unable to function because of psychological disorders enter the hospital for inpatient treatment. This chapter describes the use of cognitive therapy with this population. The focus of the chapter will be on a multidisciplinary model of treatment delivery and a problem-oriented conceptual base for therapy.

The inpatient setting is important in the implementation of any therapeutic modality. Nurses, physicians, social workers, psychologists, occupational therapists, and their students have different and often conflicting ideas on treatment. Too often, the patient hospitalized primarily for psychological reasons is confused when presented with various conflicting views of his or her problems.

This chapter is based on my experience in a university hospital with an active treatment unit as well as a mandate to conduct scientific research. The staffing is such that intensive therapy is possible and careful behavioral observations are standardly recorded.

SERVICE DELIVERY SYSTEM

In order to provide a relatively unambiguous delivery of service we use the following procedures:

1. A weekly multidisciplinary meeting (the rounds) to discuss the patient's past history, to develop a problem-oriented formula-

Brian F. Shaw. Department of Psychiatry, The University of Western Ontario, and Department of Psychological Services, University Hospital, London, Ontario, Canada.

tion (as opposed to simply a diagnosis) and to decide on the treatment plan. In most cases the patient is an active collaborator in the formulation of the problems although he or she does not attend the meeting.

2. The use of the problem-oriented record (Weed, 1968) by staff to chart progress and, importantly, to establish a feedback loop of service delivery; that is, anyone with observations of change in the patient's presenting problems notes his or her observations, then he or she offers an assessment of the meaning of the change and proposes a plan to account for the changes.

3. Daily observations of the patient's behaviors (using the Observational Behavior Scale developed by Brawley, Lancee, Allon, & Brown, in press) as an objective measure of change.

4. A relatively structured day in which patients have responsibilities to the ''community.'' Hence interaction between person and environment is maintained.

5. Weekly education meetings for staff to share ideas and recent technical advances. Videotape presentations are employed as well as reports on workshops. The most important aspect of education relevant to this chapter is the demand that staff make observations and collect cognitive data (the primary data base) while avoiding inferences (Beck, Rush, Shaw, & Emery, 1979).

The main question addressed in this chapter is: *What are the specific problems (and possible solutions) encountered when working in an inpatient setting and using cognitive therapy?* Three problem areas can be identified: (1) the nonfunctioning patient; (2) generalization outside treatment setting; and (3) the importance of continuity of care. These three areas will be illustrated by case examples including successes and failures.

THE NONFUNCTIONING PATIENT

Severe depression is one condition that is often characterized by an inability to function. There are many reasons why an individual becomes unable to function, but two of the most common are the withdrawal of social support and loss of contact with reality (psychosis).

CASE EXAMPLE 1

Mr. A. was a 64-year-old married man who was "retired" from a middle-management position of a large company. He had been depressed for approximately eight months and in the two months prior to hospitalization he remained in bed. Mr. A. had stopped communicating with his wife and two adult children during this latter period.

The initial problem list included: (1) noncommunication; (2) amotivation; (3) anemia; (4) depression; (5) family discord; (6) passive suicidal behavior (before he stopped communicating Mr. A. stated that he "just wanted to die").

The general therapeutic stance was to take a graded approach. First, the staff discussed possible misconceptions resulting from Mr. A.'s withdrawn behavior. These ideas included the possibility that Mr. A. "wanted" to antagonize others or that he "wanted" to avoid responsibility. After examining these ideas we concluded Mr. A. believed the future was hopeless and that he may have felt considerable anger and hurt. While we appreciated Mrs. A.'s statements that the family still believed in Mr. A., we were also aware of the type of "hostile" environment inadvertently created by the depressed person's family (see Coyne, 1976).

In the rounds we established a plan to document Mr. A.'s cognitions, following his interaction with each staff member, thereby providing a continuity of assessment. The number of staff interacting with Mr. A. was limited; however, a prime therapist reviewed Mr. A.'s history (obtained from family), including possible reactions (cognitions) he may have had prior to his hospitalization. Within three days Mr. A. began to express his ideas of hopelessness and loss. He believed he was unable to learn "new tricks" (i.e., new job, new lifestyle).

The treatment plan was introduced to Mr. A. gradually. The plan included specific expectations of his responsibility and an assessment of *potentially* rewarding activities. Specifically we wanted Mr. A. to increase personal care (shaving, washing, etc.) and we were initially prepared to allow him to remain in bed. We were careful not to promise that he would regain his interests, but we maintained that increased activity was essential. The nursing staff and occupational therapy staff expressed a consistent attitude that Mr. A.'s feelings of hopelessness were understandable, but that they didn't agree with him. The staff elicited his predictions of the future (e.g., "Do you think you'll be able to . . . ?") and then encouraged effort and activity to counter the depression. If Mr. A. succeeded, the staff reviewed his predictions attributing the negative ideas to the depression. They stressed that Mr. A. had functioned independently and effectively for most of his life. He was repeatedly informed that his attitude not his ability had changed.

The prime therapist, a psychiatric resident receiving supervision from the author, set out the staff's expectations. These expectations included a schedule of dates when Mr. A. would get out of bed, when he would take his meals in the dining room, how long he would spend in occupational therapy. She also coordinated the cognitive assessment (i.e., collected the predictions, followed leads from staff, integrated present behavior with past history), and therapy.

We have found that an attitude of hope (because of our experience with depression), respect for the patient's ideas, and a reasonable expectation for activity is extremely effective. We do not use concrete reinforcers (e.g., tokens) or punishers, but a social-reinforcement (praise and encouragement) program is employed.

From the staff's viewpoint it is important to set out the plan clearly and in writing (inpatient treatment occurs over 24 hours a day). The restriction of the number of staff interacting with nonfunctional patients ensures that there is a consistency in the approach. In addition, the staff's cognitions (e.g., "He's not trying; he wants to be miserable") can be anticipated and, if necessary, altered.

After six weeks of inpatient therapy Mr. A.'s progress was such that he was ready for discharge. He was able to look after his personal health needs, including eating; he had started an avocation repairing electrical appliances; and he was able to discuss his angry feelings toward his family because of their "lack of understanding and continued selfish demands."

In follow-up appointments over the next four months, Mr. A. had completely recovered from his depression and was, according to him, "finally able to enjoy my grandchildren." As an outpatient his progress continued to be significant. Mr. A. analyzed his "self-criticisms" and negative predictions characterized by his belief that you "can't teach an old dog new tricks." He became aware of high levels of anxiety and great apprehension related to his retirement. The nature of the stress (i.e., he perceived his retirement as a firing meaning that he was "over the hill"), combined with his basic beliefs about getting old, precipitated a sense of isolation and failure. There was evidence that his family didn't understand this reaction to his retirement (they avoided discussions of the area). The lack of social support added further stress, resulting in a full-blown depression and withdrawal.

At a two-year follow-up, Mr. A. had started his own minor repair business and had not experienced clinical depression. His progress is reflected in Figure 1.

CASE EXAMPLE 2

Mrs. B. was a 48-year-old married mother of two children (ages 19 and 22). She lived with her husband, a highly successful businessman. Mrs. B. had been a schoolteacher during the first five years of her marriage and she returned to teaching for six years after her own children were enrolled in school. Mrs. B. had been hospitalized on three other occasions for six, eleven, and eight weeks, respectively, each time with a diagnosis of "psychotic depression." She received electroconvulsive therapy (ECT) on each occasion.

On this admission she manifested signs and symptoms of primary depression (Feighner, Robins, Guze, Woodruff, Winokur, & Munoz, 1972) and psychotic thinking, for example, "My bowels are rotten," "It's no use eating, I'll be dead tomorrow," "I'm a sinner." There did not appear to be an environmental precipitant. The staff noted that Mrs. B. became less coherent and more agitated when her husband visited.

The problem list included: (1) severe agitation; (2) psychotic thinking (negatively self-referential); (3) depression; (4) anorexia; and (5) loss of social contact. The latter problem was added when Mrs. B.'s family informed us that she had avoided visits with friends or relatives for one year.

The treatment plan was similar to the plan for Mr. A. Specific expectations of responsibility, a series of "mini-experiments" to reality-test her thinking, an assessment of *potentially* rewarding activities, and in time, reinvolvement with her family following an assessment of her role.

The prime therapist was an intern in psychology under supervision from the author. Four nursing staff and an occupational therapist were also assigned to work with Mrs. B. The first problems treated were Mrs. B.'s hopelessness and her psychotic thinking. Initially on the unit

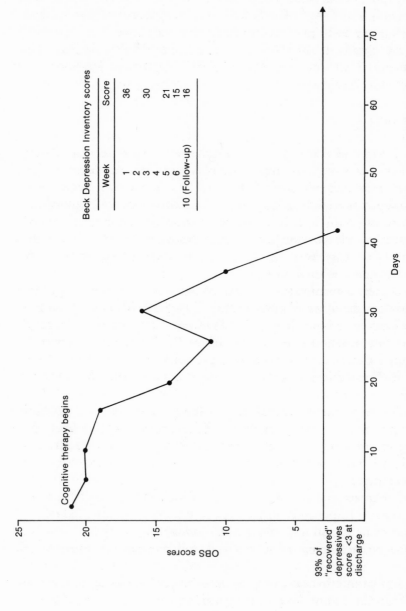

FIGURE 1. *Clinical course of Mr. A. as measured by the Observational Behavioral Scale (OBS; Brawley, Lancee, Allon & Brown, in press) and the Beck Depression Inventory.*

34

Mrs. B. was placed in an environment where there was restricted contact with others (i.e., meals in room, private room, specific schedule of daily activities). We employ this strategy to reduce stimulation of the patient in an attempt to control psychotic thinking. The therapists carefully obtained Mrs. B.'s predictions that were inevitably catastrophic in nature, for example, "I won't be able to eat. My bowels are rotted out." They maintained reasonable expectations and hope for Mrs. B. and attributed her incorrect ideas to her depression.

Potentially rewarding activities were gradually assessed and Mrs. B. began to paint, returning to an old hobby. Responsibilities were increased so that Mrs. B. could not spend more than one daytime hour in her room. She was given responsibilities on the unit (making her bed, attending the daily ward meeting). Before each program change Mrs. B.'s cognitions were obtained and the staff noted a steady improvement in her predictions as well as some reported satisfaction ("about one-tenth of what it used to be") in her daily activities.

Unlike Mr. A., however, Mrs. B. did not show the steady improvement characterized by renewed motivation and a problem-solving attitude. There continued to be occasions when her thinking would revert back to the initial idiosyncratic, overgeneralized ideas, for example, "There's no hope for me," "I'll never learn to cope." The main source of information about her "progress" was Mr. B., who constantly reminded staff that she was "as bad as ever."

After six weeks of cognitive therapy in conjunction with a range of psychotropic medications Mrs. B. was indeed judged to be only "minimally improved" (see Figure 2 summarizing the outcome). A number of the staff had lost confidence that we could help Mrs. B. via psychological approaches (interestingly, the failure of psychopharmacological approaches was not discussed in any detail, probably reflecting the disappointment given the staff time and effort). Some staff were convinced that we did not yet understand Mrs. B.'s thought process. Nevertheless, the general consensus was that ECT was indicated (given the history of a good response to this treatment).

Cognitive therapy was not stopped but there was a significant alteration in Mrs. B.'s conceptualization of treatment. She feared ECT and considerable anxiety was generalized with the result that much of her negative thinking focused on her inability to cope with the treatment. Unfortunately after seven more weeks of treatment, Mrs. B. had not improved significantly and was transferred to a longer-term facility.

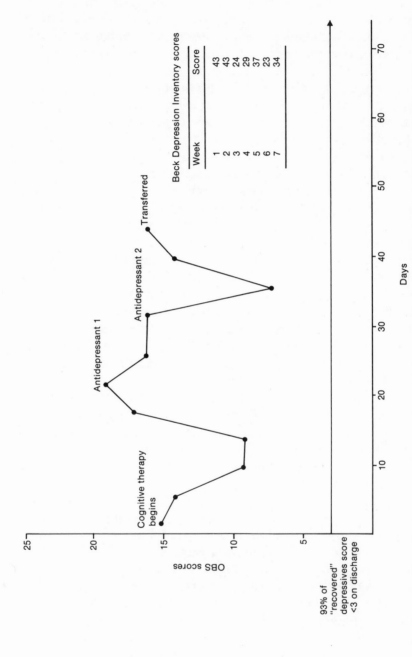

FIGURE 2. *Clinical course of Mrs. B. as measured by the Observational Behavior Scale (OBS; Brawley, Lancee, Allon, & Brown, in press) and the Beck Depression Inventory.*

Beck Depression Inventory scores

Week	Score
1	43
2	43
3	24
4	29
5	37
6	23
7	34

Days

OBS scores

93% of
"recovered"
depressives score
<3 on discharge

Transferred

Antidepressant 2

Antidepressant 1

Cognitive therapy
begins

36

What were the key factors leading to the successful treatment of Mr. A. and the unsuccessful treatment of Mrs. B.? Reviewing the charts one could consider a wide range of possibilities, including (1) patient variables—type of symptoms, past history of depression, demographic characteristics; (2) therapist variables—different personnel, fluctuating staff attitudes, possible negative cognitions toward patient; and (3) environment variables—different response from other patients, different support from significant others.

Following this procedure (which is part of our quality assurance) we realized that Mrs. B. did not speak of any particular difficulty in her environment (and there were no easily identifiable blows to her self-esteem). Yet, Mrs. B.'s condition worsened following contacts with her husband. She expressed her ideas with reference to her incapabilities and in retrospect we missed inquiring about cognitions directly related to her husband. This is not to say that we did not inquire about her relationship with her husband, but we didn't point out our observation that she worsened following interactions with her husband. We then could have elicited cognitions related to her change.

FACILITATIVE CONDITIONS

We have extrapolated our experience with "nonfunctioning patients" to propose some conditions that facilitate cognitive and behavior change. Presently we are using a stress model that dictates that external stress must be initially reduced. We want to establish conditions such that the patient gains a better understanding of his or her cognitions.

To facilitate new learning in the inpatient setting we rely on the definition of stress proposed by Lazarus and Launier (1978). Stress occurs when "external and/or internal demands exceed the individual's coping resources." One of the main goals of hospitalization is to reduce the level of stress experienced by the individual. Thus, the environmental demands made by the inpatient unit must also be managed because it can be assumed that the person's coping resources have been significantly reduced (for a review of this area see Shaw, in press).

We have found that the stress generated by family and friends is a significant factor. This finding is of course not novel as family therapists have been emphasizing similar points for a number of years (see Minuchin, 1974). For this reason, in the assessment phase we give careful consideration to cognitions related to the patient's role in the family unit. Our experience has been that the person's depression needed to be treated first, followed by a generalization period where family communications and relationships can be modified, if needed. Our experience supports Friedman's (1975) study that marital therapy does not appear to be an effective primary intervention for depression in inpatients.

GENERALIZATION

Once the patient's depression begins to lessen (as a result of decreased stress and increased coping and problem-solving skills) the second problem area emerges, the generalization of the skills to the natural environment. The average stay for depressed inpatients treated with cognitive therapy in our unit is three weeks (range from four days to six weeks). In this relatively short time period we have to provide an environment in which the patient will not only experience a reduction in stress but also learn new patterns of thinking and behavior.

During the early treatment phase of hospitalization we make extensive use of role-playing, including role reversal. The goal is to elicit a series of situations that the individual is having difficulty with. We use a graded task approach to these difficult situations. One of the primary vehicles for role-playing is the biweekly role-playing group. The actual situations frequently require assertive responses from the patient. We find the person's cognitions require modification more often than new skills need to be trained; but we are prepared to do either. For example, patients often resist making assertive statements because they believe they will insult or psychologically injure the other person. The community of patients provide an environment that may generate ''assertiveness situations'' and the staff emphasizes the importance of practicing the behavior changes in a role-playing situation first. Imagery techniques (e.g., cognitive rehearsal) are also helpful to overcome the generalization problems before the patient attempts to leave the hospital.

As patients gain an increasing understanding of what factors maintain and/or precipitate their depression, significant others may be involved in the treatment (Rush, Shaw, & Khatami, 1980). The nature of the patients' interactions may be reviewed, including their cognitions, followed by specific advice and training (see McLean, 1976, for specific types of interventions). Day and weekend passes facilitate the generalization on new skills and often provide valuable cognitive data not available because of the limitations of being hospitalized.

The prime therapist has the responsibility of coordinating the staff's and patient's efforts for generalization. Detailed planning is needed between the initial stress-reduction phase and the generalization phase. Once the patient begins the reintegration back into his or her environment, the therapist and patient must decide on a discharge date and follow-up plans. The inpatient stay is designed to return the person to a functioning level and not to do the crucial cognitive therapy work that will reduce the person's vulnerability for future depression. For this reason follow-up sessions are arranged to facilitate the transition to outpatient status and to alter maladaptive assumptions that are associated with the depression.

CASE EXAMPLE 3

Mr. C. was a 53-year-old man, married for four years, and employed as a construction supervisor. His first wife, with whom he had three children (ages 30, 28, 27), had died of cancer 14 years previously. He had no previous history of depression or other major psychological problems. Suddenly and unexpectedly he made a serious suicide attempt by shooting. He survived the wound and spent three weeks in intensive care before he was transferred to our unit. When Mr. C. was asked to detail his reasons for his suicide attempt, he pointed to "disappointments with business and worries about my wife's health" (he feared she had cancer). Symptoms and signs of depression were remarkably absent.

When interviewed, Mrs. C. described Mr. C.'s depression (apathy, crying, self-criticism) in the four months before the attempt. She corroborated his view that since his hospitalization his mood, thought process, and behavior were essentially "normal for him." The initial plan for the inpatient treatment was to assess Mr. C.'s risk for future suicidal behavior and then to review the problems that led to the attempt. His actual inpatient stay lasted ten days.

Mr. C. was asked to reconstruct the specifics of the situation in which he experienced his most severe depression. The therapist was careful to avoid the period leading to the suicide attempt, accepting the patient's statement that he was "confused and uncertain." We have found that a detailed understanding of the events and cognitions preceding suicidal attempts are valuable, but in the present care it was more important to effect some affective memories in Mr. C. Past experience with individuals like Mr. C. has taught us that their past cognitive style is characterized by emotional distancing. Thus, it was not surprising that he did not recall his "crisis." By identifying and responding to the person's cognitive set (e.g., "A man should keep his affairs to himself" and "Only weak types have feelings") the therapist can often get improved recall. Patience and empathy cannot be overestimated in these situations.

Once the therapeutic relationship was established (it took three hours to reach a comfortable stage), imagery was employed with instructions that Mr. C. try to remember the "pain and sense of hopelessness" along with the details of his actual situation. Mr. C. was able to recall a sense of "foolishness" and "deep despair" approximately two months before his attempt. The following is an excerpt of his report:

> I felt really isolated by the job. I was promoted over a year ago, but the impact of responsibility only hit me in November when I had to start layoffs [he was a construction supervisor]. I couldn't face the men and tell them they were laid off. I felt like a failure. I've never been able to hurt people. I felt I was letting everyone down. My wife married a "boss" and I was a weakling. I tried to put everything to the back of my mind, but by January the whole business was in shambles and I knew I was going to be fired. (Crying.)

This statement provided us with considerable material to pursue. What were the ideas behind his difficulty in "hurting people"? What criteria did he use to define "hurt"? What did he mean by letting "everyone" down? This excerpt also provides an example of some of the overgeneralized ideas and catastrophic predictions that are often associated with the depressed person's process of thinking (Beck, 1976). In theory Mr. C. explained that following his suicide attempt his employer had visited and expressed concern that he would take such drastic action. Mr. C. felt considerable relief from this discussion because his employer provided another perspective for the business failings, unrelated to Mr. C.'s difficulty. Furthermore, he praised Mr. C. for his decisions in the past. As a result of this interchange many of Mr. C.'s ideas about his business mistakes changed, his self-esteem was raised, and his mood improved. Thus, this disconfirming of his own negative ideas by his employer had a significant therapeutic effect, despite the fact that the business had suffered financial losses.

Inpatient therapy focused on three problem areas: (1) Mr. C.'s view of himself as a "boss"; (2) his view of himself as a "husband"; and (3) specific interpersonal skills related to anger in others. Mr. C. discussed his fear that others would "resent" his decisions and his own uncertainty in making a decision of which he wasn't "100% sure." It became apparent that Mr. C.'s attitude toward others was "If a person gets angry with me, it means I'm incompetent." Mr. C. and the therapist role-played many situations and discussed the implications of Mr. C.'s cognitions. Mr. C. began to realize that his perfectionistic attitudes resulted in excessive self-criticism and anxiety. A further consequence was that he kept his worries to himself without checking the perceptions of others (e.g., the business "failing"). Mr. C. was then seen for 12 outpatient appointments with the goals of modifying his procrastination as a coping strategy when under stress and teaching him decision-making strategies. His progress is summarized in Figure 3. A neutral observer would still consider Mr. C. to have a perfectionistic, obsessive–compulsive personality. Nevertheless, at one-year follow-up he had maintained a realistic self-appraisal, and the ability to discuss his "worries." He had also been depression-free during the year.

CONTINUITY OF CARE

The third problem area in the application of cognitive therapy to an inpatient population concerns the continuity of care. Working within an inpatient unit, especially a teaching unit, it cannot be assumed that all staff will hold the same orientation. Indeed, one view would probably be disadvantageous to the staff and patients. Nevertheless, the cognitive therapist must exert control over the treatment received by his or her patients. The conceptualization of treatment is a crucial aspect of cognitive therapy that needs to be communicated.

Meichenbaum (1974) discussed the importance of having the therapist and patient evolve a common conceptualization. One benefit is that the patient becomes an active participant and collaborator in treatment. Staff who offer premature hypotheses or speculations or who do not follow an experimental method of inquiry can do more harm than good. This problem is magnified in that an average patient in our setting has contact with at least seven members of the professional staff or students in the first week.

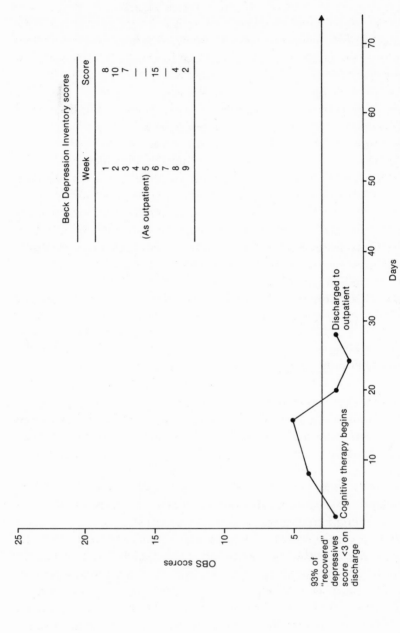

FIGURE 3. *Clinical course of Mr. C. as measured by the Observational Behavior Scale (OBS; Brawley, Lancee, Allon, & Brown, in press) and the Beck Depression Inventory.*

Once the patient is accepted for cognitive therapy, the therapist determines the priority of the problem listed with the patient and describes the structure of therapy (e.g., meeting times, homework, privileges). The patient is encouraged to convey information or thoughts related to the treatment, particularly those ideas that are negative. For example, one patient heard from another patient that "depression is genetically based and talking about it is a waste of time." He sought out one of the staff members who, in essence, agreed (not all of our staff are cognitively oriented!). Clearly, guidelines were needed to alert all staff to the importance of a common conceptualization for all treatments.

Because staff are potentially interacting with the patient 24 hours a day, communication among staff is important. We use the Problem-Oriented Record (Weed, 1968; McLean & Miles, 1974) to detail the homework assignments given to patients and the problems currently in focus. While some degree of flexibility is needed, we try to maintain the prime therapist's plan and not "sideline" the patient into other areas. For example, many of our patients present marital discord as a problem with depression (see McLean, 1976). We do not dispute the coexistence of these problems; but if the therapist and patient have a constructive plan to understand and treat the depression, intensive marital therapy is not undertaken nor suggested. Concise record-keeping and daily review of the patient's current problems facilitate the treatment and prevent "overthreatening" our patients.

The following case example is provided to illustrate the continuity of care with a multidisciplinary approach to cognitive therapy.

CASE EXAMPLE 4

Mrs. D. was a 31-year-old married mother of three (ages 11, 7, 2) hospitalized with obsessive and compulsive symptoms. The problem list included: (1) obsessive thoughts of death by infection; (2) compulsive behaviors such as excessive house-cleaning and personal-hygiene rituals; (3) angry outbursts; (4) family discord (her family could no longer tolerate her demands for cleanliness); (5) impulsive alcohol abuse; and (6) social isolation.

The primary therapist, a registered nurse with extensive therapy training and experience, was initially faced with a wide range of problem areas that increased during the first week of hospitalization. The other patients began to avoid Mrs. D. because of her rituals and inappropriate demands of them. Mrs. D. had been hospitalized at another facility where she was treated with ECT with little improvement.

The initial treatment plan included: (1) priority setting (her obsessive–compulsive behavior was first on the list); (2) cognitive assessment, including the completion of a "dysfunctional thoughts" log (Beck *et al.*, 1979); and (3) response-prevention exercises in two settings (in bathroom and in kitchen). The homework assignments were such that many different staff members (primarily nurses) worked with Mrs. D. She was encouraged to describe her goals and the treatment plan to new staff. Initially, she thought the responsibility of this communication was burdensome but in time concluded that she was indeed the person most involved in her treatment. The following vignette illustrates one intervention used with Mrs. D.

The prime therapist and Mrs. D. determined that a general area of concern was meal preparation. As a result the occupational therapist was asked to arrange a "kitchen assessment" with the following guidelines: (1) Mrs. D. agreed not to perform her ritualistic behavior. She was to report her thoughts out loud as she did various tasks. (2) The therapist insured the response prevention by her presence and discussed Mrs. D.'s cognitions during periods of tension. Interestingly, Mrs. D.'s thoughts centered on a fear of rejection from her family more than a fear of "infection." Examples were: "I hate housework but I have to do it. My family thinks I'm garbage. I just pick up after everybody. My husband said he'd never live in a dirty house."

When the kitchen assessment was completed, the occupational therapist noted a high level of anxiety (shaking hands, tremulous voice) as Mrs. D. left the area. She passed this information on to Mrs. D.'s nurse (the prime therapist was unavailable), who reviewed Mrs. D.'s cognitions about the assessment (e.g., "I've betrayed my family," "I did a terrible job"). Mrs. D. was helped to record this information in her dysfunctional thoughts log (she had started to keep the log the previous day). The nurse encouraged Mrs. D. to use the relaxation exercises aided by an audiotape of relaxation instructions. By the time Mrs. D. sat down for her biweekly session with the prime therapist, she had had three "success" experiences coping with her anxiety and preventing her compulsive behaviors.

Mrs. D.'s overall progress is summarized in Figure 4. Note that the therapy course was not a smooth one. In the early stages the prime

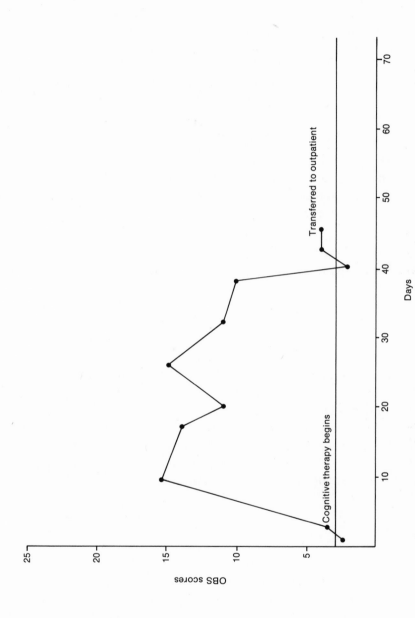

FIGURE 4. *Clinical course of Mrs. D. as measured by the Observational Behavior Scale (OBS; Brawley, Lancee, Allon, & Brown, in press).*

therapist found it difficult to communicate to other staff the importance of following the treatment plan. Hence a family assessment was associated with an increase in symptoms and a second "assessment" was again followed by increased symptomatology. While we can't assume a causal relationship, in this case we have consistently found that the timing of interventions is crucial. Treatment must follow rational decisions about priorities followed by behavioral observations as part of a feedback system.

The points to be stressed include:

1. the need for clear communication of the treatment goals;
2. the education of staff in the collection of cognitive data;
3. the importance of a central conceptualization; and
4. the view of the patient as an active collaborator in the therapy.

When we have difficulty with patient compliance in homework, we certainly review the patient's reasons for not completing the task, but we also review the possibility that we did not provide a "continuity of care."

GENERAL ISSUES

The three main problem areas, nonfunctioning patients, generalization, and continuity of care, have been discussed and illustrated. There are other practical considerations relevant to cognitive therapy with inpatients. These will be briefly presented. Please note these areas are presented as a result of clinical experience not empirical study. As a result, they are open to distortion because of the setting, population, and, most important, the author's information processing and recording system.

THE NEED FOR MULTIMODAL TREATMENT

Working on an inpatient unit demands that cognitively oriented therapists integrate their interventions with therapists from other orientations. We have stressed a problem-oriented approach that allows the identification of areas (e.g., the emotional disorders) where cognitive therapy is particularly useful. Nevertheless psychotherapy and psychopharmacology research is far from providing a detailed, empirical basis for practice. Depression, for example, may be best treated by cognitive therapy combined with pharmacotherapy. A variety of treatment approaches are needed because for any one patient we do not have predictors for the best type of therapy. It is likely that combinations of treatment in some yet unknown proportions will offer the greatest advantage (see Luborsky, Singer, & Luborsky, 1975).

THE NEED FOR A COLLABORATIVE TREATMENT

Therapist–patient collaboration as stressed by Beck *et al.* (1979) should not be underestimated. Inpatients, particularly elderly patients, may present a helplessness in their interactions with the environment that results in excessive assistance from staff. We become attentive when patients experience a decrease in stress while in hospital and obtain a sense of attachment. We begin to look for signs that the patient is fearful of leaving the hospital (the so-called dependency problem). We have found that patients who collaborate in their treatment from the beginning take greater responsibility for treatment decisions such as discharge and are less likely to become excessively dependent.

SELECTION CRITERIA FOR INPATIENT COGNITIVE THERAPY

Beck *et al.* (1979, p. 54), as one of the practical guidelines for cognitive therapy, stated, ''The amount of information that can be gained from the patient is practically infinite, but the amount of time and number of questions that can be asked is finite.'' A similar statement can be made about the availability of cognitively oriented therapists: ''The number of patients requiring therapy appears to be infinite, but the available *cognitively trained* staff is finite.''

We have found patients who are psychologically minded, of average intelligence, of average social skills, suffering from an emotional disorder, seem to respond best (i.e., earlier discharge, good follow-up contact). Initially, age appeared to be a factor (i.e., the older the patient, the less effective the therapy); but it now appears patients whose significant others are, or learn to be, accepting of the changes in the patient's style of thinking and relating have the best prognosis. Patients who have neurological problems, severe physical illness (e.g., terminal cancer), and addictions have as yet not been successfully treated with cognitive therapy on an inpatient basis; these results may be a function of our inexperience with such problems. Abnormal grief reactions, particularly prolonged reactions, have been effectively treated using the cognitive–behavioral techniques of Gauthier and Marshall (1977).

CONCLUSION

We believe it is worthwhile to employ cognitive therapy, either alone or in combination with other modalities with psychiatric inpatients. Some special considerations are needed and have been reviewed in this paper. While the present volume is designed to be a practical applied selection of experiences with cognitive therapy, it is essential that well-controlled outcome and process therapy studies are conducted. Inpatient units where knowledge, if not control, of extraneous variables is possible, should receive greater attention from researchers.

ACKNOWLEDGMENTS

This chapter was prepared while the author was supported by grants from the Medical Research Council of Canada (MA6370) and the Ontario Mental Health Foundation (777-79/80).

The author would like to thank the staff and residents on the psychiatric unit, tenth floor, University Hospital, for their active collaboration in this work. The work of Ms. Sally Groves on the preparation of the manuscript is greatly appreciated.

REFERENCES

Beck, A. T. *Cognitive therapy and the emotional disorders.* New York: International Universities Press, 1976.
Beck, A. T., Rush, A. J., Shaw, B. F., & Emery, G. *Cognitive therapy of depression.* New York: Guilford Press, 1979.
Brawley, P., Lancee, W., Allon, R., & Brown, P. A simple method of monitoring behavior change in the ward. *Research Communications in Psychology, Psychiatry and Behavior,* in press.
Coyne, J. C. Toward an interactional description of depression. *Psychiatry,* 1976, *39,* 28–40.
Feighner, J. P., Robins, E., Guze, S. B., Woodruff, R. A., Winokur, G., & Munoz, R. Diagnostic criteria for use in psychiatric research. *Archives of General Psychiatry,* 1972, *26,* 57–63.

Friedman, A. S. Interaction of drug therapy and marital therapy in depressed patients. *Archives of General Psychiatry*, 1975, *32*, 619–637.

Gauthier, J., & Marshall, W. L. Grief: A cognitive–behavioral analysis. *Cognitive Therapy and Research*, 1977, *1*, 39–44.

Lazarus, R. S., & Launier, R. Stress-related transactions between person and environment. In L. A. Pervin & M. Lewis (Eds.), *Internal and external determinants of behavior*. New York: Plenum, 1978.

Lester, D. *Why people kill themselves*. Springfield, Ill.: Charles C. Thomas, 1972.

Luborsky, L., Singer, B., & Luborsky, L. Comparative studies of psychotherapies. *Archives of General Psychiatry*, 1975, *32*, 995–1007.

McLean, P. D. Depression as a specific response to stress. In I. G. Sarason & C. D. Spielberger (Eds.), *Stress and anxiety* (Vol. 3). Washington, D.C.: Hemisphere, 1976.

McLean, P., & Miles, J. E. Evaluation and the problem-oriented record in psychiatry. *Archives of General Psychiatry*, 1974, *31*, 622–625.

Meichenbaum, D. Self-instructional methods. In F. H. Kanfer & A. P. Goldstein (Eds.), *Helping people change*. New York: Pergamon Press, 1974.

Minuchin, S. *Families and family therapy*. Cambridge: Harvard University Press, 1974.

Rush, A. J., Shaw, B. F., & Khatami, M. Cognitive therapy of depression: Utilizing the couples system. *Cognitive Therapy and Research*, 1980, *4*, 103–113.

Schless, A. P., Schwartz, L., Goetz, G., & Mendels, J. How depressives view the significance of their life events. *British Journal of Psychiatry*, 1974, *125*, 406–410.

Shaw, B. F. Comparison of cognitive therapy and behavior therapy in the treatment of depression. *Journal of Consulting and Clinical Psychology*, 1977, *45*, 543–551.

Shaw, B. F. Depression and stress: A cognitive perspective. In R. W. J. Neufeld (Ed.), *Psychological stress and psychopathology*. New York: McGraw-Hill, in press.

Weed, L. L. Medical records that guide and teach. *New England Journal of Medicine*, 1968, *278*, 593–600.

COGNITIVE THERAPY WITH CHILDREN

Raymond A. Di Giuseppe

INTRODUCTION

In the field of child psychotherapy, cognitive-behavior therapy is the new kid on the block. Nobody knows much about him and his skills are unproven. Little research exists corroborating the effectiveness of cognitive-behavior procedures with children and the clinical literature fails to provide as comprehensive a system of cognitive-behavior therapy with children as exists with adults. The treatment approaches described in the cognitive literature have either been limited to specific clinical population (i.e., hyperaggressive children) or designed for preventive purpose with nondisturbed populations. This chapter will attempt to highlight some of the key problems a cognitive-behavior therapist faces when working with a broad range of children as well as some solutions to these problems. It is therefore assumed that the reader is already familiar with the basic theories and techniques in cognitive-behavior therapy (Beck, 1976; Ellis, 1962, 1977a; Meichenbaum, 1977; Spivack, Platt, & Shure, 1976).

ASSESSMENT

Good assessment is invaluable in designing a cognitive–behavioral treatment program for children. Its importance as an initial step *and as an ongoing factor* cannot be overstated. Parents often do not provide

Raymond A. Di Giuseppe. Hofstra University, Hempstead, New York, and Institute for Rational–Emotive Therapy, New York, New York.

complete information about or even all the problems of a child when treatment begins. They may withhold mention of family conflicts simply because they do not see a connection between the discord and the child's problems. Or, they may feel too guilty, perhaps too embarrassed, to bring up parts of the child's behavior. On the child's part, the self-disclosure so vital to the assessment stage may not be sufficiently present in the personal repertoire to allow for speaking openly. Thus, months may go by before a therapist learns that a child is encopretic or school-phobic or that the father and the child do not speak to each other.

The optimal product of assessment, then, is a flexible conceptualization of the child's problem, that is, one that can change when new information presents itself. This approach sensitizes the therapist to incorporate treatment strategies as indicated. In addition, an ongoing assessment process quite naturally underscores successes achieved during treatment. Now its usefulness has doubled—it is further motivating the parents and the child; and even tripled—it is providing quality control information to the therapist.

DATA FOCUS

The following areas are recommended for inquiry in a thorough cognitive–behavioral assessment of children's problems. Not all this information needs to be assessed before an intervention is started. The more that is attained, however, the greater the likelihood the therapist will design an effective treatment program.

1. The first task is to specify the target behavior. Referrals for children often include vague comments, such as "acts out in school" or "has temper tantrums." Therapists are urged to get a clear description of exactly what behaviors comprise the summation each time. Thus, "acting out in school" can be redefined as the child gets out of his or her seat, talks to other children, makes paper airplanes, daydreams at least half of the time. "Has temper tantrums" may mean that the child cries, stamps his or her feet, throws whatever is nearby, yells at the top of his or her lungs.

Once the target behavior is thoroughly detailed, its frequency and rate of occurrence must be accurately monitored. It is equally important to identify what eliciting stimuli precede the target behavior as well as the consequences that the behavior itself elicits. For example, the child begins to cry when his or her wishes are thwarted; and at the tantrum stage the parents capitulate. Each target behavior may be maintained by independent cognitive and environmental factors. Specificity allows a more precise matching of techniques to problems and situations.

In assessing behavior, therapists are advised to seek information from as many persons as possible, especially if the problem includes behavior outside the home. When the referral involves a school-related problem, information obtained from parents, obviously secondhand, is far less useful than reporting by those who directly observed the behavior.

2. A functional cognitive analysis as described by Meichenbaum (1977) is the next step. Just exactly what thoughts are in the child's head as the target behavior is being performed? Are there self-statements? Images? Does the child guide the behavior by language? Keep in mind, too, that the absence of reported self-statements can be as important as the presence of maladaptive ones. Children with impulse-control problems may lack self-instructions as a mediator of inhibition responses (Kendall, 1978). Anxiety and depressive disorders may exist because the child has no coping self-statements to help deal with provoking incidents (Meichenbaum, 1977).

3. Therapists are advised to assess early each child's interpersonal problem-solving skills as these frequently figure in children's emotional adjustments. Research has identified two social problem-solving skills as most important in maintaining adjustment: (a) alternative solution thinking, or the ability to generate a number of solutions to a social problem; and (b) consequential thinking, or the ability to predict the social consequences of one's behavior (Spivack & Shure, 1975). Given the importance of these skills and the usefulness of problem-solving therapy techniques in the reduction of children's behavior disorders, this area should be assessed for a full picture of the child's cognitive functioning.

The skills in question can be assessed by having the child make up stories, as in the Thematic Apperception Test. As a problem arises in a story the therapist asks what solutions the child can think of to solve it. The child's responses will indicate the degree of alternative solution thinking. Consequential thinking skills can be elicited at a point where people in the story interact. Now the therapists asks the child to speculate on the reactions of the people involved. Apart from storytelling techniques, questions eliciting alternative solutions and consequential thinking can quite easily be put to the child during discussions of specific problems.

During assessment therapists should also be watchful for distorted perceptions of reality, statements the child makes about him- or herself or others that reflect unrealistic or incorrect views of the world. Errors in logic such as arbitrary inference, selective abstraction, or overgeneralization (Beck, 1976) are quite common in a child's thinking. This category of cognitive distortions would include statements that are contradicted by available data—for example, "My mother doesn't love me," "I'm stupid," "None of the other children play with me," and "No one will ever like me."

4. The assessment is not complete without investigation of the child's evaluation of personal experiences. What do the eliciting stimuli mean to the child? What value do the consequences of the behavior have? What importance does the child attach to events and people? Are these evaluations logical and rational or excessive? Note that cognitive distortions of this type do not involve thoughts that can be challenged or disputed on empirical grounds. These types of errors would fall under Beck's description of minimization / maximization errors of thinking or Ellis's irrational beliefs. In both conceptualizations such distortions reflect an exaggeration of the importance of certain elements for the child.

No evidence indicates which of the above factors are most important in the development or maintenance of various childhood behaviors or which are best stressed in treatment design. Research has focused on each of the five areas independently and there has been little, if any, collaborative or contrasting research. My hypothesis, borrowed from Lazarus (1976), is that the more modalities a therapist investigates and subsequently works in, the greater the chance for attaining behavior change and the longer lasting that change. Also, by acquiring data on all modalities the therapist can determine which modalities have deficits.

UNTANGLING THE REFERRAL

Children are often unwilling consumers of mental-health services. They arrive for therapy because they are viewed as disturbed by someone else or disturbing to someone else. The manner of referral often seems hostile or, at best, unpleasant to the child. If left unattended, it will have a braking effect on collaboration with the therapist.

The first question a therapist would do well to ask is, "Does the child know and understand the reason for the visit?" Many children report not knowing why they have come to my office. Some think, because they are coming to a doctor's office, it is for some sort of a checkup. Others see themselves as crazy, or bad. They reason: Bad kids in class are sent to the school psychologist, or on television "shrinks" only help crazy people. The initial task for the cognitive-behavior therapist then is to dispel these misconceptions and replace them with accurate information. Explanations about the role of the therapist and the process of therapy need not be complicated. I have found the simpler my presentation, the more likely it will be accepted. Following is a transcript showing how the issue might be resolved:

> THERAPIST: Johnny, I'm a psychologist. Do you know what that is?
> JOHNNY: Oh! No. Well, a kind of doctor for crazy people?
> THERAPIST: Well, that's not totally true. Psychologists are doctors who study how people learn things. And psychologists help people learn things they have been unable to learn. For example, some children have trouble learning to read. And psychologists help them learn to read better. Other children are sad or scared. They haven't learned not to be unhappy or afraid. Psychologists help them learn not to feel that way. We help children with other problems too, like anger, bed-wetting, making friends, and lots of things they don't know how to do. Do you understand that?
> JOHNNY: Yes.
> THERAPIST: Well, what problem do you think I can help you with?

Note that first a problem-solving tone is set, and second, the participants' roles are clearly defined. The child is not mislead into thinking the therapist is another friend to play with. Such deceptions are unfortunately common, and while not done with malice, a tragic result could be the eventual loss of the child's trust.

Problem ownership may present another difficulty stemming from the nature of the referral. The therapist must decide exactly who has the problem. Perhaps it is not the child at all! Two short vignettes may illustrate this.

> Mr. and Mrs. S. sought help about their children's behavior. Mrs. S. had been married twice before and the three children were the product of these previous unions. Mr. S. had no previous marriage and no children. During the two years of their marriage Mr. and Mrs. S. fought frequent-

ly about the children. Mr. S. viewed them as "destructive, unkempt barbarians." He complained they talked too much, ate too much, played too roughly, and spoke too loudly. Mrs. S. felt angry at her husband and enforced rigid rules and harsh penalties to avoid his wrath.

A total assessment involved a behavior analysis, psychological testing, and family and individual interviews. It revealed that the older daughter had mild learning disability and considerable social anxiety, and that one of the sons was encopretic and had some minor school difficulties; the other son displayed no behavioral problems at all. The children's behavior at home, which Mr. S. complained about most vehemently, appeared to be quite normal. The problem seemed more to lie in Mr. S.'s low frustration tolerance and low anger threshhold and Mrs. S.'s unassertiveness with her husband. The therapist made attempts to change some of the children's behavior (i.e., the encopretic behavior); however, most of the interventions were aimed at the parents.

Mr. and Mrs. N. were an upwardly mobile family with rather permissive child-rearing practices. Their 5-year-old son William attended a special daycare program and nursery school. The school encouraged Mr. and Mrs. N. to seek help for William since he was "intolerable and constantly fighting with the other children." Mr. and Mrs. N. had no such problems with William at home. While their son frequently attempted to test the limits placed on him, he was well-behaved and intellectually precocious.

William was placed in a children's group in my office to observe his interactions with peers and to assess his ability to follow instructions by adults other than his parents. While the youngster was restless and somewhat uncooperative in the first session, he quickly became accustomed to the group and the leader. He presented no behavior problems after the second session.

Contact with the school revealed an inexperienced first-year teacher who was easily frustrated when children acted out. More important, the teacher punished William in a most revealing way: He was sent to the program director's office for "special talks." William reported these experiences as more enjoyable than punitive, probably because there was more intellectual stimulation in the special talks than in the classroom. By helping the adults change these behavioral contingencies, William's inappropriate behavior in school was eliminated.

In situations where the problem lies outside the child, the therapist can be caught between changing what the adults wish and changing what appears to be in the best interest of the child. In both the above cases I experienced considerable difficulty convincing the "grownups" of the treatment plan. It might have been easier to change the behavior the parents or school had identified as deviant but to do so could have had iatrogenic consequences for the child. If in the first case mentioned the child perceived their behavior as normal and their stepfather's behavior as oppressive, then action on my part to change the children could have undermined their correct cognitions and taught them to believe in an incorrect view of reality.

The bottom line for the therapist then is: Who is my client? Is it the parents who pay my bill? The school that sends me referrals? Or, the child? Failure to always identify the child as your primary client will prevent you from challenging parents and schools when their views of the child are erroneous and detrimental.

GROUNDWORK FOR SELF-DISCLOSURE

Once the child has learned the appropriate roles and has more realistic expectations about therapy *and* the therapist has verified that the problem resides in the child and not in the environment, the child's ability to self-disclose will need special nurturing. Self-disclosure about the private, personal details of thoughts and actions typically occurs in children only with or in the presence of their parents. Indeed, children are often specifically discouraged from such self-disclosing to strangers. The roots of self-disclosure lie in rapport and trust. Three strategies are recommended.

1. *Don't be all business.* If your initial expectations are too high, the child may find the sessions aversive and then just not talk to you. Allow the child some time to get acquainted with you through play and off-task conversation. Shaping can be used to develop the self-disclosure and on-task conversation required in therapy.
2. *Always be honest with the child.* Children are more cautious than adults, probably because they are more vulnerable. They appear to be sensitive to deception, which they use as a measure of a person's trustworthiness.
3. *Go easily and carefully on the questions.* Children do not trust those who try to give them "the third degree."

In the initial session it is best to tell the child exactly what information you as therapist have. It has been my experience that such honesty results in open communications rather than the child's denial of the symptoms and resistance to therapy. In a recent case the parent complained of a child who was angry and aggressive, had frequent temper tantrums, and was unresponsive to any attempts to talk about these behaviors. The parents were sure that the child would not speak to anyone and the mother and father came alone to recount the child's misdeeds. When I first met the child my opening remarks consisted of telling him of my conversation with his parents and their story of his misdeeds and asking him for his position. He immediately embarked on a long conversation on why he disagreed with them and described what he actually did. At that point we were already engaged in cognitive therapy, discussing the child's perceptions of the events. *It is my specific recommendation that therapists do not start their relationships with children by asking questions.* Children may be small but they are not dumb. Once they realize why they have been brought to your office, they know that their parents have told the doctor what they are supposed to have done or that the parents have made some complaints about them. Therefore, it is unwise for the therapist to feign ignorance.

Children already in treatment are similarly sure you have the most current damaging information about them—also from their parents. Convinced that the therapist has already heard about his suspension, the child is more than uncomfortable with a parry such as, "Well, Johnny, how was school this week?" The child grasps for reasons for your pretending. "Is this a trap?" The style of questioning is flagrantly deceptive and children know it. A better opening line might be "Johnny, your mom told me that you got suspended from school today and she is really upset about it. What's your side of the story?"

The rule of not asking what you already know also applies when a child has been rightly charged with a transgression. The inquiry, "Johnny, did you take money from your mother's pocketbook?" (when you know that the cash was indeed found in his schoolbag) is an approach that burdens the child with confession. In the past the child has probably been reinforced for lying, having found that crime does indeed pay and denial of wrongdoing has previously worked. Now, in addition, the child may well be fearful of losing the therapist's approval by admitting to the transgression. Given these preceptions, most children will lie. The lie completes the cycle of distrust and deceit between the therapist and the child. Rather than chance such an interaction, it appears better to openly admit all facts: "Johnny, your mother called me this afternoon very upset. She said that she found some missing money in your schoolbag.'' This strategy allows the child to discuss rather than deny and to experience the therapist as an accepting person.

Another frequent error is asking the child the same question repeatedly. Therapists may find themselves drawn to do this when a child does not self-disclose or when they have formed a hypothesis about the behavior and are fishing for data to confirm it. A young patient who had previously been hospitalized for a suicide attempt discussed her interviews with a hospital therapist: ''The doc asked me four times if I heard voices; not once, four times! Then she came in the next day and asked me again. Every day she came in and asked me the same question over and over. Not only does she think I'm crazy, she thinks I'm a liar as well.'' Children are often very perceptive to such redundancy and will readily interpret it as distrust toward them or as incompetence on the part of the therapist. It is difficult at any age to trust a person perceived as mistrusting in return or as unworthy of trust in the first place.

ESTABLISHING ALTERNATIVES AND ATTITUDES

Since children are not self-referred they may be unwilling to cooperate in the behavior-change process. The decision to collaborate in the therapy depends on the presence of two beliefs: (1) Change is possible; and (2) change is desirable. When these beliefs are not present the therapist is advised to work on establishing them.

ALTERNATIVE SCHEMA

The inability to perceive an alternative behavioral or emotional response to the troublesome situation keeps the child from recognizing even the possibility of behavior change. For example, most children have few words for emotions and it is this narrow vocabulary that limits their ability to conceptualize situations. Recently, while discussing a child's depressed reaction to the withdrawal of some of her privileges, I made the suggestion that she could have thought or felt differently about the situation than she did. The child responded, ''What's the matter with you? Do you want me to be happy about it?'' The child only conceptualized happy or sad as possible reactions. Frequently children's schema of emotional reactions are dichotomous and are limited to happy–sad or happy–mad constructs. It will be impossible to convince a child to change his or her automatic thoughts if the child believes the therapist wants him or her to be pleased with a situation that is obviously negative.

The first step in cognitive therapy with children, then, is to provide them with a schema that incorporates a continuum of responses and feelings and contains a vocabulary for these reactions. Through anecdotal reports, parables, self-disclosure, and Socratic dialogue the therapist leads the child to change his or her schema to incorporate a range of different emotions and social responses. It may be especially helpful to role-play various emotional reactions to situations, escalating response intensity so that the child perceives a gradation in reactions to the same event. Particular attention can be applied to having the child recognize changes in facial gestures and voice intonations that arise in the different role-plays. These role-playing exercises can be done with the child as the actor so that he or she can produce different reactions, and also with the child as the observer and the therapist as the actor so that the child can learn to recognize different reactions.

Another helpful aide in teaching the idea of a continuum of emotions is a version of the SUDS (Subjective Units of Discomfort Scale; Wolpe, 1973). Children can be asked to rate their reactions in a role-playing situation with the emotional response varying along a ten-point scale. For example, a child may be asked to role-play a situation where he or she gets ten points worth of anger, etc. The same thing can be done for depression or anxiety. The purpose is to get a wide range of ratings.

Recent research has found that the ability to generate alternative solutions to social problems is positively related to behavioral and emotional adjustment (Spivack & Shure, 1975). This stage of therapy is actually emotional education and social-skill training. Once the child can imagine and conceptualize different reactions, the therapist can help the child alter his or her emotional responses to situations outside the therapy session. Providing the child with such an education may take considerable time and effort. The reader is advised against assuming that a cursory discussion of emotions and alternatives will suffice. Several sessions and much redundancy may be required to expand the child's emotional and behavioral repertoire.

ATTITUDE ADJUSTMENT

It is quite common to encounter youngsters who are totally unwilling to change their behavior and who see any change as against their interests. The failure to see behavior change as desirable can be viewed as a deficit in consequential thinking (Spivack & Shure, 1975). The child is unable to perceive or predict the results of his or her behavior. In effect, the child does not believe his or her disturbed behavior has such negative consequences and may not see that more rewards and fewer punishments are possible for new behaviors. A deficit in consequential thinking is likely to coincide with a target behavior that has multiple etiological factors and with symptoms that are strongly reinforced or modeled by significant others.

If a target behavior is strongly reinforced, there is actually not a problem with the child's consequential thinking. A payoff is an incentive to continue a behavior! In such cases the therapist can rearrange the reinforcement contingencies. Behavioral assignments are an important component of cognitive therapy with children.

When parents are reinforcing inappropriate behavior, simple behavioral instructions to change the parents' behavior may not suffice. After all, the parents' disruptive behavior patterns may be long-standing. Or, the parents may be unable to change responses to the child because of their own emotional difficulties. Frequently, it will be productive for the therapist to focus several sessions on the parents themselves, identifying and challenging the distorted thinking that produces their emotional disturbance and resultant ineffectiveness with the youngster. Parents often need special help to relinquish old destructive responses and try out new ones that will reinforce desirable behavior in their child.

A more difficult problem occurs when parents actually model the behavior they wish the child to change. The child is handicapped by the double message. While the child receives penalties for engaging in a behavior, such as yelling and fighting, the people whom the child admires fight all the time and it may pay off for them. Thirteen-year-old Mike was referred by his parents for yelling at his family whenever a problem arose and he could not have things his own way. Mike was able to identify the automatic thoughts and irrational beliefs associated with his anger and could challenge these cognitions, but he was not committed to changing. His father behaved the same way and it worked for him. Whenever Dad was confronted with a problem he yelled and the family acquisced. Given the success modeled by his parent the behavior seemed "O.K." to the child. I have never successfully changed a child's behavior when significant family members behave similarly. The most helpful solution appears to hold family sessions that focus on getting all family members to change.

COGNITIVE POTENTIAL IN YOUNG CLIENTS

With the above issues well in hand, the therapist moves along to the crucial step in cognitive therapies, challenging or disputing the child's troublesome beliefs. Beliefs and attitudes can be changed by experience, modeling, or instruction. While cognitive therapists rely on all three strategies, it is the last, instruction, that takes up the bulk of the treatment session and is the most difficult for *both therapist and child to learn*. Not surprisingly, then, some therapists wonder if a child can actually benefit from a cognitive intervention. Specifically, they ask whether children have the intellectual ability to understand the process and reach logical conclusions. The answer depends very much upon the child. Intelligence and maturity greatly affect the ability of a child to reason. Therapy techniques may be best viewed along a continuum of procedures that can be used with children of different cognitive ability.

For children age 7 or below, who are still in Piaget's preoperational stage of cognitive functioning, simpler procedures are more appropriate. With this group therapists can utilize direct self-instructional training. The child's maladaptive thoughts can be replaced by more appropriate coping statements that will help the child manage a specific problem.

The following case illustrates the use of self-instructional training. Six-year-old Paula was reported by her mother as deeply depressed about her parents' divorce two years earlier. Paula's father visited the child every Sunday. When the visits ended Paula cried about missing her dad. Also, she cried frequently during the week, often giving the same reason. Coping statements were devised to help Paula ward off depression and crying. If she felt near tears Paula was instructed to say, "My daddy loves me and I'll see him next week." Using dolls and puppets the therapist played scenes where a father and daughter said goodbye and went away from each other. At each separation the child puppet used the coping statement and followed the appropriate behavior of no crying. Paula was then asked to take the role of the child character and use the coping statement in similar scenes. After only two sessions Paula's crying after her father's visit stopped completely and had not reoccurred at the three-month follow-up.

A disadvantage of the self-instruction technique is its low generalization, since coping statements are a cognitive skill that does not easily transfer to new situations. In the case of Paula, there were other situations that elicited crying as well and each was dealt with separately with its own coping statement. I have also used specific self-instruction to inhibit anxiety, anger, stealing, and fire-setting in young children of this age. Self-instructional training was the sole treatment with Paula. But there is no reason why the procedure cannot be used with other behavioral strategies such as extinguishing the response or rewarding more appropriate behavior. It is, in fact, advisable that such integration be done in all cases since such experience will strongly influence the cognitions in the desired direction.

Older children, who have passed Piaget's preoperational stage and are functioning in what Piaget terms the stage of concrete operations, are better able to reason. Their cognitions are more likely to change with more Socratic and didactic methods since their thinking is more logical. Disputing and challenging disturbing cognitions rely on critical thinking skills. It is erroneous to assume that children have such skills or that they value the rules of logic. While some children may be intermittently aware of the rules of inference, most will require some didactic teaching in how to think. Many children, for example, do not understand the difference between facts and opinions.

Children frequently fret when others make disparaging remarks toward them. They become upset when Johnny calls them stupid because they identify themselves as stupid. The cognitive therapist will focus on assessing the validity of Johnny's statement. Johnny's belief need not represent reality and the client is equating the truth of the statement based on the fact it was said or by whom it was said. This type of belief is one of the most common cognitive distortions in children's thinking. The therapist's job is to convince the child that regardless of the strengths of others' convictions, believing cannot be used as evidence for the truth or falsity of a hypothesis.

The therapist may also have to teach the child the importance of empirically testing hypotheses. This can be done by talking about ideas that people believed in the past but that we now know are different. For example, people once believed that the earth was flat and that the sun revolved around our planet, but through theory building and testing we know differently. Whenever the therapist tries to teach critical thinking skills or challenge a belief it is important to point out the benefits of critical thinking, repeatedly showing the child how these new reasoning habits can benefit him or her and will strengthen this new mode of thinking.

COGNITIVE STRATEGIES

Beck (1976) and Ellis (1977b) have focused on two types of cognitions that lead to emotional disturbances. Simply put, the first consists of distorted perceptions of reality, and the second, of evaluations about that perceived reality. When a client erroneously exaggerates the probability of occurrence and the degree of aversiveness, emotional disturbance will occur. For example, 8-year-old Linda sadly reports that the other children do not like or want to play with her. Linda's perception of her peers' feelings and behaviors may or may not be true. Compounding it destructively, though, is Linda's further belief that she needs the other youngsters' approval and that it is indeed terrible when they dislike her. The overall cognitive set is disastrous; the result is a depressed child.

Ellis (1977b) recommends a twofold challenge of such beliefs. The first set of beliefs can be disputed by asking Linda to engage in empirical analysis. Together Linda and the therapist can design a simple experiment to measure how children respond toward her after she asks them to play. The therapist has led the client to challenge that a specific event has occurred or will occur. The experiment will either support, weaken, or discredit entirely Linda's notion of being ostracized by the other children. Ellis labels this type of disputing empirical or inelegant.

It is important here, not only if the experiment seems to support Linda's perception of peer rejection *but also* when such a perception is partially or completely discredited, for therapist and client to continue on the second set of beliefs: the assumption that the event is so terrible. This is challenged by what Ellis calls philosophical or elegant disputing.

A third therapeutic strategy exists: Teach young clients problem-solving skills (alternative solutions) so that they come to believe they can avoid or cope with the event. In the case of Linda, I helped her think of alternative strategies to make new friends as well as accurately predict the outcome of these attempts.

No experimental evidence exists to prove which of these strategies or combination thereof is most successful. My own clinical experience suggests it is best to start with the simpler strategies, problem-solving and empirical disputing, even through the remaining strategy, elegant disputing, may be more prophylactic. The first two strategies usually provided more rapid symptom relief. The third, challenging basic philosophical assumptions, is difficult with children because of their less developed reasoning ability. Two recent cases serve as examples.

Curt, an articulate 12-year-old, was referred because of his difficulty with peer relations at school. Specifically, he became involved in a fight whenever he was teased. A cognitive assessment revealed that immediately after a taunt was tossed at him Curt thought, ''This kid doesn't like me—no one likes me—it's terrible not to have any friends.'' With the degree of aversiveness so exaggerated, Curt could match no other response to the teasing than a swing at his tormentors. He failed to conceptualize that this reaction only worsened his popularity.

The primary strategy was to teach Curt to develop a plan before fighting. First, he was to list the consequences of fighting. He would get in trouble, possibly be hurt, probably become more unpopular. Then he was helped to consider other responses and to imagine their consequences. He could ignore the behavior, or he could retort with a similar comment. Once equipped with situation-specific responses, Curt was led to challenge the idea that teasing meant someone didn't like you. He was asked to observe the behavior of other children and found that children tease each other frequently. The idea that someone doesn't like you is the same as no one will like you was also empirically challenged. Curt and the therapist drew a diagram of the friendships in his class. In the model some children had a more elaborate network of chums than others but no child came up a total isolate.

This treatment plan produced rapid behavior change. Well aware that 12-year-olds have an exaggerated belief in the need for approval, I avoided elegant disputing. No attempt was made to challenge Curt's belief that it was terrible not to be liked. Attacking this belief would have required considerable more time and effort. In my opinion the strategy would have been appropriate only if for some reason Curt could expect a great deal of unavoidable social rejection in the future.

Paul, a 10-year-old, displayed temper tantrums, specifically, yelling and arguing with his parents. A behavioral analysis revealed these behaviors occurred whenever his parents discussed an issue about which they held differing opinions, even if their disagreement was amicable. A cognitive analysis revealed Paul held two troublesome beliefs: first, that disagreement leads to divorce; and second, that he could not survive if his parents separated.

I asked Paul to set up an experiment to test his hypothesis that disagreement leads to divorce. He was willing to do so and we designed a questionnaire for this purpose. Paul polled his teacher and principal, several storekeepers, a police officer, and others about whether they decided to divorce every time they argued with their spouses. Paul found that disagreements were common in marriage and rarely resulted in divorce. His symptoms ceased.

This strategy would not have provided Paul with the coping skills if his parents did divorce, but that possibility was remote in this case. Most children strongly believe they need both parents. While this may not be true, it is a chore to change such a pernicious cultural belief. When a more practical strategy exists, it would be inefficient to spend time providing Paul with coping skills for an event that was unlikely.

There are times, however, when children are faced with unchangeable, unavoidable events that are undeniably aversive. In such cases the problem-solving or empirical disputing strategies will provide little relief and the best tactic is helping the child assess and accept the degree of risk or loss. Such a situation typically arises when significant others behave uncaringly toward a child. Some therapists try to protect the child from this awareness. Their therapeutic strategies may involve helping the child see the good qualities in the significant other or providing the child with a substitute relationship with the therapist. The cognitive therapist would reject these tactics and be concerned that the child perceive the situation accurately and develop coping strategies to deal with the stress.

The following case may illustrate this point. Junior was a 10-year-old boy referred by his school because he ran away from home and had been threatening suicide. In the initial session Junior said he wanted to die because nobody cared about him, especially his stepfather. Junior and I began to discuss the definition of caring and I asked him to describe how one could tell whether or not a person cared about you. Then I asked him to consider the people in his life and apply his criteria to each. In the course of a lengthy discussion Junior was able to compile a list of 12 people who cared for him. Junior's mood improved dramatically during this session. After reviewing the names he had written, however, again Junior became morose; his stepfather was not on the list.

I focused the next discussion on the stepfather and asked Junior to apply his criteria to him. The stepfather failed to meet Junior's expectations. He spent more time with Junior's siblings and at times said he loved his own son more. The therapist asked Junior to monitor his stepfather's behavior in the following days to verify whether or not it met the criteria. Several attempts were made to reach the stepfather but he refused to come in and discuss the issue.

At the next session Junior reported that his stepfather had indeed failed to meet the criteria and Junior drew the inevitable conclusion that Dad did not care for him. The therapist then focused on evaluation of this fact. The therapist was able to show Junior that he didn't really need more caring behavior from his stepfather and that life could be happy with such a deficit. This point was discussed in the subsequent sessions with the resultant lifting of Junior's depression and an improvement in his behavior at school and home.

CONCLUSION

This chapter has outlined some of the ways cognitive therapy can be applied to the emotional problems of children. While this approach is new and little experimental support for its effectiveness exists, it appears to be successful enough to warrant optimism and continued investigation. Many problems exist in translating cognitive techniques to use with children. The largest of these difficulties seems to be the therapist's underestimation of the child's abilities to reason. I have found that children can indeed think about their thinking. My hope is that we as therapists can help them think more clearly.

REFERENCES

Beck, A. T. *Cognitive therapy and the emotional disorders.* New York: International Universities Press, 1976.
Beck, A. T., Rush, A. J., Shaw, B. F., & Emery, G. *Cognitive therapy of depression.* New York: Guilford Press, 1979.

Ellis, A. *Reason and emotion in psychotherapy*. New York: Lyle Stuart, 1962.

Ellis, A. *Humanistic psychotherapy*. New York: McGraw-Hill Paperback, 1977. (a)

Ellis, A. Rejoinder: Elegant and inelegant RET. *The Counseling Psychologist*, 1977, 7, (1), 73–82. (b)

Kendall, P. On the efficacious use of verbal self-instructional procedures with children. *Cognitive Therapy and Research*, 1977, 1, 331–341.

Lazarus, A. *Multimodal behavior therapy*. New York: Springer, 1976.

Meichenbaum, D. *Cognitive-behavior modification*. New York: Plenum Press, 1977.

Spivack, G., Platt, S., & Shure, M. *The problem-solving approach to adjustment*. San Francisco: Jossey-Bass, 1976.

Spivack, G., & Shure, M. *The social adjustment of young children*. San Francisco: Jossey-Bass, 1975.

Wolpe, J. *The practice of behavior therapy*. New York: Pergamon, 1973.

THE APPLICATION OF COGNITIVE THERAPY TECHNIQUES WITH ADOLESCENTS

Richard C. Bedrosian

INTRODUCTION

Adolescents, like adults, suffer from symptoms of anxiety and depression. Clinical experiences indicate that many of the typical cognitive therapy techniques developed for adults can be applied profitably with teenaged patients. Nonetheless, the cognitive therapist needs to be aware of the unique difficulties associated with the treatment of adolescents. The purpose of this chapter is to suggest ways in which cognitive methods can be modified for effective use with younger patients.

For the sake of convenience, adolescence will be defined as the period that begins with the onset of puberty and ends with graduation from high school, at about age 18. Due to constitutional, psychological, and subcultural differences, the age at which adolescence begins will vary considerably across individuals. Similarly, some patients in their 20s will seem to share many of the attributes of their teenaged counterparts. The interested reader can consult an excellent volume by Conger (1973) for a broad overview of the psychology of adolescence.

WHO SEEKS TREATMENT?

As any mental-health professional who works with involuntary hospital patients can verify, psychotherapy with hostile or resistant patients can

Richard C. Bedrosian. Leominster Mental Health Clinic, Leominster, Massachusetts.

be a fruitless endeavor. Most adolescents do not voluntarily seek treatment. A concerned parent, school counselor, probation officer, or other member of the community generally refers the teenager for psychological treatment. Consequently, the first responsibility of the therapist who aspires to treat an adolescent is to clarify the nature of the presenting problem. It is advisable to conduct the initial interview with the entire family present. Haley (1976) offers a useful format for the first family interview.

It is not enough for the therapist to understand the nature and history of the adolescent's presenting symptoms; he or she should also obtain a clear understanding of the *context* in which the symptoms occur. Consider, for example, the adolescent who experiences symptoms of anxiety at school. The therapist should obtain a picture of the presenting problem from parents, siblings, and other significant persons in the adolescent's environment. The following will require answers: What is the significance of the presenting problem for the parents? How does the school see the problem? Are there disparities in the two viewpoints? Are the adolescent's social difficulties at variance with the social adjustment of the rest of the family, or is there a pattern of social anxiety among other family members as well? How has the family attempted to solve the problem in the past? How does the adolescent relate to his or her parents and siblings? Are there other problems in the family or in the immediate social environment that seem to exacerbate the adolescent's symptoms? Does race, religion, economics, or some other aspect of his or her background make it difficult for the adolescent to obtain social support in the school setting?

The therapist may decide in some instances against treating the adolescent individually. There may be a problem between the adolescent and authorities in the school, or the school placement itself may be inappropriate for the patient. Alternatively, the therapist may decide to treat the family as a whole, in order to correct dysfunctional interaction patterns in the home.

In some instances, ongoing family interactions either exacerbate or impede the rapid amelioration of individual symptoms. The therapist will then need to implement changes within the family system before he or she can help the adolescent with individual problems. A school psychologist referred a 15-year-old male for treatment because of the young man's academic underachievement, social isolation, and inability to control his anger. The therapist diagnosed the young man as suffering from a chronic state of depression, which involved low self-esteem, apathy, anhedonia, and a sense of helplessness. The initial treatment plan involved seeing the boy individually and utilizing the parents to help engineer mastery and pleasure experiences for their son. Somehow the parents found it difficult to follow even the most simple directives from the therapist (e.g., "Call me on Thursday at 4:30"), despite their evident concern for their son. Moreover, a series of violent arguments in the home, involving an 18-year-old daughter, disrupted the therapist's initial efforts to focus on the young man's school difficulties. It was clear that the son's individual problems reflected both pervasive lack of structure and a highly charged emotional climate in the home. Given the distressing conflicts that had become a way of life for the entire family, the therapist believed that the prognosis for the identified patient was poor unless other changes in the household could occur. Consequently, he began to work more closely with the parents, in an attempt to bolster their minimal leadership skills and to cultivate a higher rate of cooperation between them. For additional information on family interventions, see the subsequent chapter on the use of significant others in cognitive therapy, as well as the relevant texts by Papp (1977) and Minuchin (1974).

Perhaps since the developmental concerns of the adolescent, such as competence and sexuality, are often difficult areas for adults as well, parents are often "primed" to perceive problems in their teenaged offspring. The therapist may need to differentiate, therefore, between the adolescent symptoms and the distorted perceptions of parents or other family members. Consequently, the therapist's task in some cases will involve modifying the *parents'* cognitive distortions. For example, a highly perfectionistic business executive sought a therapist's advice about difficulties with his 17-year-old son. The businessman considered himself a failure as father, citing as evidence his son's failure to complete various household chores and his recent disinterest in attending family functions. Moreover, he was certain that the young man despised him and that his wife held him responsible for alienating their son.

The therapist, who had not met the young man, began questioning the parents about their son's overall level of functioning. They indicated that his grades were excellent and that he socialized readily with peers of both sexes. Neither parent worried about the use of alcohol or drugs. Their only complaint seemed to involve the young man's passive–aggressive avoidance of household responsibilities. Mother was quick to point out that she was far from dissatisfied with her husband's performance as a father. To her husband's surprise, she cited several vignettes that indicated that the teenager actively admired his father. Further questioning revealed that despite the recent tensions and the young man's extensive peer-group involvement, father and son still enjoyed a number of recreational activities together. It became clear to the father that the son's oppositional behavior, limited as it was to minor matters, was relatively normal for a teenager and that his concerns about parenting reflected his own perfectionistic tendencies. The therapist continued to work with the businessman individually and in conjunction with the wife, but never included the son in subsequent treatment.

Even when the therapist decides that it would be appropriate to treat the adolescent individually, the young man or woman may simply refuse to become involved in treatment. The adolescent who declines to cooperate severely constricts the range of therapeutic options. However, the therapist *can* elect to meet with the parents, in order to offer support or to conduct other interventions within the family. Moreover the therapist can always remain available to the family should the adolescent experience a change of heart concerning treatment.

COGNITIVE DISTORTIONS IN ADOLESCENCE: SOME COMMON THEMES

The theoretical framework underlying cognitive therapy holds that the pattern of dysfunctional ideation may be quite idiosyncratic to the particular patient (Bedrosian & Beck, 1980). Nonetheless, the cognitive distortions of adolescents often focus on a number of common themes. The sections below offer the therapist several potential leads for investigating the adolescent patient's cognitions.

PHYSICAL APPEARANCE

The physical changes that accompany adolescence are extreme and often disorienting to the individual. The adolescent growth spurt, which can occur at any time, creates wide differences in physical appearance among peers at any particular age level, particularly during the early teenage years. Likewise, the onset of secondary sexual development is extremely variable across individuals. Reactions to physical changes are quite idiosyncratic. One young man may delight in towering over his peers, while another may feel gangling and awkward. Similarly, one young woman may feel more "feminine" due to the onset of menses, while another may feel frightened and bewildered. Peer contacts, from the playground to the school showers, provide the opportunity for invidious comparisons and at times, public ridicule. Like their adult counterparts, teenagers often selectively attend to their physical deficits, real or imagined, and thereby make distorted estimates of self-worth (e.g., "No one could be attracted to me because my breasts are too small"). Even more extreme distortions of body image can accompany severe forms of psychopathology such as anorexia nervosa.

Sexual Identity and Sexuality

Most observers would agree that society in general and parents in particular do an incomplete job of preparing adolescents for the rapid onset of sexual responses that accompany puberty. Moreover, many adolescents are too inhibited to discuss their sexual concerns with responsible adults, while they may be quick to consult their peers, who often provide them with a fund of misinformation and distorted attitudes on sexual matters.

Any number of dysfunctional ideas can accompany masturbation, such as "It's evil," "It will damage me," or "No one else does this but me." Like their parents, adolescents sometimes find it difficult to reconcile personal or subcultural norms with religious mores, and experience guilt or anxiety as a result. One young adult reported that as a teenager she felt tremendous shame over masturbation, which she found extremely pleasurable nonetheless. Time and again, she broke her solemn resolutions to end the practice, and thereby intensified her sense of shame. Finally, the young woman went to confession with a youthful parish priest. Fortunately, the priest eased her conscience by telling her that masturbation was a common and natural occurrence. The teenager continued to masturbate, but no longer castigated herself for doing so.

On a broader level, teenagers are apt to hold distorted conceptions regarding what it means to be masculine or feminine. As alluded to above, the adolescent may focus selectively on physical attributes and suffer a certain amount of gender confusion as a result. Likewise, the teenager's perception of his or her "manliness" or "womanliness" can be based upon myths and stereotypes fostered by the mass media, parents, or peers. In some cultures, athletic prowess or physical courage are considered prerequisites of masculinity. Many societies and subcultures view academic or professional achievement as incompatible with femininity. The therapist should probe for dysfunctional beliefs that take the form of "I'll never be a man unless . . ." or "I can't be feminine if I. . . ."

Finally, some teenagers experience homophobia, which can be the result of all-or-nothing thinking. Thus, a young man who experiences one sexual episode with another male, or who fails to lose his virginity soon enough may then conclude "I'm a homosexual," and become anxious or depressed as a result.

COMPETENCY AND PEER STATUS

Adolescents in treatment may experience low self-esteem as a result of concerns about competency. Like their adult counterparts, some teenagers may make unrealistic and/or excessively stringent demands upon themselves. Parents and other authority figures often stimulate and maintain perfectionistic or self-punitive attitudes on the part of the teenager. In some instances, it may be necessary to modify the expectations of both the adolescent and the parents. Unlike adults, adolescents generally function in a social environment that does not offer a broad range of roles and potential areas of competency. Social reinforcement in the peer group can be contingent on attributes such as physical attractiveness and athletic ability, which may or may not be necessary for successful adjustment later in life. The peer group may reinforce some behaviors such as drug abuse and petty crime, which can exert a detrimental effect on the individual. On the other hand, studying, practicing a musical instrument, and other activities that can enhance the possibility of effective adult adjustment may offer the industrious teenager little in the way of social support from peers. In fact, the teenager may experience overt rejection from peers as a result of engaging in behaviors that are highly esteemed by adults. Moreover, events that adults view as rewarding may have little or no positive valence for adolescents.

One young man spoke of the day when, as a 14-year-old, he won first prize in the school science fair for an unprecedented third year in a row. He had fantasized that winning the award would bolster his status in the eyes of a young lady whom he idealized. Instead, as he left school with his trophy he saw her walking arm-in-arm with one of his more "street-wise" classmates. Thereafter he ceased to be interested in scientific pursuits and maintained a fairly mediocre school adjustment. He based his subsequent behavior on the assumption that it was all-important to achieve respect in the eyes of his peers, regardless of the opinions of adults.

Some teenagers become so discouraged about their ability to succeed in school, athletics, or other areas that they simply stop trying. By the time they reach treatment, these adolescents may seem apathetic or resistant when discussing their abilities, interests, or goals. The therapist should recognize that adolescents often respond to feelings of inadequacy by assuming a facade of defiance or disinterest. Gentle probing combined with an empathetic, nonthreatening attitude may be effective in eliciting the teenager's self-deprecating cognitions.

Success experiences in the natural environment seem to do more for low self-esteem than any interventions in the consulting room. The therapist who wishes to bolster an adolescent's sense of competence will need to investigate the relevant cognitions, the mores of the subculture or peer group, and the resources available in the environment. Consequently, it often will be necessary to become familiar with the appropriate agencies (e.g., Girl Scouts, YMCA, Police Athletic League, Catholic Youth Organization, Big Brothers) in the patient's community. With very rare exceptions, most young men or women can come to feel competent at *something*. Moreover, the therapist who actively inquires will find that even the most disadvantaged communities offer training and support for a wide variety of skills. The therapist can then work with the youth to facilitate increased mastery and socialization.

AUTONOMY AND CONTROL

Despite the physical or intellectual maturity that they may possess, adolescents are expected to submit to the controls imposed by an adult world. We ask adolescents to renounce sexual gratification, to postpone marriage and childbearing, and to abide by the rules of school and family. The young person who enters professional school, the armed forces, or a religious order must experience a more prolonged period of pronounced external control. On the other hand, most adults also expect adolescents to achieve increasing degrees of physical and psychological independence as they grow older.

It is no wonder then that the issue of autonomy can be a major concern for adolescent patients (and their parents). Some teenagers will respond in a highly emotional manner to adult limits (e.g., "Be home at 11:00") on their behavior, in part due to their own cognitive distortions. Some teenagers will perceive *any* adult control, however innocuous, as a major threat to their personal freedom. Other teenagers believe that adults see them as immature or inadequate and feel personally attacked when an older person attempts to set limits. Lastly, some adolescents who hold dysfunctional beliefs about fairness and justice may become upset and ultimately symptomatic in response to conditions at home or in school that cannot be changed. Writers such as Minuchin (1974) and Haley (1976) have theorized that extreme symptoms such as anorexia nervosa represent the adolescent's attempt to exercise autonomy in his or her family of origin.

Since many adolescents do not spontaneously seek psychotherapy, power and control issues are likely to surface quite early in their treatment. The teenager may view the therapist as another agent of the home or school, while distrusting the therapy situation as a result. The therapist must monitor the adolescent's interpretation of his or her actions by attending carefully to verbal and nonverbal responses and, of course, by eliciting the relevant cognitions (e.g., "You're trying to talk me into something," "You'll put me in a hospital if I don't do what you want," and so on) whenever the patient cooperates.

ALTERATIONS IN THE TREATMENT FORMAT FOR ADOLESCENTS

The Therapeutic Contract

Cognitive therapy proceeds most smoothly when a spirit of collaboration and a specific treatment contract exist between the therapist and the patient, whether he or she is an adult or an adolescent. Unlike adults, however, adolescents generally do not enter treatment with a clearly articulated set of complaints. Even the teenager with a fair degree of insight into his or her problems may need some time to "warm up" to the therapist and the whole notion of psychotherapy. Moreover, initially the therapist may not want to limit treatment to individual meetings with the identified patient. Consequently, it is frequently useful to propose a rather nonthreatening, time-limited arrangement to the adolescent, as illustrated in the following quotation:

> Now your parents (school counselor, etc.) are concerned about the way things have been going for you, and they feel there may be a problem that needs attention. You don't seem too happy about things either but you're not sure if you're the one who has the problem and I know you're not very pleased about coming in to see me. I can't read minds; all I can do is ask a lot of questions and try to find out what's going on with you, or with your family, and I'm not sure if I can help or how. I'd like you to come back to see me two or three more times, so I can talk to you and maybe to your parents. We'll see how we get along and if there are any problems we could work on together.

Note that the therapist's statement to the adolescent includes the following points:

1. He or she does not necessarily accept the parents' (or the adolescent's) account of the problem.
2. The adolescent is not necessarily to blame for the problem.
3. He or she understands and accepts the adolescent's negative feelings about treatment.
4. He or she does not pretend to be omnipotent or clairvoyant, but can admit to being confused or making errors.
5. He or she wants the adolescent to feel comfortable about treatment and has no intention of force-feeding therapy to an unwilling individual.
6. He or she will try to gear treatment to the adolescent's needs.

As the relationship grows over succeeding visits, the therapist can then propose a more symptom-oriented contract with the adolescent, provided individual treatment still seems appropriate.

One further aspect of the therapeutic contract deserves comment, confidentiality. The therapist should be familiar with state and federal regulations regarding the treatment of adolescents, as well as the implications of relevant court decisions on confidentiality and the rights of children. He or she should inform the adolescent that the contents of the therapy sessions will remain confidential under ordinary circumstances and that he or she will inform the adolescent in advance if any material is to be revealed to the parents.

ESTABLISHING RAPPORT

The treatment of adolescents requires a broad range of interpersonal skills on the part of the therapist, who must work to inspire trust and minimize apprehensiveness during the early interviews. The therapist can begin to build rapport by encouraging the patient to discuss his or her sports, friends, school subjects, hobbies, pet peeves, and the like. In discussing topics of interest with the adolescent, the therapist avoids a condescending manner, but also makes no pretense of abdicating the adult role. Teenagers will ultimately distrust a professional who approaches them on a peer level. If an adolescent finds it difficult to discuss his or her problems, the therapist may help to minimize threat in the interview situation by alternating symptom-oriented dialogue with periods of more informal conversation.

Since face-to-face discussions can be uncomfortable for some adolescents, the therapist may wish to include other activities as part of the interview. Card games and other competitive pursuits with adolescents can provide the therapist with information that could not have been obtained through other means. The therapist will find that some adolescents will discuss sensitive topics such as sex only over a deck of cards. In addition, games can serve as "projective" devices, in that they may reveal the youth's attitude toward competition, his or her ability to behave in a task-oriented manner, and so on.

At a later point in treatment, games and other diversions can serve as a foundation for therapeutic interventions. For example, a very shy and inhibited 15-year-old male maintained eye contact and displayed appropriate affect only when he and his therapist played blackjack or spoke about sports. As part of a program to encourage risk-taking behavior, the therapist subsequently placed a series of small bets with the young man on various sporting events and blackjack hands. A different sequence of events occurred in the case of a 13-year-old who over the course of several sessions had nearly convinced his therapist that he had no interests. One day the teenager walked into the interview with a beer-can collector's catalogue rolled up under his arm. After the therapist asked to see the catalogue and began to show some interest, the patient freely discussed his hobby. Later, the therapist explored the young man's belief that no one else could share his interests.

MINIMIZING CONFLICT AND THREAT

Once the therapist has established rapport with the adolescent, he or she needs to confront the target symptoms while minimizing unproductive reactions on the part of the patient. Parents and teenagers often engage in "mutual selective attention" in that they fight for control over a relatively insignificant matter such as hairstyle, dress, and so forth. In other families, behaviors such as smoking pot or dating unacceptable partners, which may reflect other, more significant difficulties and/or may pose minimal long-term danger to the adolescent, can occupy center stage for weeks or months at a time. Consequently, the therapist must model a different style of information processing for the young patient. In essence the therapist's *actions* must communicate the following to the teenager:

1. I can't necessarily condone your actions, so please don't ask me to.
2. I know that I can't control your behavior, and I don't intend to try.
3. I intend to separate my evaluation of you as a *person* from my reaction to some of your *behaviors*.

At times discussion of rather crucial topics such as suicide can lead to conflict with the teenage patient. The therapist may be able to focus on the relevant issues while avoiding an unproductive power struggle, as illustrated by the following vignette. A young man was admitted to an inpatient unit after he had attempted suicide by ingesting a quantity of Valium. Although he appeared depressed and apathetic, he participated willingly in activities on the unit. Whenever the clinical staff attempted to discuss the suicide attempt, the youth would become hostile and assert, "I'm going to kill myself sooner or later and there's nothing you can do to stop me." It seemed that the more the staff tried to discuss suicide with the young man, the more he expressed his determination to take his life.

The inpatient unit arranged for a consultation with a cognitive therapist, who agreed to interview the adolescent. The therapist found the young man to be cooperative and fairly communicative—as long as suicide was not the topic of conversation. The adolescent began to discuss his interest in films, an interest that the interviewer shared. The therapist and the young man swapped lists of their favorite films and shared their impressions of various directors. Despite his suicidal wishes, the patient did have vague hopes of a future career as a film director, which he disclosed freely. The therapist explored ways in which the young man might find out how to pursue such a career and touched on some of the dysfunctional cognitions (e.g., "The only place you can learn to be a director is Paris, and I don't speak French") that prevented him from making the appropriate inquiries. Notice that the discussion of films and film-making was hardly irrelevant to the issue of suicide, since it dealt directly with hopelessness, a major component of suicidal intent (Bedrosian & Beck, 1979), self-esteem, and apathy. The young man seemed to become more alert and involved as the interview progressed, but if the discussion drifted toward suicide, he withdrew into belligerent silence. Following the interview, the therapist recommended that the inpatient unit capitalize on the young man's interest in cinema by encouraging him to attend films, to select movies for his peers to watch, and to inquire further into a career as a director. He also suggested that someone *other* than the youth's primary therapist take responsibility for keeping him in the hospital until the suicidal risk diminished.

Even the most cooperative adolescents may hold a number of dysfunctional beliefs that lead them to feel intimidated in the therapist's presence. Some teenagers believe that the therapist can pry into their innermost experiences without their consent, while others may suspect that the therapist's goal is to obtain damaging information from them in order to report it to their parents. It is vital, therefore, for the therapist to give the youthful patient a sense of control over the flow of information in the session. The therapist should emphasize that he or she is neither willing nor able to read the teenager's thoughts. Questioning of the adolescent should proceed in the gentle, nonintrusive manner. When the patient balks at disclosing sensitive information, the therapist may respond by saying, "I know it's hard for you to talk about some things, so I'm not going to push you. You may want to talk about this subject sometime later on." Later in treatment, the teenager may well raise the issue spontaneously, particularly if the therapist has maintained an empathetic, nonpunitive position. On the other hand, the therapist who tries to stimulate self-disclosure through intrusive methods may arouse distrust and drive the adolescent out of treatment altogether.

STRUCTURING THE SESSION

The need for the adolescent to experience a sense of control over the structure of the interview was discussed above. The therapist should insure that even the highly passive teenager contributes to the agenda at the beginning of each session. As mentioned previously, the therapist can maintain rapport and reduce threat in the interview by alternating between task-oriented discussion and more informal conversation. Protracted periods of silence in the therapy session are counterproductive. If the therapist encounters frequent lulls in discussions with an adolescent patient, he or she should generate and test out a number of hypotheses. Some examples would include:

1. The adolescent is not sufficiently involved in treatment.
2. The treatment contract requires renegotiation.
3. The adolescent finds it difficult to disclose pertinent information.
4. The adolescent is troubled by a problem of which the therapist is unaware.
5. The adolescent is experiencing negative reactions to the therapist.
6. The sessions should be shorter or less frequent.

Adolescents may find it difficult to sustain intense self-disclosure and self-exploration for an hour at a time. Clinical experience indicates that adolescents make good use of shorter sessions (e.g., 30 minutes). If the therapist desires, he or she can use the rest of the hour for family meetings and other relevant interventions. Another option available to the therapist is to schedule shorter sessions at more frequent intervals.

The therapist can monitor negative patient reactions by attending to nonverbal cues during the session and by asking near the end of the interview, "Was there anything I said or did today that made you angry?" However, like adults, adolescents will not always be open about their negative reactions. Consequently, the therapist may unexpectedly receive a call from a parent informing him or her that the adolescent no longer wishes to be involved in therapy. Whenever possible, the therapist should arrange to see the adolescent one more time, if only to elicit the reasons behind the termination.

PURSUING LIMITED GOALS

Throughout this chapter, adolescents have been described as more easily threatened and less self-disclosing in the therapy session than adults. The teenage patient who experiences recognizable symptom relief may prefer to terminate rather than go on to examine additional life problems or modify more basic dysfunctional assumptions. Unless the individual is grossly symptomatic or poses a threat to self or others, the therapist should not attempt to pressure an adolescent into remaining in treatment. Individuals of all ages who end treatment on a positive note are more likely to make use of the therapist if a need arises in the future.

Even when the therapist correctly identifies a cognitive pattern that renders an adolescent psychologically vulnerable, he or she must wait until the patient decides to work on the problem. Unfortunately, motivation for treatment may reappear only when the teenager begins to experience symptoms again.

The following case illustrates the importance of respecting the adolescent's "latitude of acceptance" (Beck, 1976). A 16-year-old male suffered from severe anxiety in social situations, which led him to behave in a withdrawn, grossly immature manner. His rather intrusive, overprotective parents often behaved in a way that seemed to underscore their son's lack of self-esteem. The therapist divided his time between family interviews and individual sessions with the young man. While he worked to disengage the parents (particularly the mother) from their son, the therapist proceeded slowly but steadily to win the confidence of the identified patient. As the son grew more comfortable in the therapist's presence, he began to discuss his boredom and his alienation from his peers. Eventually, the therapist was able to use the Weekly Activity Schedule (Beck, Rush, Shaw, & Emery, 1979) to increase the young man's involvement in pursuits that gave him a sense of mastery and pleasure, such as playing hockey and going to the movies. The youth gradually revealed some of the dysfunctional cognitions that prevented him from socializing with his peers (e.g., "They'll think I'm a 'queer,' " "I won't have anything to talk about''). The therapist encouraged the young man to test out some of his beliefs, and used role-playing to improve the patient's social skills. To the surprise of his parents, the son began participating in intramural athletics at school and attended several sporting events with some of his male classmates.

Buoyed by the gain, the therapist then became more grandiose in his approach to treatment. He knew from the parents that the son had no social contacts with the opposite sex and felt extremely anxious around females his own age. The therapist decided unilaterally to make the heterosexual anxiety the focus of treatment. Despite the patient's reluctance, the therapist began discussing girls and dating during the individual meetings. The young man responded to the therapist's attempts to control the agenda by "clamming up." He subsequently lost interest in therapy and refused to come to the clinic any further.

The therapist should remember that distorted cognitions and other psychological problems can be corrected by an adolescent in the course of maturation, without the help of a professional. The adolescent has many years ahead in which to work out his or her problems, and over time, "corrective emotional experiences" can come from a variety of sources. The therapist, much like a parent, may have to be content to let the adolescent "leave the nest" and go on to learn from his or her mistakes, painful as they may be.

HOMEWORK

Adolescents are generally less compulsive or conscientious than adults in completing therapeutic homework assignments. Even the young man or woman who behaves in an enthusiastic manner during the interview may find it difficult to follow up on tasks assigned by the therapist between sessions. Since a low level of productivity seems to be the norm, the therapist must adopt flexible standards regarding the amount of work he or she expects from the adolescent between interviews.

The more straightforward, concrete, and finite (as opposed to open-ended) the assignment, the greater the chances of compliance by the teenager. Likewise, behavioral tasks, such as activity scheduling and behavioral experiments, have a greater chance of completion than more abstract assignments, such as recording dysfunctional cognitions.

The similarity between academic and therapeutic homework

assignments can stimulate evaluation anxiety, fear of failure, and other dysfunctional attitudes on the part of the adolescent. Consequently, the therapist should set up extratherapeutic tasks as "no-lose" situations for the patient. If the therapist makes assignments that demand proficiency in reading, writing, or other academic activities, he or she should make sure that the teenager has already mastered the skills required for the task; otherwise the youth will fail.

CLOSING COMMENT

One of the goals of the current chapter was to acquaint the reader with the special problems associated with applying cognitive therapy techniques to adolescents. Perhaps it was inevitable, then, that a good deal of the preceding discussion stressed the pitfalls and frustrations involved in treating teenaged patients. Nonetheless, many adolescents are capable of dramatic changes in the course of therapy, particularly if the environment is a supportive one. Because it is a direct, structured form of treatment, cognitive therapy offers a great deal of the mental-health professional who experiences a sense of challenge and excitement in confronting the problems of adolescence.

REFERENCES

Beck, A. T. *Cognitive therapy and the emotional disorders.* New York: International Universities Press, 1976.

Beck, A. T., Rush, A. J., Shaw, B. F., & Emery, G. *Cognitive therapy of depression.* New York: Guilford Press, 1979.

Bedrosian, R. C., & Beck, A. T. Cognitive aspects of suicidal behavior. *Suicide and Life-Threatening Behavior,* 1979, 9, 87–96.

Bedrosian, R. C., & Beck, A. T. Principles of cognitive therapy. In M. J. Mahoney (Ed.), *Psychotherapy process: Current issues and future directions.* New York: Plenum Press, 1980.

Conger, J. J. *Adolescence and youth: Psychological development in a changing world.* New York: Harper & Row, 1973.

Haley, J. *Problem-solving therapy.* San Francisco: Jossey-Bass, 1976.

Minuchin, S. *Families and family therapy.* Cambridge: Harvard University Press, 1974.

Papp, P. (Ed.). *Family therapy: Full-length case studies.* New York: Gardner Press, 1977.

COGNITIVE THERAPY WITH THE ELDERLY

Gary Emery

INTRODUCTION

The elderly have traditionally underutilized mental-health services, despite a higher-than-average incidence of emotional disorders (Eisdorfer & Stotsky, 1977). This situation exists largely because of neglect by mental-health workers and a skeptical attitude toward therapy by many older people. There are signs of a change as increasing numbers of elderly seem to be seeking counseling and therapy. Cognitive therapy, with its emphasis on the practical, has a number of features that makes it a particularly attractive approach for working with the aged. This chapter will provide some general guidelines for applying cognitive therapy to this population.

TREATMENT SOCIALIZATION

In order to carry out effective therapy with the elderly, the therapist must first become aware of his or her own distortions about this group of patients. Negative stereotypes of the aged abound in our society, and it is nearly impossible to avoid incorporating some of these beliefs. For example, it is not uncommon for therapists to attribute a younger patient's negative view of the world to his or her depression while attributing similar symptoms of an elderly patient to the belief that "old people just like to complain." Experience alone doesn't prevent this

Gary Emery. Department of Psychiatry, University of Southern California Medical School, Los Angeles, California.

type of negative stereotyping; those who work with minority groups are often the worst perpetrators of myths and stereotypes.

The therapist has to question him- or herself to discover whether he or she holds any underlying assumptions about the old that could interfere with therapy. Common dysfunctional beliefs are: "Old people can't learn new behaviors"; "The elderly are inadequate and need to be cared for"; "There is something inherently inferior about old age"; "They are going to die soon, so why bother?" Some assumptions can lead to task-irrelevant reactions such as "Society shouldn't treat the elderly this way." This belief can lead the therapist to commiserate with the patient, thereby blocking constructive measures. These assumptions are the other side of the coin and can be just as counterproductive.

By spending some time with healthy, well-functioning older individuals, the therapist can correct his or her own erroneous assumptions; and by maintaining a cognitive perspective on the patient's disorder, improve his or her ability to be task-relevant in therapy. The elderly person is feeling and acting as he or she does largely because of the way he or she is viewing his or her world, not because of some inherent quality of aging. From this perspective, it follows that the therapist's job is to help this person change those thoughts and beliefs that are maintaining negative feelings and maladaptive behaviors.

The older patient, particularly if this is his or her first course of therapy, will often hold misconceptions about therapy. The patient may feel that there is a stigma attached to coming for therapy or that it may indicate he or she is crazy and ready to be institutionalized. These beliefs are more likely to be present if a family member coerced the patient into coming. By careful questioning, the therapist can elicit these beliefs, and can correct them by being concrete and specific in explaining therapy. Many of these beliefs can be nullified by the presentation of therapy as an educational model: a systematic way to learn more effective ways to adjust to this stage of life. If the therapist is successful in socializing the patient into treatment, the problems caused by the patient's having been pressured into treatment can be overcome.

One of the purposes of treatment socialization is to teach the patient to label correctly the symptoms of the emotional disorder. (The therapist should refer the patient for a physical exam if there is any doubt about the nature of these symptoms.) The elderly patient often mislabels these symptoms as "signs of aging"; many perceive nervousness, lack of energy, sleep difficulties, appetite disturbance, hopelessness, and dysphoria as inevitable aspects of the natural aging process. This misperception may have been reinforced by others with whom the patient has come into contact. Throughout therapy, whenever the patient uses these symptoms as evidence that he or she is old and useless, the therapist can raise the point that these symptoms are also manifestations of an emotional problem.

DIAGNOSIS

The correct diagnosis of the elderly patient's symptoms is an important aspect of therapy. The therapist can keep the following points in mind when evaluating older patients:

1. The aged usually have a conservative bias about taking tests and are apt to give socially desirable answers. For example, they may underreport sexual concerns and problems with alcohol.
2. The elderly patient tires easily when taking tests. For this reason, test batteries should either be kept short or extended over two days.
3. The patient's emotional problems may be due to a physical disorder or to a drug reaction. These possibilities must be checked out. Because many elderly patients take medication without knowing its name or dosage, they are asked to bring in all of their medications at the time of the evaluation.
4. There can be a problem in separating depression from organic brain syndrome because the symptoms are similar. The Mental Status Questionnaire and the Face–Hand Test are good screening devices for detecting intellectual deficits associated with impaired brain function among the elderly (Zarit, Miller, & Kahn, 1978). Patients' complaints about memory are more often associated with depression than with impaired performance (Kahn, Zarit, & Hilbert, 1975).
5. The evaluator should inquire into the pattern and history of the patient's symptoms; the history is often more important than the symptoms. The therapist may obtain more reliable information on the developments, if necessary, from significant others.
6. Frequently, there are physical as well as psychological factors

involved in the etiology of the older patient's problem, and many of these factors are unknown (Eisdorfer & Stotsky, 1977). Consequently, the diagnosis may remain open until after a course of treatment has been tried.

THERAPEUTIC RELATIONSHIP

From the first session the therapist has to work to develop a collaborative relationship with the patient. A collaborative relationship is particularly crucial with the older patient who is skeptical and mistrustful of therapy. It may take time to develop this relationship; but if the therapist and patient move toward working together as a team for solving problems, such a relationship will develop.

The patient may have a set of beliefs that work against the establishment of a collaborative relationship. For example, he or she may equate being old with being inadequate and in need of care. The alteration of this belief in favor of development of the patient's self-reliance may be one of the treatment goals. However, it is important to clarify this issue between the patient and the therapist early in treatment. In addition to discussing this issue, the therapist can help by not trying to do too much for the patient. For example, one patient wanted to do some volunteer work with children. The therapist knew the contact person, but instead of making the call for the patient, he had the patient carry through with this on her own. There is evidence that trying to do too much for the older patient is counterproductive and even shortens the life span of the older person (Bloom & Blenker, 1970).

As therapy evolves, the patient takes an increasingly active role in setting agendas, generating solutions to problems, and designing homework assignments. The therapist can further counter the development of patient dependency by stressing that therapy is time limited and by contracting for a specific number of therapy sessions.

A therapist's low expectations of an older person puts the patient in a one-down position that can hamper therapy. Even if the therapist doesn't have low expectations, he or she has to be careful not to convey that impression. The therapist's tone of voice and manner of speaking to the elderly patient is one way this impression is often conveyed. In our society, the elderly are frequently patronized and told what to do rather than consulted. The therapist should speak to his or her older patient in the same manner he or she uses with younger patients. As a general rule, the therapist should address the patient by first name only if the patient calls the therapist by his or her first name. If the patient addresses the therapist more formally, this style should be reciprocated.

Gerontologists have found that the aged in Western societies are involved in a chronic conflict between stereotypes of the elderly as weak and incompetent and their own concepts of themselves as being active and competent (Thomae, 1970). Typically, the aged resolve this conflict by adopting more negative concepts of themselves. Another way they resolve this conflict is by forming negative attitudes toward those perceived as the source of this unfriendly stereotype. Given this situation, it is not surprising that many older patients enter therapy with the belief that in order to maintain their independence and integrity they have to fight the therapist and resist his or her suggestions.

The elderly patient's resistance may take the form of telling the therapist, "You are too young to help me." The therapist should avoid a power struggle with the patient and instead can say, "What do you think about taking an experimental approach toward this? We can try working on some of these problems together and see if we can get anywhere with them. If I don't seem to understand something because of the difference in our ages, please tell me and we'll work it out."

The patient may be self-absorbed and unwilling to let another person help with his or her problems. In these cases, the therapist can try to convey in a variety of ways the notion that "two heads may be better than one" in trying to solve these problems. For this patient, as with the overdependent patient, a therapeutic goal is to help the patient learn more adaptive ways of relating to others.

PROBLEMS IN FOCUSING

Many patients have trouble staying on a topic during the session, and the problem becomes exaggerated for some elderly patients. Some patients tend to drift from topic to topic, to globalize, and to exhibit a general difficulty in staying on target. In these cases, the therapist should listen intently to ascertain the patient's major problem areas. The therapist then sets a specific agenda for the session. When the patient starts to drift from the area under discussion, the therapist should not hesitate to bring the patient back to the topic. If straying from the task is a chronic problem with the patient, the therapist can begin each session by saying he or she will interrupt the patient whenever the patient wanders from the topic. By directing the patient to stay on target, the therapist not only makes the session more productive, but also helps the patient learn better concentration skills.

With patients who ramble, the therapist should try to make therapy as concrete as possible. The content of the session should be very specific. The patient can keep lists of what to discuss in the session, and homework assignments are written out.

BEHAVIORAL BLOCKS

A number of elderly patients suffer from a paralysis of the will that prevents them from initiating new behaviors. The decision to start therapy was probably a great struggle for them. The patient's lack of initiative is usually due to strongly held beliefs that any new activity is too difficult, fearful, or complicated, or that he or she is too vulnerable and weak to handle the task.

The therapist's job is to plant the seed of doubt that the patient's appraisal might be inaccurate, and to spark the patient's interest in trying a new activity. The therapist can use a range of cognitive–behavioral techniques to induce the patient to try some new activity, which includes:

1. setting up a test of the patient's hypothesis that he or she cannot perform the activity;
2. assessing with the patient what is to be lost versus what is to be gained by trying the activity;
3. breaking down the task into small steps that can be taken gradually;
4. cognitively rehearsing the task in the office first;
5. getting feedback on assigned tasks; and
6. teaching the patient to use self-instruction.

In addition to such techniques, the therapist's encouragement and expectations that the patient can do the new activity are extremely important.

An example of countering a patient's low activity level was a

72-year-old woman who sought treatment for depression. She had retired five years earlier after an active career as an associate editor on a newspaper. She had no children, and her husband had died three years earlier. One of the first goals of treatment was to raise her low activity level. She had enjoyed going to concerts in the past with her husband, but had not gone for several years. Two sessions were spent on inducing her to go to a concert.

The reasons that she gave for not going to the concert were that she couldn't go there alone and there was no one with whom she could go; it was too much of a bother to get tickets—they would probably be sold out, anyway; even if she went, she wouldn't enjoy herself. These ideas were set up as hypotheses to be tested out. During the therapy session she reserved tickets over the phone for the next concert, and she was able to call and ask a friend to go with her.

Through testing out her beliefs she discovered that she could still enjoy herself and that she still had friends with whom she could attend events of interest. This initial step helped eventually to bring her out of her depression.

Many of the older patients, like the woman discussed above, have in their repertoire adequate coping skills that are temporarily blocked by anxiety or depression. In such cases, the therapist's major job is to help the person reactivate these skills. With some elderly patients this process can occur rather rapidly. One woman, for example, came for treatment after her husband died. She said that her husband had supported her her whole life, and she didn't know how she could manage without him. After three sessions, the woman realized that she in effect had been running the family business for the last few years, and that if she would try, she could continue to operate it without her husband. After coming to this realization, her depression lifted and she required no further therapy.

DYSFUNCTIONAL THEMES

There are more similarities than differences between older patients as a group and younger patients. However, certain clusters of cognitive distortions and dysfunctional assumptions are frequently found among older patients. These maladaptive ideas and beliefs involve the aging process, lifestyle changes, health issues, and relationships with others. Each of these areas will be discussed briefly.

AGE-ISM

One of the most unfortunate aspects of prejudice is that the members of the prejudged group frequently begin to believe the negative judgments that others hold about them. The aged are victims of such a process. Further, as individuals grow older they are more inclined to adopt age-related norms, norms that are even more restrictive for the elderly. This tendency to adopt a negative attitude toward one's aging and more restrictive behavioral norms is often exaggerated in those seeking treatment. The patient may believe he or she is too old to have sex, to try new experiences, or in general to enjoy him- or herself. The therapist can help the person question some of these arbitrary beliefs and standards.

The arbitrariness of age-related beliefs is highlighted by the tendencies of some patients to drastically alter their self-concept after an age change that ends in zero or five. One patient believed that after a person turned 65, there was nothing else to do but wait for death. She functioned quite well up until her 65th birthday, at which time her belief became a self-fulfilling prophecy. She curtailed her activities and began to say ''no'' to life. Her attitudes created a vicious cycle—the less she did, the more inadequate she believed she was. The following dialogue illustrates one of the best ways in which the therapist helped her see the arbitrariness of her belief.

> PATIENT: As I told you, things have gone downhill since I turned 65.
> THERAPIST: How were you the year before you turned 65?
> PATIENT: Things were going all right then.
> THERAPIST: Well, then, actually you did well in your 65th year. After you turned 65, you entered your 66th year.
> PATIENT: I hadn't looked at it that way. But society says when you turn 65, you're old.
> THERAPIST: Well, *old* is a relative concept. Do you think there is a greater difference between 20-year-olds than between two 65-year-olds?
> PATIENT: Well, I guess between two 20-year-olds.
> THERAPIST: This is what researchers have found out: There are greater differences, both psychologically and physiologically, among older individuals.

The patient was eventually able to realize through repetition of similar dialogue that she had drawn an arbitrary line for old age, and that this judgment was bringing her more disadvantages than advantages.

Many of the elderly patients' automatic thoughts that precede their anxiety and depression are related to age-ism, that is, the belief that the old are inferior. Patients are taught to become aware of these thoughts and to supply more balanced interpretations. One woman, for example, was extremely anxious at social gatherings. She discovered she was having thoughts such as "People will think I'm trying to act younger than I am because I wear bright clothes." Later she was able to answer this type of thought with "I have no evidence that they think such things. And even if they do, I'm not going to wear dowdy clothes just to please them." This coping technique of answering her thoughts helped her control anxiety in a number of social situations.

At times the patient's dysfunctional thoughts related to aging are implanted and reinforced by others. For example, prior to coming for therapy, one 67-year-old male had consulted his doctor about occasional impotence. The doctor said he was "lucky" to have any sex drive at his age. As part of therapy he was given reading material on sex and the elderly that pointed out that while it may take an aging male a longer period of time to reach an erection, he can go longer periods of time without ejaculating. Further research indicated that the majority of married men have active sex lives up to the 75th year, and many men have active sex lives to the eighth decade and beyond. This educational approach alleviated his concerns.

LIFE REVIEW

Many people go through a period of life review as they move from one developmental stage to another. This retrospective tendency is frequently characteristic of the elderly. Problems arise, however, when a person abstracts selectively a negative aspect of his or her life from which he or she overgeneralizes to an estimate of his or her total worth as a person. When this distortion occurs, the person becomes in a sense stuck and has difficulty moving on to the next life-stage.

A good example of this process was the case of a 68-year-old male who was treated for depression. His depression was precipitated by his conclusion that his life was a total failure. Over several sessions he revealed this self-appraisal was based on his belief that he had been a terrible husband. His wife had died several years earlier. The major reason he believed he was a bad husband was that once during a fight he had hit his wife and she had required hospitalization. This issue had to be discussed numerous times before the patient was able to reappraise his judgment. He finally realized that his marriage was basically a good one, and that his role of husband was only one of the many roles he had filled in his life. He also came to the conclusion that he had paid enough for this one incident in terms of his own suffering and that any further guilt over it would serve no purpose. This issue was at the center of his depression and once he resolved it his depression lifted.

ADJUSTMENT REACTION

Growing older requires making a number of real adjustments and while many personal resources are diminishing, society continues to change and place new demands on individuals. Many of the elderly patients have problems in making lifestyle changes. Thomae (1970) has developed a framework for successful age adjustment that has implications for cognitive therapy.

Thomae postulates that a person's *perception* of growing older rather than any internal (biological) or external (social) objective change determines the mode of adjustment to aging. He cites a number of longitudinal studies in support of this position. For example, how a person perceives retirement in the years prior to retirement is significantly correlated with adjustment to retirement. If a person perceives retirement as a negative experience, he or she is likely to have a negative adjustment. And while researchers have found a clear evidence of the relevancy of health and economic issues to retirement, the perceived quality of the situation is more often correlated with actual adjustment behaviors.

Thomae's second postulate is that a person perceives his or her aging in terms of his or her dominant concerns and expectations. The satisfaction or frustration of these dominant concerns accounts for the motivational aspect of adjustment to aging. His third and final postulate is that successful adjustment to aging is related to a balance between a person's cognitive structure (how he or she perceives the situation) and the motivational structure (what the person wants). To support this he cites research studies that find workers' successful retirement is related to a high degree of congruence between achieved and desired goals.

Thomae writes that achieving this balance must be done by "a restruction of the cognitive schemata defined 'desired' or 'achieved' goals or it must be achieved by continuation of active work." (p. 10) Because of the internal and external limitations placed on the older individual, he or she has to maintain this balance mainly by altering his or her cognitive system. In line with Thomae's model, a therapist with skills in helping a person correct cognitive distortions and change dysfunctional thinking could play a key role in a person's adjustment to old age.

Most of the elderly patients with adjustment problems are misperceiving the situation; they overgeneralize, jump to conclusions, see the situation in black or white terms, tune out positive factors, and tend to put the worst possible construction on the situation. In addition to helping the person recognize and change these thoughts, the therapist can help the patient in another way to maintain a balance between desired and achieved goals. This process involves helping the person extend his or her concept of self. Through identification with children and grandchildren, the patient can learn to equate children's and grandchildren's economic and occupational achievement with his or her own. The patient can also extend him- or herself in a similar way to identify with the achievement of a social group or movement and with mankind in general.

PRACTICAL PROBLEMS

The therapist does not want to be or appear to be Pollyannish about the older patient's concerns. The aged in our society face numerous real problems: loss of income, serious health problems, such as loss of sight and hearing, the death of close relatives and friends, and increased vulnerability to the hazards of modern society.

The more the therapist knows about community resources for the elderly, the stronger will be his or her position in helping them with these practical concerns. These resources include social agencies that provide housing, health and legal services, Social Security benefits, and transportation. The therapist should also familiarize him- or herself with special programs for the elderly, such as the foster grandparents program and athletic programs.

Frequently, the therapist has to help the patient with these practical concerns. One patient, for example, was extremely anxious over the loss of income from his impending retirement. After a detailed discussion of his budget, it became clear that he and his wife would have enough money to live on if he would curtail a regular allotment he was giving to his two grown children. While it was painful for the patient to tell his children he could no longer provide them with this money, this act alleviated his anxiety.

HEALTH PROBLEMS

The patient should see his or her family physician for any undiagnosed physical complaints, but the therapist can help the patient with the psychological aspects of the ailment. The importance of psychological factors has been acknowledged in the successful management of a wide range of physical disorders in the elderly, including diabetes, strokes, and other neurological disorders (Eisdorfer & Stotsky, 1977).

The therapist can help the patient manage these physical problems by teaching the patient:

1. to recognize and modify dysfunctional ruminations, exaggerations, and catastrophic thoughts about the ailment;
2. to limit discussion of the problem and stop other activities that may be reinforcing the patient's attention to the disorder;
3. to learn coping skills, such as imagery and relaxation techniques that can divert the patient's attention from the discomfort; and
4. to carry out the prescribed medical recommendations on dietary management, medication, and exercise programs.

Cognitive therapy works best, as would be expected, for those elderly patients with a history of good adjustment. The approach is least successful for those with a fixed delusion of a health impairment or with a fixed belief that their emotional problems can be cured only with medical treatment. For example, one patient at the evaluation attributed her depression to a pain in her vagina. Although she had undergone two extensive medical examinations that could find nothing physically wrong with her, she refused treatment when told it would be primarily psychological.

The therapist does not have to give up on a patient that holds firmly onto dysfunctional beliefs. Given enough disconfirming experiences, many are able to modify such beliefs. One example was an 83-year-old woman who was treated for anxiety and loneliness. She had moved to a new city to be close to her son; but shortly after she arrived, her son had died and she was left alone in a strange city. She was remarkably active and alert.

Her major dysfunctional belief was that there was something wrong with her balance that would cause her to fall when she left her apartment. Her physician had told her that there was nothing wrong with her balance and that she should get out and walk. Although she never completely changed her belief, she responded quickly to therapy. She joined several clubs and began making friends. At this point therapy ended. She called, however, several months later and said she hadn't left her apartment for a week for fear she would lose her balance and fall.

The therapist, in two telephone sessions, was unable to persuade the patient to try a short trip out of her apartment to test out her belief. Consequently, a paraprofessional home counselor was sent to her home. (For further information on *in vivo* therapy, see Chapter 15, this volume.) The home counselor was able to have the patient try a trip down to the lobby of her apartment building. This "experiment" was successful and they eventually went shopping together that day and even stopped for drinks. This one intervention was enough to start the patient moving again. At a three-month follow-up, the patient indicated she was doing well.

SIGNIFICANT OTHERS

The therapist should make a point of seeing significant others in the patient's life at least once. During these contacts the therapist can introduce him- or herself, explain the purpose of therapy, and gain more information about the patient's environment. With the patient's consent, significant others can also act as helpers in therapy.

Friends and relatives play an auxiliary role most frequently when the patient is suffering from agoraphobia. In these cases, the person accompanies the patient on short trips from home. Significant others are also used to help the depressed patient. One elderly lady, for example, believed she was unable to find any pleasure in life. To disprove this thought, her daughter helped her keep a record of the times when she actually did enjoy herself.

When the therapist uses significant others in therapy, he or she has to structure the situation to avoid creating resentment between the patient and the helper, and also has to guard against increasing the patient's sense of dependency. The therapist should gradually phase out the significant other as a helper, and if possible, the patient should help the significant other with a personal problem to provide some balance in the relationship.

The aged patient may be involved in some type of family conflict, usually with his or her children. In these cases, the therapist may choose to have one or more sessions with the children alone. In one case the therapist saw the son and daughter of the patient. Both children felt extremely guilty about their father, who lived alone. The son handled his guilt by avoiding contact with his father, while the daughter responded to her guilt by being overprotective. She insisted that he move in with her family, although neither she nor her father actually wanted this. The therapist worked to alleviate their guilt so that they could start acting on ''wants'' rather than ''shoulds.''

Older patients in turn frequently have dysfunctional beliefs about the role their children should play in their lives. These patients grew up in the period prior to Social Security when older people were mainly cared for by their children. Some patients believe their children are selfish for not doing more for them; others believe that because their children call or visit infrequently they must have failed as parents. The therapist can discuss with these patients the changing nature of the American family and help them correct any specific misattributions they have about their children.

The older patients' beliefs about how others should treat them often lead to self-defeating behavior patterns. Some examples are: A person fails to speak up when slighted because he or she believes others should know enough to treat the elderly with respect. A mother becomes angry at her children when they call because they do not call often enough, and thus causes them to call even less frequently. An elderly man doesn't initiate social contact because he believes he is entitled at his age to have people come to him.

The therapist can use role-playing, information gathered from others and *in vivo* therapy experience to determine whether the patient needs help with any social behaviors. Once the therapist can pinpoint the problem, he or she can help the patient learn to respond to others more effectively. One 72-year-old woman had moved back to her hometown to be near her relatives. Initially her relatives were quite attentive to her, but gradually spent less time with her. She became depressed and came for treatment. The therapist had a consultation with the patient's daughter and granddaughter. The daughter said her mother didn't listen to others, that she only wanted to talk about herself, and that she didn't acknowledge gifts and attention when they were given to her. These facts were confirmed by the granddaughter.

After the therapist had established a good relationship with this patient he was able to work with her on improving her social skills. The therapist told the patient that social interactions that are rewarded or rewarding tend to be repeated. She should therefore reward those who spend extra time with her by acknowledging their thoughtfulness, and she should make her conversation more rewarding to others by asking questions to let them know she is listening. These skills were practiced in role-playing until there was noticeable improvement. At a six-month follow-up her daughter said that there had been a remarkable improvement in her mother's way of relating to her and other family members.

CONCLUDING COMMENTS

This chapter has outlined a number of problems that are encountered in conducting therapy with the elderly, but few of the benefits. There are many; not the least are the insight and wisdom the therapist can learn from the elderly.

REFERENCES

Bloom, M., & Blenker, M. Assessing functioning of older persons living in the community. *Gerontologist, 10,* 1970, 31–37.

Eisdorfer, C., & Stotsky, B. A. Intervention, treatment and rehabilitation of psychiatric disorders. In J. E. Birren & K. W. Schaie (Eds.), *Handbook of the psychology of aging.* New York: Van Nostrand Reinhold, 1977.

Kahn, R. L., Zarit, S. H., & Hilbert, N. M. Memory complaint and impairment in the aged: The effect of depression and altered brain function. *Archives of General Psychiatry, 32,* 1975, 1569.

Thomae, H. Theory of aging and cognitive theory of personality. *Human Development, 13,* 1970, 1–16.

Zarit, S. H., Miller, N. E., & Kahn, R. L. Brain function, intellectual impairment and education in the aged. *Journal of the American Geriatrics Society, 26,* 1978, 2.

SPECIFIC CLINICAL PROBLEMS

The five chapters in this section represent case studies focusing on cognitive–behavioral interventions with specific disorders other than depression. Much of the early work associated with the development of cognitive therapy has been based on intervention with depressed populations. In this section, a variety of alternative types of difficulties are considered.

Two of the chapters, that by Ronald E. Coleman on agoraphobia (Chapter 6) and Steven D. Hollon on drug-induced anxiety states (Chapter 7), focus on problems revolving around anxiety states. Coleman argues that the symptoms of agoraphobia are mediated by catastrophic cognitions about the implications of experiencing anxiety. In a sense, agoraphobia is seen as a "fear of fear," the individual's own innate mood states serving as cues for the cognition–affect–avoidance behavior cycle.

Hollon's description of drug-induced anxiety states similarly revolves around generalized panic reactions, either with or without specific avoidance behaviors. In a sense, drug-induced anxiety states can be seen as a special case of an agoraphobialike syndrome. The key distinction lies in the apparent etiology. In many cases, agoraphobia develops in the aftermath of the loss (or anticipated loss) of some major interpersonal relationship. Drug-induced anxiety states appear to be initiated by a misinterpretation of an unpleasant drug experience.

Chapters by Jeffrey E. Young on loneliness (Chapter 8) and Sonja Fox and Gary Emery on sexual dysfunctions (Chapter 9) focus on dysfunctions in interpersonal spheres that may or may not involve anxiety mediation. In some cases, these interpersonal difficulties are based on maladaptive cognitive processes. In these two chapters, it becomes clear that techniques must be adjusted to discern and deal with a wide range of cognitive distortions; while only some lead directly to distress, all lead directly to interpersonal dysfunction.

Gary Emery and Sonja Fox's chapter on alcoholism (Chapter 10) continues this theme of multiple cognition–affect–behavior sequences. Some of the sequences may involve distressing emotions—for example, anxiety or depression—but many others may not; all involve cognition–affect sequences that lead to alcohol abuse. Even more than for loneliness and sexual dysfunctions, treatment interventions must begin with careful assessments of the nature of the cognitive processes underlying and maintaining maladaptive drinking behavior.

Each of the five chapters describes cognitive assessment and intervention strategies flexibly adapted from the range of cognitive techniques to fit the nature of the various dysfunctions. All encompass basic principles such as cognitive–behavioral functional analyses, collaborative empiricism, self-monitoring procedures, behavioral interventions, and cognitive restructuring.

What clearly emerges is a picture of cognitive therapy as a flexible system of therapeutic interventions, capable of being brought to bear on a wide range of clinical problems, rather than a simple collection of various techniques and procedures. When implemented in conjunction with a thoroughgoing cognitive–affective–behavioral functional analysis, and in the context of a systematic cognitive formulation of psychopathology, cognitive therapy can provide a broad-spectrum system of clinical intervention.

COGNITIVE–BEHAVIORAL TREATMENT OF AGORAPHOBIA

Ronald E. Coleman

INTRODUCTION

The following account of the cognitive–behavioral treatment of agoraphobia was refined by myself and my trainees' experience in clinical practice and research. The present theoretical model, clinical syndrome, and treatment package for agoraphobia is supported by our continuing clinical treatment trials. Controlled research that evaluates the cognitive–behavioral approach to agoraphobia treatment remains necessary, obviously. However, the present chapter depicts the details of a more complete and realistic treatment package than many research reports imply need be employed.

IDENTIFICATION OF SYNDROME

Agoraphobia is seen often in patients who have gone from doctor to doctor with multiple symptoms and who may have been treated for depression, other psychiatric disorders, or a host of specific physical complaints related to signs of anxiety rather than for agoraphobia. Initially, agoraphobia seems to develop from specific seemingly spontaneous panic attacks that become associated with many situations and lead to anticipatory anxiety attacks. Due to the intensity, chronicity, frequency, or lack of apparent logic of their anxiety responses, frequently agoraphobics exibit other psychiatric symptoms in addition to panic. These symptoms may include serious depression, hopelessness,

Ronald E. Coleman. Department of Psychology, Friends Hospital and University of Pennsylvania, Philadelphia, Pennsylvania.

obsessive–compulsive behavior, depersonalization, and insomnia. Agoraphobia is also seen in individuals who have avoided doctors and treatment. These individuals, whose lives may have become increasingly constricted, may be coming for consultation for the first time, fearing the worst. Frequently, these individuals worry that they are "going crazy," because of the subjective experience of helplessness and dreaded expectations associated with their panic attacks. Agoraphobics are usually female and their relationships often are marked by dependence and/or passiveness–aggressiveness with their spouse or loved ones. This dependence may be a function of premorbid personality characteristics or may result from patients' seeming inability to function on their own.

The presence of critical adjunctive symptoms that may have been treated by physicians and mental-health professionals as primary symptoms ought not mislead the clinician. The central feature to be identified is the patients' experience of anxiety and their physical withdrawal from situations in order to protect themselves from their panic and expectation of catastrophe. As mentioned above, initially, agoraphobics experience a panic attack or series of panic attacks that, though seemingly spontaneous, are quickly associated with various situations. To protect themselves they withdraw to the point that they are reluctant to venture from the safety of their homes. If they do go out of the house it may be only if accompanied by a loved one.

Our clinical experience is similar to that of others (Chambless & Goldstein, 1980; Goldstein & Chambless, 1978) who find that agoraphobics are afraid of their experience of anxiety (fear of fear) and what it can do to them. The strength of cognitive interventions are in their ability to elicit, evaluate, and modify beliefs regarding the supposed consequences of anxiety that maintains fear-avoidance behavior. Thus, agoraphobics maintain irrational beliefs regarding the dreaded consequences that may follow from the experience of anxiety, such as going crazy, or losing control. These anxiety may become associated strongly with situations and agoraphobics may then maintain irrational beliefs about the potential trauma that situations may elicit. However, agoraphobics differ from other phobic patients in that phobic patients anticipate potential trauma associated primarily with objects or situations whereas agoraphobics are primarily concerned with expected consequences of their own experience of anxiety. The agoraphobic syndrome also may be distinguished from primary depression. In the depressive, the patient's avoidance of situations stems from loss and low motivation regarding future success. The agoraphobic, on the other hand, avoids situations because of the potential trauma associated with their own experience of anxiety and situations that have been associated with it.

To achieve some sense of relief for the patient, and to enlist the patient's collaboration in therapy, it is important that the clinician identify the agoraphobic syndrome accurately. The clear suggestion to patients that many of their symptoms stem from anxiety, their anticipation of it, and worry about its consequences helps reduce the patient's concern over his or her plight.

Communication with the patient about the treatment program proceeds from clear-cut identification of the syndrome. In the treatment program the clinician assists the patient in analyzing cognitions that suggest impending disaster. The clinician invites the patient to see that experiencing anxiety more fully rather than avoiding it and that approaching feared situations are necessary and inevitable if agoraphobia is to be overcome.

Patients often agree that they at some time believed that the most useful attitude would be to face their anxiety and situations associated with anxiety. They often report, however, that they tried this technique usually for too brief a time. Consequently, they found that they either had low tolerance for their experienced anxiety and/or that their catastrophic expectations frightened them away. They are frequently heartened by the idea that approach to feared situations is recommended and that their expectations of catastrophe may be unrealistic. Reading assignments such as Weekes's (1978) account of agoraphobia help the patient understand his or her symptoms and the need to examine and explore the anxiety response. Of course, the clinician needs to rule out any possible physical basis for the anxiety experienced by these patients.

The cognitive therapist's emphasis on evaluation of subjective experience is an excellent aid in identification of the agoraphobic syndrome. The agoraphobic patient who has multiple symptoms needs to be evaluated to determine that anxiety symptoms are the central feature as compared to either depression, passive–dependent personality disorders, or psychosis. Examination of thoughts and personal meanings underlying anxiety behavior enables the differential diagnosis to be made. For instance, avoidant behavior due to thoughts that the experience of anxiety or exposure to certain situations has high threat value indicates the presence of phobia. Careful exploration of the type of automatic thoughts associated with anxiety will enable a determination between agoraphobia and simple phobia. The agoraphobic will be found to have catastrophic thoughts of doom associated with the internal experience of anxiety itself. For instance, a 27-year-old married female patient complained that she could not take public transportation or enter crowded stores. Exploration of the spontaneous thoughts she had on entering these situations in the past revealed that mild anxiety symptoms led to the fear that she might faint. She was overwhelmingly afraid that this would lead to a trip to a hospital, a consequence that she irrationally believed would lead to worse physical problems or to death. Note that any anxiety symptom signaled the possibility that a dreaded internal event would occur that would be uncontrollable. This may be differentiated from simple phobia patients whose worry is that specific stimuli pose threat value to the patient. For example, a middle-aged man was seen because of his avoidant behavior and anxiety over public transportation and driving in automobiles. Upon exploration of the threat value of these circumstances, it was determined that his wife had been involved in a serious car accident and that the patient had developed specific fears about the consequences regarding physical harm possible from being in these situations. Note that though this involves avoidant behavior and response to anxiety symptoms it is a response to the consequences posed by an external threat.

COGNITIVE–BEHAVIORAL MODEL OF AGORAPHOBIA

Agoraphobics are particularly sensitized to the fear of the anxiety experience itself. They tend to be hypervigilant to internal signs indicating the onset of anxiety. This is to prevent the occurrence of expected, impending panic and the overwhelming and frightening loss of control to which it might lead.

A vicious cycle may ensue in which signs of panic appear and become newly associated with previously neutral situations. Later, rational justification of why that situation might be unsafe seems to be added on. Even more tertiary and circular explanations are offered by patients as to the potential danger of situations based on beliefs that one must not at all appear foolish or out of control. Then patients explain that "No one should see my hands tremble," or "People will think I'm weak or crazy," etc., justifying further avoidance. A generalized account of the cognitive model of anxiety may be found in Beck (1976), Beck, Laude, and Bohnert (1974), and Beck and Rush (1975).

Why does the agoraphobic develop hypervigilance to the experience of anxiety while the phobic develops hypervigilance to avoidance of specific external threat stimuli? It is generally agreed that the agoraphobic is a dependent unassertive individual (Chambless & Goldstein, 1980; Goldstein & Chambless, 1978; Zitrin, Klein, & Woerner, 1978). From a cognitive point of view this may be stated as a generalized set held by agoraphobics that the world has threat value if confronted independently. Agoraphobics, then, view the world as a dangerous place. Security from danger may be ensured through the availability of a loved one, and/or by being cautious in the world. Either willful or unexpected autonomous action (e.g., desire to separate from spouse or death of a loved one) may lead therefore to the experience of self-in-the-world-alone that has been associated with helplessness and loss of control (panic). Thus, agoraphobics have present a constellation of attitudes about self (cognitive schema) involving inadequate self-efficacy that surfaces when the agoraphobic is faced with environmental demands for autonomy. Anxiety seems to serve as a signal that, unless avoidant action is taken, the individual will be overwhelmed by helplesness and loss of control (panic). Indeed, the clinical experience of therapists working with agoraphobics is that their anxiety is associated with cognitions of impending heart attack, going crazy, and running amuck. Agoraphobics are afraid of the expected effects of their own panic based on a constellation of cognitions regarding need to be cared for and need to be cautious in the world.

Simple phobics, on the other hand, are afraid of some external event that may occur, based on an obviously experienced or observed traumatic event or series of events in their past. Why environmental demands for autonomy result in agoraphobic symptoms for some (i.e., anxiety) and depression for others requires additional theorizing and research.

Theoretical and clinical accounts of the early years of agoraphobics support the view that agoraphobics learn that the world is a dangerous

place. Patients' mothers may be anxious and view the child's autonomous action as threatening (Bowlby, 1973). The mother's style of overprotective interaction may lead to the patient's own fear that she may
be in harm if autonomous. This is consistent with the cognitive viewpoint that at an early age, preagoraphobic individuals develop irrational generalized attitudes about the extent of danger in the world.
These attitudes are rarely subject to clear examination but may lead to
tentativeness regarding being in the world and to self-attitudes of
cautiousness, and of requiring control or certainty regarding events.
These cognitive attitudes are important for the cognitive therapist to
investigate with the patient.

The agoraphobic patient previously mentioned exemplifies the
present theoretical point of view. Though panic attacks seemed to occur spontaneously, this patient was passive and dependent. She was
afraid to go out unless accompanied by husband or mother and was
timid interpersonally. Her mother was agoraphobic. The patient re-
members that as a child she worried over her mother's panic attacks,
feared for her mother's health, but felt inadequate to do anything.
Mother's frequent method of obtaining cooperation was to threaten
loss of safety by telling the child she would be left behind if she got
ready slowly. A traumatic event occurred at age 9 when, in fact, the patient was left at a hospital for treatment of an ulcer, confirming the
mother's threat.

OVERVIEW OF TREATMENT

The course of treatment follows from the theoretical model just
described. First, identification and communication that symptoms experienced conform to the agoraphobia syndrome reduce patients'
worry. Second, agoraphobics' fear of their own fear is explained.
Because agoraphobics are phobic of their own anxiety, they fail to experience or examine it fully. As a result they maintain their irrational
beliefs about the dreaded consequences of strong anxiety. Thus, the
treatment program, which involves facing the experience of anxiety, is
stated in the first session to ensure the cooperation and understanding
of the patient.

Stated generally, the treatment tactic is to ask the patients to give up their control of anxiety, to accept their experience of anxiety, and to expose themselves to situations in which they would heighten their anxiety. Obviously, patients are reluctant to do what they dread. The strength of the cognitive therapist is her or his ability to work with the patient in examining the patient's irrational beliefs about the dangerous consequences of anxiety. The agoraphobic may begin to see, initially, that the personal meanings he or she assigns to the outcome of anxiety may be theory rather than fact.

Initially, then, the cognitive therapist explores those categories of the patient's thoughts that have to do with the experience of anxiety itself. The need to control anxiety and to avoid the feared consequences of anxiety are first explored. For instance, patients have specific unrealistic expectations that when in panic they may fail to be able to walk, talk, breathe, swallow, may faint or may lose control and run amuck, or may "go crazy." It is critical to note and identify for the patient those beliefs regarding his or her expectancies of the concomitant of panic. With self-observations patients may keep logs of their dysfunctional thoughts associated with anxiety on specially prepared forms (triple-column technique, see Figure 1, below) between sessions.

Patients are encouraged to enter situations *in vivo* as soon as possible. They are enabled to do so with the initial cognitive interventions. An interaction between examination of irrational cognitions during approach–avoidance to real-life situations is then a major part of the subsequent course of therapy. Between sessions homework to enter feared situations exposes the patient to the potential experience of anxiety while he or she may examine the validity of catastrophic cognitions regarding that situation. The patient may ascertain experientially the difference between catastrophic expectations and events as they actually proceed. The achievement of specific behavioral goals, mutually arrived at by patient and therapist marks the course of treatment.

Early on in therapy cognitive therapists emphasize cognitive interventions that lead to initiation of approach behavior and then later to maintenance of approach behavior. While initial cognitive interventions entail evaluating catastrophic thoughts regarding the consequences of anxiety, cognitive interventions that lead to maintenance of approach involve cognitive restructuring techniques which allow the anxious patient a new view of a situation so he or she may remain in it. Frequently, as agoraphobics respond with less panic, maintenance cognitions involve the identification of automatic thoughts related to personal inadequacy and unassertiveness in difficult situations. These types of interventions will be discussed below.

FEAR OF FEAR: ENCOURAGING EXAMINATION OF CATASTROPHIC THINKING REGARDING ANXIETY

Agoraphobics believe that they cannot tolerate anxiety. This may have been confirmed for the patient by a single or several prior episodes in which the patient panicked and ran from a store, a social encounter, or a meeting. By the time the patient consults a therapist he or she may experience depersonalization, feeling faint and other concomitants of severe anxiety. By this time the agoraphobic's response to the physiological concomitants of anxiety is to believe that (1) panic is imminent, (2) dreaded consequences will occur, and (3) anxiety must be controlled or the individual must flee to safety.

An important initial aspect of the treatment plan is to convey the following. Didactic information regarding anxiety is offered. In order to assist the patient to accept his or her experience of anxiety rather than to fight to control it, he or she is asked to consider the hypothesis that he or she can experience anxiety without dire consequences. The patient is asked to consider the restructured logic that worries about not coping with anxiety actually lead to an increment in levels of panic generated by the worry itself. The patient is asked to consider the faulty logic inherent in his or her catastrophic thinking. The therapist's intention is to assist the patient to restructure his or her view on anxiety in order to lead the patient to accept the experience rather than fight to control it.

The following is an example of such an interchange between patient and therapist. In this example the therapist indicates that the patient can physically cope with anxiety. In addition, the patient's catastrophic cognitions regarding anxiety are identified.

> THERAPIST: What is it that you are afraid of when you think about entering the store?
> PATIENT: Well, a year ago I was in _____ Department Store. I panicked and ran out. My heart was beating fast and I couldn't stand it. I ran out of there.
> THERAPIST: Do you expect that might happen again?
> PATIENT: Yes.
> THERAPIST: What do you think of when you consider entering a store now?

PATIENT: Well, I seldom think about it but when I do seriously, I immediately think that I wouldn't be able to handle it.

THERAPIST: Notice that you panicked once. Yet, now you always consider that you'll panic. Now, do you think your expectation is the same as what might happen if you actually went?

PATIENT: I don't know. Maybe not. But I'm afraid to try it.

THERAPIST: O.K. Let me focus on the experience of panic, then, when you entered.
Tell me what you feel, or felt then.

PATIENT: O.K. I noticed that my heart was racing. I felt a tightness in here (*points to abdomen*).

THERAPIST: Can you remember what happened next?

PATIENT: Then I thought I couldn't take it.

THERAPIST: What did you do next?

PATIENT: I became really scared and became fearful that I'd faint or couldn't leave so I ran out of there.

THERAPIST: What did you think or decide between the time you felt the panic and when you decided to run out?

PATIENT: I thought about that a lot. I think I was worried that if I fainted I would come-to babbling and people would think I was crazy.

THERAPIST: Did that actually happen?

PATIENT: No, I never got to fainting.

THERAPIST: Would you be willing to entertain the notion that despite your experience of your racing heart and other feelings of anxiety, it was your mind's reaction to them that is what you thought caused you to panic? That is, it's what you added on to your feelings that catastrophized the situation?

PATIENT: You know I do worry over every little thing that happens; every little thing in my body.

THERAPIST: I want to differentiate between your initial experience of anxiety at any given time and the things you say or catastrophize to yourself that add on to that experience.

PATIENT: Go on.

THERAPIST: Well, I have found that patients who realize that the physiological symptoms you experience are anxiety and can be experienced without hurting them can begin to accept the experiences and relax with them. It is the worry or catastrophizing about the meaning that exaggerates the anxiety into panic. Do you see what I mean?

PATIENT: I think I do.

THERAPIST: Would you be willing to enter the store for a while and notice that you are capable of experiencing anxiety and also notice what catastrophe or dread statements you add on to your feelings?

PATIENT: I don't know. I'm not sure I can take it if my heart starts up like that. I really panic.

THERAPIST: Well, I can see that your expectation is that you will panic. Will you be willing to see if you can enter the store, if you can experience some anxiety, and if your experience is different from your expectations?

Also, notice if you add any thoughts on to what you feel.
PATIENT: I'll give it a try.

The therapist in the interview was interested in having the patient consider approaching her own anxieties. To accomplish this, several cognitive techniques were employed. Notice that the therapist identified the faulty logic inherent in the idea that one panic experience means that it will happen again (overgeneralization). The therapist also elicited and identified those automatic catastrophic thoughts that probably kept the patient out of department stores (she thought she would faint and wake up babbling). Note finally that this aspect of the initial treatment interview encouraged the patient to enter the situation again. She could begin to differentiate those experiences of anxiety from her catastrophic thoughts.

Once the patient is willing to enter feared situations he or she may differentiate fact from expectation. Then the patient is instructed additionally in identification of automatic thoughts, that is, those thoughts and images that increase the patient's concern about his or her ability to cope with anxiety. During sessions, identified automatic thoughts are examined for faulty logic and coping plans to handle anxiety are devised. Initially, the task of observing automatic thoughts and the experience of anxiety *in vivo* is often sufficient to afford the patient some distancing from the situation, resulting in a drop in anxiety level. The patient is also instructed to relax as best they are able when anxious. They are instructed in Claire Weekes's (1978) concepts regarding acceptance of anxiety. In this approach the individual is encouraged to decontrol the response to anxiety by "floating" with it and by "letting time pass." The patient is asked to log in his or her observation using the triple-column technique in between sessions. One column identifies the situation, a second column identifies the level of anxiety experienced, and a third column identifies any automatic thoughts the patient has observed in the situation. Later, rational responses to the automatic thoughts are discussed, initially during therapy sessions, then later on by the patient only, between sessions. An example of a triple column from one session is provided in Figure 1.

COGNITIVE INTERVENTIONS WITH EXTREMELY AVOIDANT PATIENTS

Sometimes patients, though they agree to enter therapy, refuse to expose themselves to anxiety. They refuse to leave safety (house, presence of loved one) to venture into feared situations in order to evaluate their

DATE	SITUATION Describe: 1. Actual event leading to unpleasant emotion, or 2. Stream of thoughts, daydream, or recollection, leading to unpleasant emotion.	EMOTION(S) 1. Specify sad/ anxious/angry, etc. 2. Rate degree of emotion, 1–100.	AUTOMATIC THOUGHT(S) 1. Write automatic thought(s) that preceded emotion(s). 2. Rate belief in automatic thought(s), 0–100%.	RATIONAL RESPONSE 1. Write rational response to automatic thought(s). 2. Rate belief in rational response, 0–100%.	OUTCOME 1. Rerate belief in automatic thought(s), 0–100%. 2. Specify and rate subsequent emotions, 0–100.
	Enter store.	Very anxious. 100	Felt trapped. Knees feel weak, worried that I won't be able to stay. I feel I'm going to faint. Something may happen to me. No one will help me if I faint.	I will not faint. I haven't fainted in a store yet. If I faint people will help me. Someone will come to my aid.	

Explanation: When you experience an unpleasant emotion, note the situation that seemed to stimulate the emotion. (If the emotion occurred while you were thinking, daydreaming, etc., please note this.) Then note the automatic thought associated with the emotion. Record the degree to which you believe this thought: 0%=not at all; 100%= completely. In rating degree of emotion: 1=a trace; 100=the most intense possible.

FIGURE 1. *Daily Record of Dysfunctional Thoughts.*

catastrophic cognitions. Then it is necessary to explore the meaning of present catastrophic cognitions with these patients in greater detail to reduce their catastrophic potency and to encourage approach in real-life situations. Guided fantasy is employed that re-creates feared situations to elicit a rich set of automatic thoughts central to avoidance behavior.

With reluctant patients it is often the case that their present catastrophic beliefs about anxiety have been held since childhood though they are not always remembered clearly. The following illustrates the use of guided fantasy with a young woman reluctant to enter feared situations. Her anxiety symptoms exacerbated soon after she married. By then she could travel from her house and attend work only if her husband was present. Fortunately, they were employed with the same company. Her catastrophic expectation was that should she be left alone, she would faint and then die. Or, she might faint, be taken to the hospital, and left there to die. Though she acknowledged the irrational nature of this construct she firmly acted on the belief that if she was without a loved one, she would be helpless and would be somehow struck down.

Efforts to have her enter actual feared situations raised this patient's anxiety level. She could not accept her anxiety because of the consequences she expected. Guided fantasy in which she was instructed to experience an event in which she was left alone elicited cognitions of abandonment. When she was asked to associate attitudes and memories to this event she remembered experiencing her mother's anxiety attack when a young girl. The mother thought she was dying and cried out for help. The patient's memory of this was captured and vividly remembered. Soon, events were remembered that indicated that the patient had become school phobic. The association of her present dysfunctional cognitions with these earlier traumatic fears regarding abandonment, death, and the modeling of her mother led to more effective cognitive restructuring during subsequent guided fantasies. Soon the patient was able to approach actual feared situations.

BEHAVIORAL ACHIEVEMENTS

The patient is asked to expose him- or herself to situations that lead to anxiety arousal as soon as possible. However, the cognitive–behavioral therapist does not utilize real-life exposure techniques as a method to obtain extinction of the physiological aspects of the anxiety response, as does the more purely behavioral therapist (Marks, 1978). Real-life exposure within the cognitive therapist's strategy allows for reevaluation by the patient of the validity of his or her catastrophic expectations. Comparison of the experience of anxiety with their dreaded expectation is possible while in a real-life situation. Homework assignments repeatedly request the individual to remain in a feared situation to test the comparison between these expectations and what actually occurs.

Real-life exposure has an additional value to the cognitive therapist. Experience in actual feared situations elicits and releases important associations, memories, and cognitions that may be additional bases for catastrophic thinking. The retrieval of these automatic cognitions and their rational evaluations leads to additional therapuetic gains.

The set of circumstances that the agoraphobic is aware he or she avoids vary. These circumstances serve as the unique treatment goals for that patient. One patient may not be able to leave the company of a spouse. Another may not be able to go out to socialize but may be able to shop. Another may not be able to enter stores but may be able to drive on streets and highways. Many cannot venture far from their house. In this way they avoid the experience of anxiety. After determining what is generally avoided in life, the patient can usually tell the therapist what it is necessary to first accomplish. The patient has usually entered treatment because of the discomfort of having to avoid this situation. This will be the first thing worked on. Agoraphobics often are not aware of the full extent of their avoidance until treatment helps them once again enter situations. As they approach feared situations, additional circumstances that they had avoided come into their sights.

The patient is instructed to enter feared situations and to compare their expectations regarding anxiety with their experience of it. The patient is encouraged to remain in a situation until his or her anxiety diminishes, if possible. Patients are instructed that the more frequent and the longer time a phobic person spends in a feared situation the greater the likelihood of additional attitude change, approach behavior, and fear reduction.

Initially, patients are allowed whatever minimal aid they require to help them enter real-life situations. Usually patients are unwilling initially to enter feared situations without a loved one until additional cognitive restructuring is accomplished. These types of aids are faded as soon as possible, however. Patients are told that they need to identify successful real-life exposure as due to self-mastery rather than based on association with a protective other (Smith & Coleman, 1977).

COGNITIVE INTERVENTIONS THAT MAINTAIN BEHAVIORAL APPROACH

Once behavioral goals are determined and tried out, the agoraphobic requires ongoing support for maintenance of approach behavior. Without support the agoraphobic might easily be guided by the personal philosophy that the world is a dangerous place. Therefore, painstaking week-by-week repetitions of cognitive interventions that maintain approach behavior slowly bring about more pervasive attitude change (these will be discussed shortly).

Frequently, reevaluations of the most serious intrusive beliefs, that is, "I am going to die from anxiety," and/or "I am going crazy from anxiety," need be made. Therefore, the cognitive therapist working with agoraphobics requires patience and persistance in reapplication of the steps of (1) identifying these automatic thoughts (2) noting their relationship to panic and anxiety, and (3) making logical evaluations. These types of intervention strategies are similar to those described with depressives (Beck, Rush, Shaw, & Emery, 1979) and with individuals with anxiety problems (Beck & Emery, 1979). Cognitive strategies specifically useful with agoraphobics are described below. These tactics enhance the agoraphobics' ability to accept anxiety while engaging in independent activity (behavioral maintenance).

Agoraphobics are encouraged to engage in more autonomous behavior with the following informational and cognitive restructuring strategy. Patients are introduced to the idea that they use *props* and *safeguards* in order to venture into feared situations. The safeguard may be the presence of a loved one, for example, child, spouse, or parent. Patients are instructed that it would be useful to wean themselves from this dependency. Initially patients may be somewhat unaware of the pervasiveness of their reliance on others. Careful questioning about the security of such props and safeguards always yields dysfunctional thoughts that may be evaluated, however. Patients reply to this line of questioning that they would need help if they fainted, would become lost if confused, would not be aided by strangers if they got into trouble. Evaluation and logical analysis of this category of automatic thought can lead to the beginning of autonomous behaviors. Examples of useful cognitive interventions are as follows. The cognitive therapist might evaluate the *probability* at which fainting (or getting lost, or getting hurt) might occur. This is found usually to be at negligible rates, if ever, compared to what the patient believed, initially. At this point, *"what-if "* techniques that ask the patient to explore the worst possible outcome, and how they would deal with them, may be employed. The therapist may ask, "Well, what if you became confused and felt lost?" Most frequently, what follows is analysis into how to handle the problem of being lost. Patients are then encouraged to enter situations between intervening sessions to test out this new information and cognitive restructuring.

A second general tactic, useful early in therapy, helps the patient perceive that he or she has control over behavior. Their belief is that because of the perception of pervasive avoidance the patient has no control over feared events. A useful strategem is to evaluate with the patient that choice is really available. This technique of choice evaluation is adapted from a process called owning one's action, utilized by Dr. Jay S. Efran (1978, personal communication). In it, the patient is asked to decide which situations he or she wants to avoid because of the likelihood of associated anxiety, and which situations he or she would be willing to enter. Then, the therapist may focus on the notion that the patient chooses specific situations in which he or she is able to stay or wishes to leave. Invitations or allowances by the therapist that it is O.K. to avoid if they choose provides a measure of control. It allows the patient to "own this action," too. Subsequent choices regarding entering situations are the patient's to make also. Inevitably, patients who "choose to enter" most frequently choose to stay, partially through their observations that they are in control. Patients invariably find out that they are able to persist, exist, and even function in feared situations despite their expectancies to the contrary.

A third useful strategy is the *critical-incident* strategy developed by Gary Emery (Beck & Emery, 1979). This strategy further restructures cognitions regarding fear that controls the agoraphobic patient, versus the patient controlling his or her behavior despite fear. The critical-incident strategy conveys the notion to the patient that fear avoidance may be examined and pinned down to a particular difficult moment in a situation. At that moment the patient becomes afraid and makes a decision to avoid or flee based on the automatic thought, "I don't know what to do now," or "I can't handle these feelings," or "If I become more anxious I will be out of control." The patient is instructed in how to become more aware of such moments and is offered the option of choosing to cope, approach, or "hang-in."

Important to the decision whether to stay or flee is the perception by the patient as to whether they are emotion-oriented or task-oriented. The choice to flee follows from attention and response to their catastrophic upset-producing automatic thoughts. Task-oriented thinking stems from answering the question, "What do I need to do now to get through this situation the way I want to, or can do?" Patients learn to apply this decision process, and self-talk during subsequent forays into difficult situations.

Patients' tentative and cautious style of being-in-the-world requires attention throughout therapy. The agoraphobic fails to place him- or herself thoroughly at risk in the world but consistently is vigilant for difficulty that might arise in almost any situation. Therefore, the cognitive therapist needs to be always vigilant for anxiety-engendering cognitions that indicate that the patient requires protection. Typical cognitions of the agoraphobic patient related to their cautious approach to the world are beliefs that they need to handle themselves perfectly in situations and the related belief that they ought to avoid looking foolish. Thus, agoraphobics frequently heighten their anxiety by attempting to hide signs of their anxiety.

The following case illustrates this point. One young male agoraphobic refused to enter department stores for fear that the clerk would see his shaky hands as he completed a purchase. Evaluation of task-oriented versus task-irrelevant emotion-oriented cognitions were useful in leading this patient to view this situation more positively. In the case of this young man, fearful of being observed shaking, the following interchange was found useful. He was asked what he needed to accomplish in any venture into a store. He said, "I want to buy something, but I would be embarrassed if I couldn't sign my name when I charged things." Further discussion revealed his concerns about having to "look good" and his worry about what others thought of him. These concerns were weighed against the possibility that he could successfully accomplish a task, however inadequate were aspects of the performance. After repeated intervention with various such examples, this patient became more willing to be task-oriented and less focused on emotion-arousing dysfunctional thoughts.

THE COURSE OF THERAPY

As therapy continues, homework in which patients engage in approach behavior is central. From this flows a rich lode of cognitions. For each patient a particular set of protective catastrophic cognitions keeps the patient sensitized and avoidant of situations in which the person believes he or she cannot cope. These cognitions tend to cut short the patient's self-maintenance in the feared situation. These are continuously identified by patient or therapist and countered with rational restructuring and additional real-life experiments to evaluate the reality basis of these beliefs. Over time, the therapy proceeds from identification of the specific dysfunctional thinking to the generalized basic assumptions that support behavioral avoidance and fear.

The course of therapy inevitably leads to an attack on an agoraphobic's basic assumptions. He or she learns that being-in-the-world is not necessarily catastrophic, but exciting. Basic assumptions related to being in control, having to be perfect, fear of abandonment, and fear of separation are necessarily confronted if approach behavior is to continue. As improvement and *in vivo* approach continue, basic assumptions are reviewed, frequently spontaneously by the patient.

The course of therapy for an agoraphobic patient is arduous. Approach behavior will have anxiety associated with it for a long period throughout treatment. Nevertheless, continued effort at approach is necessary. Treatment of one to two years individually or in group is frequently the term of treatment necessary to attain diminished fear and independent approach behavior for seriously incapacitated agoraphobics.

The clinician need be aware of at least two pitfalls that patients encounter. Upon the initial entrance into actual situations the patient may experience little anxiety and think that it won't again be experienced. Strong anxiety may then reappear. Or, later on in therapy, after a situation seems anxiety-free after long work, anxiety may appear once again. At these times, patients may become discouraged and self-pitying. Therapists need to point out that therapy is uneven in progress and that high levels of anxiety might periodically return. Patients may resume reliance on self-protective evaluation of events, or may reestablish old avoidance behavior. Additional attention to examination of cognitions and continued emphasis on actual exposure is to be emphasized at these times.

Clinical levels of depression may appear when the patients notice early on or in the middle of therapy that continued experience of anxiety will be necessary for a period. This occurs when patients have not accepted their anxiety as egosyntonic. Renewed effort by the therapist at examining egodystonic cognitive assumptions regarding anxiety are helpful.

Antianxiety and antidepressant drugs are typically not used by us if patients are seen to be making progress. Antianxiety drugs are sometimes recommended to aid in unusual situations but are not encouraged for general use with agoraphobics. Antidepressants are sometimes prescribed to deal with the effects of depression when a patient is midway through treatment. When treated with antidepressive medication the chronic depression associated with chronic anxiety may improve, raising the agoraphobic's motivation for additional treatment.

Klein and his colleagues (e.g., Zitrin et al., 1978) utilize imipramine in low dosages for the purpose of controlling the spontaneous panic attacks associated with agoraphobia. This group describes success in controlled experiments comparing a regimen of imipramine and behavior therapy versus placebo plus behavior therapy. However, no study directly indicates that imipramine, in fact, controls panic attacks. Our experience is that on imipramine, or other antidepressants, patients do not have a dramatic reduction in their panic attacks. This is consistent with Chambless and Goldstein's (1980) observation with agoraphobics on antidepressants.

DEPENDENT RELATIONSHIPS

Marital relationships will inevitably be strained when an agoraphobic is treated. Agoraphobics typically are dependent on their spouses. Spouses frequently may be seen as holding back the patient's increasingly independent behavior. The agoraphobic may require training in assertive responses and in identifying marital obligations versus consideration of his or her own needs. Later, as therapy succeeds in allowing the patient independent approach in feared situations, the spouse may communicate directly or passive-aggressively that he or she (i.e., the nontreated spouse) feels some loss in the relationship. Consultation with the couple by the therapist that identifies assumptions about their marriage and fosters effective communication is helpful to the marital partners.

The present view that the agoraphobic is dependent on a loved one (or loved ones) is consistent with Goldstein's (Chambless & Goldstein, 1980; Goldstein & Chambless, 1978) view of the onset of agoraphobia. He views the onset of agoraphobia as occurring in an atmosphere of interpersonal conflict in which the relationship is threatened. We frequently observe this in our work with agoraphobics. As patients are successful in learning how to be more autonomous they frequently refocus on imagined and real interpersonal difficulties that seem to stem from the lack of assertiveness. Therapy frequently involves encouragement and evaluation of dysfunctional thinking regarding assertive behavior in old and new relationships.

REFERENCES

Beck, A. T. *Cognitive therapy and the emotional disorders*. New York: International Universities Press, 1976.

Beck, A. T., & Emery, G. *Cognitive therapy of anxiety and phobic disorders*. Philadelphia: University of Pennsylvania, 1979.

Beck, A. T., Laude, R., & Bohnert, M. Ideational components of anxiety neurosis. *Archives of General Psychiatry*, 1974, *31*, 319–325.

Beck, A. T., & Rush, A. J. A cognitive model of anxiety resolution. In I. D. Sarason & C. D. Spielberger (Eds.), *Stress and anxiety* (Vol. 2). Washington, D.C.: Hemisphere Publishing Corp., 1975.

Beck, A. T., Rush, A. J., Shaw, B. F., & Emery, G. *Cognitive therapy of depression*. New York: Guilford Press, 1979.

Bowlby, J. *Attachment and loss* (Vol. II): *Separation*. New York: Basic Books, 1973.

Chambless, D. L., & Goldstein, A. The treatment of agoraphobia. In A. Goldstein & E. Foa (Eds.), *Handbook of behavioral interventions*. New York: Wiley, 1980.

Goldstein, A. J., & Chambless, D. L. A reanalysis of agoraphobia. *Behavior Therapy*, 1978, *9*, 47–59.

Marks, I. Behavioral psychotherapy of adult neurosis. In S. L. Garfield & A. E Bergin (Eds.), *Handbook of psychotherapy and behavior change*. New York: Wiley, 1978.

Smith, G. P., & Coleman, R. E. Processes underlying generalization through participant modeling with self-directed practice. *Behaviour Research and Therapy*, 1977, *15*, 204–206.

Weekes, C. *Hope and help for your nerves*. New York: Bantam Books, 1978.

Zitrin, C. M., Klein, D. K., & Woerner, M. G. Behavior therapy, supportive psychotherapy, imipramine and phobias, *Archives of General Psychiatry*, 1978, *35*, 307–316.

COGNITIVE–BEHAVIORAL TREATMENT OF DRUG-INDUCED PANSITUATIONAL ANXIETY STATES

Steven D. Hollon

INTRODUCTION

The experience of anxiety can be overwhelming. When it occurs in the absence of external threat, it can be particularly devastating, largely because of the potential for misattribution regarding its source.

This chapter describes two case studies involving the use of cognitive–behavioral techniques in the treatment of drug-induced panic states. In both cases, the patients first experienced severe panic states while under the influence of drugs, panic states attributed, in each case, to the fear that they were losing their minds. In both cases, episodic panic attacks persisted for extended periods (up to three years) after the initial episode, maintained in large part by the stability of the belief that each had suffered irreparable psychological damage. A variety of procedures, including the self-monitoring of anxiety levels, situations, and ongoing cognitions, cognitive hypothesis testing, and enactive graded exposure, were used to evaluate each patient's erroneous belief and correct his misattributions of experienced anxiety.

CLIENT 1: CLIFF

Cliff was a 31-year-old black male seeking treatment for severe anxiety attacks. Never married, Cliff had been homosexual since his first sexual awareness, and had been living with the same companion for several

Steven D. Hollon. Department of Psychology, University of Minnesota, Minneapolis, Minnesota.

years before entering treatment. At the time treatment began, Cliff was working as a typing instructor.

Cliff's symptoms had begun approximately two years prior to referral. He reported "getting high" on marijuana at a party (not his first drug experience), then becoming increasingly anxious. He reported feeling light-headed and anxious, his heart starting to pound, his palms becoming sweaty, and his beginning to hyperventilate. He felt as if he could "fly across the street"; that he was "out of control." He reported becoming fearful that he was "going crazy" and had a friend drive him to a hospital emergency room. At the emergency room, he was evaluated by a psychiatrist, given a tranquilizer, and released after his mother's arrival helped calm him down.

For the next several months, panic attacks occurred several times monthly, with ongoing chronic anxiety of lesser intensity present between episodes. Cliff began to experience depressive episodes of several days duration, typically occurring after one of the specific panic attacks. Following a second visit to the emergency room, Cliff was referred to a local community mental-health center, where he was seen on an outpatient basis. Treatment involved pharmacologic (Mellaril) and brief supportive contacts. Treatment appeared to produce little, if any, benefit. Cliff reported becoming somewhat more lethargic and depressed on the Mellaril, but continued on medication for over a year. Although reportedly not particularly fearful prior to the initial onset of symptoms, he developed strong fear of high places, being alone, catching diseases, being attacked, attempting suicide, or harming someone else. Typical was his description of his fear of knives: "I get nervous having knives around. . . . I mean, what happens to those other people that they picked up a knife and attacked someone? . . . I mean, do they just 'lose control' or something? How do I know that won't happen to me?"

He continued in treatment throughout the remaining year, then discontinued, generally unimproved. Within two weeks, he experienced another particularly severe panic attack, again after smoking marijuana. He states that since his "treatment" had proven largely unsuccessful, he had decided at a friend's urging to smoke again, thereby "confronting his fears of going crazy." He was again seen in the hospital emergency room, evaluated, provided a minor tranquilizer, given a referral to the outpatient service of the University Medical School, and released in his mother's care.

At the subsequent evaluation for treatment, Cliff was seen as an engaging, if somewhat overly dramatic, individual. He presented himself in a warm and friendly way. The evaluating psychologist saw no evidence of any thought disorder, and diagnosed Cliff as evidencing an anxiety neurosis. In keeping with the general dynamic orientation of the service, Cliff's panic attacks were formulated as being the result of an inability to effectively express and channel unconscious anger toward his (presumably) domineering lover. Cliff was referred for expressive depth psychotherapy with supportive hypnotherapy, with the goal of providing insight into the dynamics underlying his overt symptomatology.

FIRST TREATMENT SESSION

At our first therapy session, approximately two weeks after evaluation and one year, nine months after the onset of symptoms, Cliff described being overwhelmed with fears that he was losing his mind, or, more accurately, had already experienced at least one or more major episodes of psychotic decompensation in association with drug usage. He saw himself as "hanging on to my sanity by my fingernails." The absence of any psychotic symptomatology, age of onset in the late 20s, and clear association of panic attacks with thoughts *about* going crazy were all more consistent with a nonpsychotic *phrenophobia*, or fear of fear, as described by authors such as Beck (1976), Raimy (1974), or Weekes (1969, 1972). We discussed this possibility; Cliff was not impressed. He was, however, willing to test the possibility, particularly after he learned that I was neither able nor willing to hypnotize him to learn "what was in his subconscious."

To test the notion that his panic derived from his misattribution of normal anxiety to incipient decompensation, he agreed to conduct three tests. The first involved the use of imaginal-scene presentation, initially imagining his companion forgetting a luncheon date, then imagining himself going crazy. He experienced feelings of irritation as he sat back, closed his eyes, and described the first image, but not anxiety. When he imagined himself "going crazy," he became visibly upset, and insisted on stopping the scene. After some coaxing, he tolerated going through several brief trials of thought stopping, first introducing the image to himself, then dismissing the image when, as the therapist, I clapped my hands loudly.

The second test of the hypothesis involved leaving the office and proceeding to the roof of the hospital. Cliff had indicated that he had developed a strong fear of heights, something he had never experienced before the first drug-related panic attack. Once on the roof, located on the 11th floor, Cliff began again to show visible signs of anxiety, and would proceed no farther than about 10 feet from the edge, despite the presence of a safety screen. When asked to report what he was thinking, he replied that he was afraid that he might try to jump, actually experienced as "How do I know I won't try to jump?" When asked if he wanted to jump, he replied, "No, but how do I know I can trust myself, how do I know I'm not crazy?" We then discussed other instances of fears that he experienced; in each instance, the underlying theme was that, after his drug-related experience, he could no longer trust his own capacity to control "crazy" impulses. These were typically experienced as undesired acts in a "what if I . . . ?" format, leading to unwanted outcomes.

The third test involved keeping a "fears" diary, consisting of recording situation, affect level, and cognition whenever he found himself becoming particularly anxious or panicky (see also Beck, Rush, Shaw, & Emery, 1979). Cliff agreed to keep the "diary" between sessions, but did insist on an understanding that I arrange for him to be hypnotized if "things don't start working out after several sessions." He also requested that we not hold subsequent sessions on the roof.

SECOND TREATMENT SESSION

Cliff returned for his second session two weeks later reporting that he was feeling much better. During the first week, he had charted his anxiety levels (including two panic attacks), and found that although the situations varied, his thoughts evidenced striking commonality. Typically, Cliff would find himself ruminating about his capacity to control his own behavior. Frequently, such episodes were as likely to be triggered by the absence of external cues as by their presence; Cliff found that on several occasions on breaks at work he found his attention wandering to his "problems," with a consequent increase in his anxiety level.

He also identified a strong tendency for the experience of anxiety to be related to the self-application of a "should" statement (Horney, 1965). Table 1 lists examples of cognitions recorded by Cliff between the two sessions. The remainder of the session was spent discussing the various beliefs, for example, why should he read his Bible more?, why

TABLE 1. *Examples of cognitions associated with increases in anxiety for Client 1*

Situation	Affect	Belief
Walking to my car on fifth level of the parking lot	Anxious	What if I jump off? . . . What if I drive my car over the edge?
At church	Anxious/ depressed	I should read my Bible more. . . . If I really loved myself this wouldn't be happening to me. I should love myself, then God wouldn't be punishing me. I'm immoral.
On break at work, having a cigarette	Anxious	Why does this happen to me? Maybe this is a punishment for being gay.
On break at work	Anxious	What am I going to do? I'll have all this time on my hands, I'll just get depressed.
Meeting my ex- for lunch	Anxious/ guilty	I shouldn't be here, I shouldn't be taking a chance.

shouldn't he have lunch with a former lover?, what kind of punishment did he expect?

During this discussion Cliff described his uncertainty and conflict over his religious beliefs on the one hand (he was a devout fundamentalist Baptist) and his sexual orientation and *avant-garde* lifestyle on the other. He pointed out that while he was basically comfortable with his lifelong homosexual orientation (he had long since informed friends and family, and described a close, accepting, supportive family system), he had never reconciled his sexual orientation with his rather fundamentalistic "fire-and-brimstone" religion.

THIRD AND FOURTH SESSIONS

Two subsequent weekly sessions were largely uneventful, taken up largely with reviews of Cliff's efforts at hypothesis testing (rational restructuring) using the triple-column (ABC) format.[1] The reduction in

---

1. This triple-column format, also called the Dysfunctional Thought Record, is described at length in Beck *et al.* (1979).

symptoms first evident in the second week between the first and second sessions continued to accelerate; Cliff reported no panic attacks and only occasional episodes of mild to moderate anxiety. He attributed this improvement to his increasing sense of predictability; while he could not always tell when he would begin to ruminate he became increasingly certain that it was the content of his thinking that largely determined his anxiety level, rather than any disturbance in his capacity to "think straight" or control his impulses. He also became increasingly comfortable with respect to testing his capacity to control his behavior, for example, voluntarily introducing thoughts that he did not want to act on, simply to prove to himself that he could think about "scary" actions and still choose not to act on those thoughts.

Fifth Session

By the fifth session, Cliff was initiating enactive tests of his capacities, for example, going to a nearby amusement park to ride the ferris wheel, encouraging his roommate to take a weekend trip so that he could practice being alone and dealing on his own with feeling jealous and fearing abandonment. He also reported consciously acting so as to please himself, even if it meant not meeting someone else's expectations. He reported having usually tried to "play up to people so they would like me," and he found his newfound capacities "exhilarating." He described being intrigued by the notion that his beliefs were "like gossip" that required "checking out" (a concept introduced several weeks earlier in an effort to communicate the basic theory of a cognitive approach in everyday terminology), and stated that he found himself using the approach to examine beliefs that he had "just always taken for granted."

Sixth and Final Sessions

By the sixth session (seven weeks after beginning treatment), Cliff had been largely symptom-free for close to three weeks. He reported himself able to stand on high places, able to handle sharp objects, able to spend the night alone, and able to disagree with his roommate without experiencing distress. He further reported that the quality of his relationships had improved, particularly with his roommate, but also with his family, in that although feeling more independent and outspoken, he was less moody, or in his terms, "bitchy." He further described having smoked marijuana at a party earlier in the week. He again began getting anxious, but "talked myself out of it," reminding himself that some anxiety was reasonable, since he viewed his exposure as a "test." He described calming himself down by reminding himself that he was not likely to be going crazy and reviewing the evidence he had generated for himself over the last several weeks about his ability to tolerate "scary" situations without "going crazy." He reported staying at the party without further distress. After reviewing progress made during the previous sessions we agreed to terminate regular sessions. Table 2 describes the course and nature of symptoms before and during active treatment.

FOLLOW-UP

Follow-up contacts were held one month and ten months later. Cliff described himself as being essentially symptom-free throughout the entire period. He even described, with evident pride, going to visit a relative hospitalized in a psychiatric unit, pointing out that he used to get anxious even thinking about an inpatient facility. He volunteered that he had regarded that visit as the "biggest feat of all," since he had come to believe that it was his fear of losing his mind, triggered by his misattribution of his drug experience, that lay at the root of his problems.

DISCUSSION

In the previous case history, a cognitive–behavioral approach was utilized to help the client first understand, then alter, his presenting symptomatology. The program of intervention, adhering to a strategy of collaborative empiricism (Hollon & Beck, 1979) in which client and therapist worked jointly to formulate empirical tests of the client's beliefs, was carefully integrated with the process of assessment. Rather than attempting to decide, via traditional diagnostics, whether or not the patient was presenting with a major thinking disorder, the therapist moved rapidly from imaginal to *in vivo* tests as a means of assessing the integrity of the patient's thinking. Throughout treatment, the therapist consistently formulated the following questions: (1) What's

TABLE 2. *Sequence of symptoms and treatment for Client 1*

Time	Symptoms	Treatment
October 5, 1974	*Onset:* panic attack following exposure to marijuana	First visit to hospital emergency room
December 1974	Continued symptoms; panic attacks followed by depression, chronic anxiety between episodes with multiple phobias	Second visit to hospital emergency room
January 1975	Continued symptoms as above	Begin outpatient pharmacotherapy plus brief supportive contacts
May 1976	Continued symptoms as above	Terminate outpatient treatments
June 1976	Exacerbation of symptoms following second exposure to marijuana	Third visit to hospital emergency room
June 7, 1976	Continued symptoms as above	Evaluation: referral for depth psychotherapy with adjunctive hypnotherapy
July 20, 1976	Continued symptoms as above	*First session:* test beliefs, trip to roof, assign "diary"
August 5, 1976	Remains largely symptomatic, but some reduction of frequency of panic attacks	*Second session:* introduce triple-column technique, assign *Coping with Depression,* review diary
August 13, 1976	Occasional symptomatic episodes, but marked decrease in frequency and intensity	*Third session:* review triple-column technique, discuss *Coping with Depression,* evaluate beliefs
August 20, 1976	Largely asymptomatic; no panic attacks, only infrequent anxiety	*Fourth session:* continue triple-column technique, assign behavioral tests
August 27, 1976	Symptom-free	*Fifth session:* review behavioral tests
September 15, 1976	Symptom-free	*Sixth session:* plan termination, review progress
October 1976	Symptom-free	Follow-up session
July 1977	Symptom-free	Follow-up session

the evidence for that belief? (2) Is there any other way of looking at that incident? (3) What new evidence would help us decide between your initial, and our new hypothesis? (Hollon, 1980).

CLIENT 2: DAVE

The second client, Dave, was a 26-year-old white male, employed as a maintenance worker at a local factory.

At the time of intake, Dave had been married for one-and-one-half years, and had an 8-year-old daughter by an earlier marriage. Dave presented for treatment complaining of frequent severe spells of nervousness and dizziness. The episodes were marked by extreme anxiety, hot and cold flashes, light-headedness, and feelings of shakiness and exhaustion.

The episodes had begun approximately four years earlier. The initial episode had occurred during a "bad trip" on LSD. The patient reconstituted readily, but retained the fear that he had almost "lost his mind." Several months later, while driving back from a weekend trip with several friends, the patient began to experience an overwhelming fear that he wouldn't be able to control his actions. Panic episodes continued, with considerable frequency, up to several times a week. At the time of our initial interview, the patient had received extensive medical treatment and neurological evaluation, with little effect.

During the first session, it became apparent that, like Cliff, the patient seriously believed that he had suffered a drug-induced psychotic episode during his first drug exposure. His current symptomatology, consisting of sudden, overwhelming panic states, heart palpitations, dizziness, tremors, sweating, and hot and cold sensations, was attributed by Dave to his earlier drug experience. From Dave's perspective, these attacks were totally unpredictable. They appeared to overtake him without warning and, when they arrived, to be totally incapacitating. Dave reported having developed a variety of phobic avoidant behaviors, for example, not driving over bridges or not going up on the roof of the building at work. These situations were viewed as ones in which the onset of the panic states (which he believed to be drug-related "flashbacks" in which he was on the verge of psychotic decompensation) could lead to real physical danger to himself or others. Typical of his beliefs was his questioning "How do I know I won't drive the car right off the bridge?'' He described vivid visual fantasies (which he labeled "hallucinations") of himself doing exactly that, with the car crashing over the railing and plunging to the ground.

FIRST TREATMENT SESSION

At the initial session, it was possible to ascertain that a consistent set of cognitions typically accompanied the panic states. It was not as clear that there was any consistency as to when the attacks occurred. It was also not clear that Dave was not experiencing a more malignant drug-related or schizophrenia-related thinking disorder.

The client was instructed in self-monitoring procedures, recording events, activities, and anxiety level on an hourly basis throughout the week (see Beck et al., 1979, or Hollon & Kendall, 1981, for extended discussions of self-monitoring procedures). Table 3 presents one of Dave's weekly records from early in treatment.

SECOND TREATMENT SESSION

At the second session, it became evident from the self-monitoring data that the primary cue for the onset of the panic attacks was the anticipation of exposure to a situation in which Dave thought it would be physically dangerous to experience such an attack. One such situation involved driving his car over bridges. Figure 1 presents a summary of anxious "high-points" when driving. In essence, the beliefs that (1) he might decompensate and lose control over his actions and (2) if he did, he would kill himself invariably covaried with the panic states.

This suggested a different formulation from that held by Dave. Rather than experiencing decompensation that led to panic, he appeared to be thinking that he *might* decompensate, which led to panic. In the former case, the fear is viewed as the product in incipient insanity, and thus appeared to confirm that fear. In the latter case, the anxiety could be viewed as a fairly rational consequence of a mistaken notion.

Dave was interested in, but far from convinced by, this reformulation. We attempted two maneuvers in that session. First, I suggested that Dave voluntarily make himself as anxious as possible in the office at that moment, as an experiment to test Dave's corollary hypothesis that extreme anxiety would push him into a full-blown decompensa-

TABLE 3. *Client-generated self-monitoring of activity events and anxiety level (0—none to 50—extreme)*

	M	T	W (10/20)	Th (10/21)	F	S	S
9–10			Drive, 36 Work in wheel, 20 Walk to brake, 32 Light head	Drive, 30 Work on roof of wheel, 15			
10–11			Work in wheel, 20	Ride on cart, 20			
11–12			Lunch 11:40–12:30, 30 Dizzy walking back from lunch	Lunch, 38 Nervous for 15 min.			
12–1			Walk, 30	21			

1–2	Work wheel, read paper, 15	Read paper at wheel, 20
2–3	Work wheel, 15	Drive truck, 23
3–4	Walk back 3:30, shop, 30	25
4–5	Worked O.T., cut weeds, 30	Drive home, 40 Nervous
5–6	Worked, cut weeds, 30 Little dizzy	Home Feel better out of car, 20
6–7	Work over, 30	Listen to stereo, 15
7–8	Ride home 8:00, 33	At bar till 10:00, 20
8–12	Watch TV, 20	20
AVERAGE	26.25	24.83

Note. Grade activities M for mastery and P for pleasure.

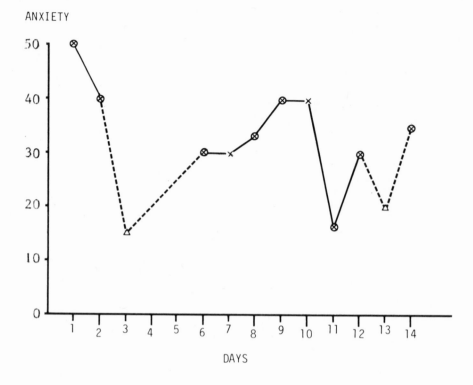

ANXIETY

FIGURE 1. *Self-monitoring of anxiety: Relation to driving.*

Key: × Highest anxiety rating for day occurs while not driving

⊗ Highest anxiety rating for day occurs while driving

△ Highest anxiety rating - did not drive this day

Days driving highest: 8 of 12 = 67%

(Excluding days not driving: 8 of 10 = 80%)

% of hours spent driving: 20 of 129 = 16%

tion. While Dave was initially reluctant, he finally agreed after a period of discussion. It was pointed out that his efforts at self-protection had essentially crippled him over the last several years, and that if he were ever going to finally break down, he might as well do it in a hospital in the presence of a psychologist.

As might be expected, Dave was able only to make himself

extremely anxious. He was not able to make himself "crack." Interestingly, he used exactly the kinds of thoughts and fantasies that spontaneously accompanied his panic states to induce his "experimental" panic state.

The second maneuver involved asking for reports of other instances in which he had become highly aroused in a positive fashion. Dave reported an intramural football game in which he had caught the winning pass. When asked to describe his physiological state, he reported similar kinds of sensations as during his panic states, although his mood was one of exhilaration rather than dread. We then discussed the body's generalized capacity for arousal, with similar physiologic processes occurring whether the eliciting situation was pleasurable or threatening, external or covert. This discussion helped to undercut his attribution of his panic-related arousal states to some drug-induced decompensation.

SUBSEQUENT SESSIONS

Dave continued self-monitoring over the next several sessions. Explicit cognitive restructuring, using Beck's Dysfunctional Thought Record (Beck *et al.*, 1979) was also instituted and proved to be helpful in the process of identifying, challenging, and disconfirming beliefs.

Perhaps most helpful, however, were two additional maneuvers added to the treatment package. First was the use of guided fantasy. The vivid images of impending loss of control and subsequent disaster appeared to play a particularly large role in the panic attacks. It was explained to Dave that while humans appear to have little direct control over their passive fantasy processes, they could choose to guide their fantasies actively. Dave began to train himself to alter his spontaneous fantasies. When approaching a bridge in his car, for example, he would begin to experience a spontaneous visual image in which he would lose control and steer the car toward the rail. He would then remind himself, "Its only an image. What's more, its my fantasy. I can change it if I want to." He would then guide his own fantasy in a more positive direction, for example, guiding the car back to the center of the road in his imagination.

The second therapeutic maneuver involved Dave's growing recognition that his capacity to induce (and, to a lesser extent, reduce) anxiety made the whole process less mysterious and less formidable. Dave treated these instances as experiments; he was helped to regard himself as an investigator discerning the true nature of causality with regard to his symptoms rather than as a victim of those symptoms.

Figure 2 depicts the relationship between anxiety and driving in the first versus the last two weeks of therapy. As can be seen, there was a considerable change in the intensity level of self-reported anxiety in the client's 50-point intensity-of-anxiety scale.

TERMINATION AND FOLLOW-UP

Treatment lasted over five months, with the frequency of sessions dropping from once weekly initially to biweekly in the last two months. Dave was virtually asymptomatic at termination. Follow-up visits at six months and one-year posttermination indicated that Dave remained essentially asymptomatic.

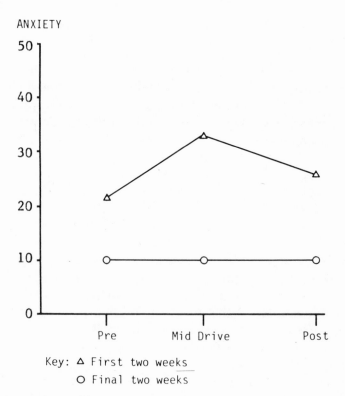

FIGURE 2. *Relationship of anxiety to driving: First versus last two weeks of therapy.*

DISCUSSION

Like Cliff, Dave appeared to be symptomatic largely because of a basic misattribution of panic states to earlier drug experiences. Treatment that essentially involved identifying and disconfirming beliefs about the etiologies and implications of panic states was strikingly successful in both cases.

While there is no reason to think that *all* cases of drug-related psychopathology follow this pattern, there are several points of commonality between the two clients that may facilitate identification and treatment efforts. Essentially, these points are the following:

1. Both clients had been essentially free of psychiatric disorder prior to the drug-related episode and each had evidenced a fairly rich and satisfactory set of interpersonal relationships.
2. Both attributed initial anxiety states to drug-induced decompensation, and both attributed subsequent attacks to psychic damage induced during those initial episodes.
3. Both believed that they were in imminent danger of total decompensation.
4. Both believed that, during one of these decompensations, they were quite capable of losing control of aggressive or self-destructive impulses.
5. Both had been misdiagnosed by a series of mental-health professions, either by omission or commission, and both had received several years of inappropriate interventions.

Figure 3 depicts a cognitive–behavioral functional analysis of the etiology and maintenance of this syndrome. As can be seen, it is the misconception, "I'm losing my mind," in the initial drug episode that leads to the development of the panic states and avoidance behaviors. Once set in motion, this syndrome is maintained by a sequence of beliefs in which various cues (S^D's) trigger the expectation that "I may not be able to control my impulses, what happens if I . . ? ," which is based on the belief that "I have the capacity to go crazy," which results from the misattribution of panic states to the physiological effects of that earlier drug experience.

Diagnostic and treatment interventions similarly evidenced several points of congruence. These similarities included:

ETIOLOGY:

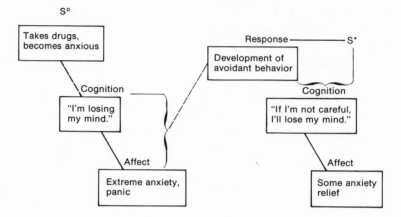

MAINTENANCE:

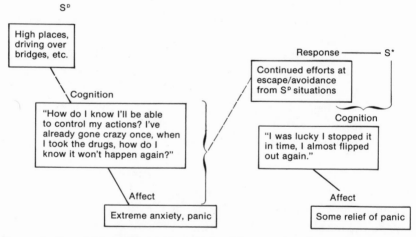

FIGURE 3. *Cognitive–behavioral analysis of drug-induced pansituational anxiety states.*

6. the use of *in vivo* self-monitoring procedures to detect a lawful relationship between specific cue cognitions and subsequent panic states,

7. the effect that the detection of this predictability of onset had on each client's beliefs about the causes and implications of

the symptoms; that is, there seems to be no good reason why someone should begin to decompensate only when one thinks about decompensation although it is eminently "normal" to become frightened if you believe that something awful is about to happen,

8. the benefit derived from the process of being provided with a reasonable alternative explanation for their symptoms, especially when,

9. both engaged in mini-experiments that directly pitted their new, more benign explanation against their original, more malignant, decompensation notion, and, finally,

10. the benefit derived from an intensive regime of *self-applied* self-monitoring, cognitive restructuring, guided fantasy, and enactive hypothesis testing. After some initial training and guidance, both clients invested considerable time and energy in the process of self-change. Both became, in effect, their own therapists.

SUMMARY

In the two case studies described, two young male clients were successfully treated for drug-induced pansituational anxiety states via cognitive–behavioral means. In both cases, treatment results exceeded the therapist's initial expectations, and, in both cases, diagnosis and treatment grew directly out of a careful cognitive–behavioral functional analysis. This underscores the fact that neither therapist nor client need necessarily know the "exact" nature of the disorder being dealt with nor the "best" type of intervention to select. Even in the absence of such knowledge, a careful program of hypothesis generation and hypothesis testing should lead, ultimately, to an empirically grounded set of solutions. In the cases described, such a process helped discern the basis of, and led to the reversal of, drug-induced pansituational anxiety.

ACKNOWLEDGMENT

An earlier version of this chapter was presented at the Annual Meeting of the American Psychological Association, New York, New York, September 1979, under the title, "Cognitive therapy in drug-induced pansituational anxiety states."

REFERENCES

Beck, A. T. *Cognitive therapy and the emotional disorders*. New York: International Universities Press, 1976.

Beck, A. T., Rush, A. J., Shaw, B. F., & Emery, G. *Cognitive therapy of depression*. New York: Guilford Press, 1979.

Hollon, S. D. *A component analysis of systematic cognitive restructuring*. Unpublished manuscript, University of Minnesota, Minneapolis, 1980.

Hollon, S. D., & Beck, A. T. Cognitive therapy of depression. In P. C. Kendall & S. D. Hollon (Eds.), *Cognitive-behavioral intervention: Theory, research, and procedures*. New York: Academic Press, 1979.

Hollon, S. D., & Kendall, P. C. *In vivo* assessment techniques for cognitive-behavioral processes. In P. C. Kendall & S. D. Hollon (Eds.), *Assessment strategies for cognitive-behavioral interventions*. New York: Academic Press, 1981.

Horney, K. *Collected works*. New York: Norton, 1965.

Raimy, V. *Misunderstandings of the self*. San Francisco: Jossey-Bass, 1974.

Weekes, C. *Hope and help for your nerves*. New York: Hawthorn Books, 1969.

Weekes, C. *Peace from nervous suffering*. New York: Hawthorn Books, 1972.

COGNITIVE THERAPY AND LONELINESS

Jeffrey E. Young

INTRODUCTION

Few psychologists or psychiatrists have written specifically about the treatment of loneliness. This observation is remarkable in light of its estimated high incidence rate in both general (Bradburn, 1969; Shaver & Freedman, 1976) and psychiatric (cited in Rosenbaum & Rosenbaum, 1973) populations. Loneliness has also been implicated as one possible causal factor in other disorders, including depression (Ortega, 1969), suicide (Wenz, 1977), and serious medical problems such as cardiovascular disease (Lynch, 1977).

In this chapter, I will outline a comprehensive psychotherapy for loneliness based on the principles of cognitive therapy. I will describe seven stages of treatment: diagnosing loneliness, gathering baseline data, planning activities to improve the experience of being alone, initiating nonintimate relationships, self-disclosing in nonintimate relationships, initiating intimate relationships, and deepening intimate relationships. For each stage, I will elaborate on specific dysfunctional cognitions and behaviors that lead to difficulties in attaining the stated goals and I will suggest appropriate therapeutic strategies. Finally, I will illustrate the application of cognitive therapy for loneliness by describing an actual case.

DIAGNOSIS

Perhaps one reason loneliness has been neglected as a problem warranting serious attention is that many patients suffering from it either do

Jeffrey E. Young. Department of Psychiatry, University of Pennsylvania, Philadelphia, Pennsylvania.

not recognize loneliness as an important aspect of their problem or do not want to use the label because they are ashamed of their feelings or the perceived inadequacies underlying these feelings. Therefore, it is essential for clinicians to have diagnostic criteria for assessing the presence of loneliness that do not depend solely on patients' spontaneous use of the "lonely" label.

I define loneliness as the absence, or perceived absence, of satisfying social relationships, accompanied by symptoms of psychological distress. According to this definition, I will define as lonely either those people who specifically label themselves as lonely and dissatisfied; or those who report they are not currently experiencing most of the benefits of social relationships that nonlonely people typically enjoy and who are showing signs of psychological distress or maladjustment (e.g., anxiety, depression, insomnia, drug abuse, alcoholism). Thus, an individual who rejects the label might nevertheless be termed "lonely."

I developed the Young Inventory to diagnose loneliness (Figure 1). The inventory is comprised of 18 items dealing with specific benefits obtained from social relationships and with some typical attitudes lonely people express about their relationships. The items were derived from interviews with college students, a research study contrasting lonely moods with happy moods (Young, 1979a), and therapy sessions with lonely patients. (For information regarding reliability, validity, and norms, see Young, 1979b.) The inventory is based on the following composite picture of lonely individuals as being without:

1. a "caring" person to depend on;
2. someone who understands them;
3. the opportunity to express their private feelings to another person;
4. a close group of friends they feel part of;
5. someone who needs them and wants their love;
6. other people who share their values and interests;
7. friends to share enjoyable activities;
8. friendships they had at another point in their lives and have been unable to replace;
9. a particular person they lost;
10. collegial relationships at work;
11. a sense of trust with close friends; and
12. physical intimacy on a regular basis.

It has proven useful to distinguish lonely individuals on the basis of how long they have been experiencing unsatisfying relationships. *Chronic loneliness* refers to people who have not been able to establish satisfying relationships for a period of several years, across at least two developmental stages (e.g., adolescence and early adulthood). *Transitional or situational loneliness* involves individuals who had had adequate relationships until they were confronted either with a specific crisis (e.g., death, divorce) or with a predictable developmental change (e.g., leaving home for college, dealing with old age). *Transient loneliness* includes the everyday variety of brief and occasional lonely moods. Transient loneliness will not be discussed in this paper since individuals classified here are unlikely to present themselves for treatment. And, when they do, the loneliness usually subsides rapidly leading to early termination.

GATHERING BASELINE DATA

I and other therapists at the Center for Cognitive Therapy of the University of Pennsylvania have been applying cognitive–behavioral techniques to the problem of loneliness in the context of treating depression. Our experience with lonely patients suggests that most people we see who feel lonely do, in fact, have friendships that would be unsatisfying to most of us. They do not seem to be significantly more demanding than other people; their loneliness usually involves more than unreasonable expectations. Therefore, the focus of treatment will usually have to involve specific behavioral changes in the way lonely people initiate and deepen relationships.

The first step in treatment is to obtain detailed baseline data regarding the patient's social relationships, both currently and before the onset of the problem. A chart such as the one depicted in Table 1 is often helpful.

Patients are asked to list across the top of the chart the names of all friends and close family members during a given period of time. They then rate each friend on a scale from 0 (low) to 10 (high) for frequency, disclosure, caring, and physical intimacy. The *frequency* rating indicates the amount of time the patient and friend spent together. For *disclosure,* patients rate the extent to which they and the friend were able to discuss private thoughts and feelings: the more private the issues that were disclosed, the higher the rating. The *caring* score

On this questionnaire are groups of statements. Please read each group of statements carefully. Then pick out the one statement in each group that best describes you. Circle the number beside the statement you picked. If several statements in the group seem to apply equally well, circle each one. Be sure to read all the statements in each group before making your choice.

Name _____ Date _____

1. 0   I have someone nearby I can really depend on and who cares about me.
    1   I'm not sure there's anyone nearby I can really depend on and who cares about me.
    2   There's no one anywhere I can really depend on and who cares about me right now.
    3   For several years, I haven't had anyone I could really depend on and who cared about me.

2. 0   There is someone nearby who really understands me.
    1   I'm not sure there's anyone nearby who really understands me.
    2   There's no one who really understands me anywhere right now.
    3   For several years, no one has really understood me.

3. 0   I have someone nearby I could talk to about my private feelings.
    1   There's no one nearby I could talk to about my private feelings.
    2   There's no one I could talk to about my private feelings anywhere right now.
    3   For several years, I haven't had anyone I could talk to about my private feelings.

4. 0   I have a close group of friends nearby that I feel part of.
    1   I don't feel part of any close group of friends nearby.
    2   I don't have a close group of friends anywhere right now.
    3   For several years, I haven't had a close group of friends.

5. 0   There is someone nearby who really needs me and wants my love.
    1   I'm not sure anyone nearby really needs me and wants my love.
    2   There isn't anyone anywhere who really needs me or wants my love right now.
    3   For several years, no one has really needed me or wanted my love.

6. 0   I have a lot in common with other people I know.
    1   I wish my values and interests, and those of other people I know, were more similar.
    2   I'm different from other people I know.
    3   I've felt different from other people for several years.

7. 0   When I want to do something for enjoyment, I can usually find someone to join me.
    1   Often I end up doing things alone even though I'd like to have someone join me.
    2   There's no one right now I can go out and enjoy things with.
    3   There hasn't been anyone I could go out and enjoy things with for several years.

8. 0   There are no groups I'd really like to belong to that won't accept me.
    1   There is a group of people I know that I'd like to belong to but don't.
    2   It bothers me that there is a group of people I know right now who don't like me.
    3   For the past several years I've felt excluded by group(s) of people I've wanted to belong to.

9. 0   I rarely think about particular times in my life when my relationships seemed better.
    1   I sometimes wish my relationships now could be more like they were at another time in my life.
    2   I am often disturbed about how unsatisfactory my relationships now are compared with another time in my life.
    3   I cannot stop thinking about how much better my relationships once were.

FIGURE 1. *Young Loneliness Inventory.*

10. 0   I don't miss anyone in particular right now.
    1   I miss someone who isn't here now.
    2   I often think about a particular person I was close to.
    3   I cannot stop thinking about someone I lost.

11. 0   I feel like a part of a "team" with the people I work with.
    1   I am not employed at the present time.
    1   There is little team feeling where I work.
    2   There is a team feeling among the people I work with, but I do not feel I fit in.
    3   Most of the people I work with don't like me.

12. 0   I can usually talk freely to close friends about my thoughts and feelings.
    1   I have some difficulty talking to close friends about my thoughts and feelings.
    2   I feel like my thoughts and feelings are bottled up inside.
    3   I cannot seem to communicate with anyone.

13. 0   The important people in my life have not let me down.
    1   I'm still disappointed at someone I thought I could trust.
    2   As I look back at my life, many people I trusted have let me down.
    3   I find I can't trust anyone anymore.

14. 0   I can almost always enjoy myself when I am alone.
    1   I can sometimes enjoy myself alone.
    2   I can rarely enjoy myself alone.
    3   I can never really enjoy myself when I am alone.

15. 0   I rarely wish that my relationships could be more like other people's.
    1   I sometimes wish that I could have relationships that satisfied me the way other people's relationships satisfy them.
    2   I often wish that I could have relationships that satisfied me the way other people's relationships satisfy them.
    3   I cannot stop comparing the satisfaction other people get from their relationships with my own lack of satisfaction.

16. 0   There is someone I am physically intimate with now on a regular basis.
    1   I am not physically intimate with anyone now on a regular basis.
    2   I am often disturbed that I am not physically intimate with someone on a regular basis now.
    3   I have never been physically intimate with anyone on a regular basis for several months.

17. 0   I haven't felt lonely during the past week (including today).
    1   I've felt somewhat lonely during the past week (including today).
    2   I've felt very lonely during the past week (including today).
    3   I could barely stand the loneliness during the past week (including today).

18. 0   Loneliness has never been a real problem for me.
    1   There have been times in my life when I've felt quite lonely, but not during the past few months.
    2   I've felt lonely regularly during the past few months.
    3   I've felt lonely regularly for more than a year.
    4   I've felt lonely for several years.
    5   I've always felt lonely.

TABLE 1. *Sample friendship chart*

	Friends' names (1976–1978)	
	John	Judy
Frequency rating (0–10)	8	5
Disclosure rating (0–10)	8	1
"Caring" rating (0–10)	9	5
Physical intimacy rating (0–10)	0	0
Date relationship began	January 1975	March 1978
Date relationship ended or weakened	June 1978	May 1978
Reason for ending or weakening	He moved away.	I lost interest.

represents the patients' evaluation of how much each friend could be trusted and depended upon, especially at times of crisis. Finally, the *physical intimacy* rating includes both the regularity of intimate physical contact and the satisfaction patients obtained from the physical element of each relationship.

There will probably be a considerable degree of overlap among these four ratings. Nevertheless, they provide important clues regarding the nature of the patient's loneliness. First of all, we are interested in determining whether the patient is lonely primarily because of difficulties in *initiating* relationships or problems in *deepening* them. The tentative focus of treatment will follow from this analysis. Patients who list very few friends of either sex, or who report spending very little time with the friends listed (frequency rating), should probably begin with the initiating phase of treatment, which I will describe shortly. Patients who name friends of both sexes and who have frequent contact with them, but who indicate limited disclosure, caring, or physical intimacy, are probably more appropriate for the *deepening* phase of therapy.

PLANNING ACTIVITIES

Let us begin by assuming that our patient has been living in relative isolation from other people, spending most free time alone for several years. The chronically lonely patient such as this one often reveals many symptoms of depression, especially inactivity, lack of energy, and loss of pleasure in activities that once were enjoyable. Sometimes lonely patients do not want to do anything if they have to do it alone. Nevertheless, we find that engaging in activities, even alone, is often an essential first step in treating loneliness. Therefore, inactive patients can be given a rationale such as the following:

> I don't believe that simply learning to enjoy being alone will be enough to solve your problems. In fact, I feel strongly that we will have to work together to help you initiate and deepen relationships. However, we have found that being active is very helpful *as a first step,* to get you moving again, even if this means doing things alone for a while.

To help isolated patients "get moving again," we often use the techniques of *activity scheduling* and *pleasure therapy,* described elsewhere (Beck, Rush, Shaw, & Emery, 1979). This strategy involves helping the lonely patient plan activities for each day's free time. Patients are first asked to list hobbies, sports, and other interests that they once found enjoyable, concentrating especially on activities that involve vigorous movement, that require leaving the house, or that place them in contact with other people. The therapist should incorporate in this schedule one specific assignment involving a potential friend. The assignment should be one the patient considers manageable. Depending on the individual's willingness, it may be as simple as calling an old friend and having a conversation or as "advanced" as asking someone out for a date.

Patients are asked to write down any problems they have in carrying out the assignment, especially any thoughts they are aware of having as they anticipate initiating the relationship. As we shall see, this early attention to cognitions is of great importance, although these cognitions may not become the focus of treatment until later in therapy. The emphasis on thoughts, beliefs, and expectations is a major difference between a cognitive–behavioral and a strictly behavioral approach to loneliness.

INITIATING NONINTIMATE RELATIONSHIPS

Once the patient has begun following a more active schedule of activities, the emphasis in treatment changes to the development of a satisfying friendship involving companionship and self-disclosure, usually with someone of the same sex. This stage is usually initiated during the activity-planning period when the patient is asked to contact a potential companion and do something with that companion.

PATIENTS REACTING TO AN UNRESOLVED RELATIONSHIP

The first group of patients who often have difficulty initiating nonintimate relationships are those who have been involved in a previous intimate relationship that they have not been able to resolve satisfactorily. This is especially common among patients who have recently been divorced or separated and cannot seem to achieve a sense of closure. Some of their typical automatic thoughts might be: (1) "She left me because I don't know how to communicate." (2) "I don't know how to show my feelings." (3) "I'm just not worth loving." (4) "I don't know if I will ever be able to trust anyone again."

With patients such as these, it may be necessary to review the entire relationship to understand why the relationship did, in fact, end, thereby helping the patients challenge their maladaptive automatic thoughts. A helpful assumption for the therapist to hold and try to communicate to patients is that many relationships end because of either (1) some unrecognized basic incompatibility between the patient and the partner, or (2) changes that took place in one or both partners, making it increasingly difficult for them to function together. Even when patients remain convinced that a relationship ended because of a flaw in their behavior, it is still not true that any future relationship is doomed. When some flaw does exist, it is usually correctable, but detection and change proceed best when the client is working in the context of a new relationship.

PATIENTS WITH A SERIES OF TRANSIENT RELATIONSHIPS

A second belief that prevents some lonely patients from initiating new relationships (even with someone of the same sex) is that it is safer not to get involved with anyone because eventually the relationship will falter, as others have. This general pessimism may arise from unreasonable expectations about how long most relationships "should" last, or the degree of commitment one can expect from friendships. Some patients cannot accept the fact that many friendships are transient.

The therapist may need to point out that relationships are constantly in a state of transition; that simultaneous relationships may vary in their level of caring and commitment, yet can still be valid. Some friendships may even be based primarily on convenience: Two people may enjoy pursuing activities together over a period of a few months and then separate. In short, patients may need help lowering their expectations in order to initiate casual friendships that will reduce their loneliness.

PATIENTS WHO BELIEVE THEY ARE UNDESIRABLE

Many lonely patients avoid social contact because they believe they are unattractive, unlikable, dull and boring, stupid, or unable to carry on a friendship. Assuming these patients are not extremely deficient in social skills, the therapist can help them review past relationships to refute the hypothesis that most people avoid them because they are unlikable, dull, etc. Specifically, the therapist can point out that (1) they are inappropriately generalizing from one or two bad relationships, and (2) they have had friends who accepted them in the past. If the therapist feels, after observing the patient, that he or she probably is driving people away, then the therapist and patient should reconceptualize the problem. The patient is not cursed with a "basic flaw," but rather lacks a particular social skill that the therapist and patient can work to develop. Some of the common socially unacceptable behaviors are: trying too hard to make an impression, self-disclosing too much too soon, being too passive, self-effacing, cynical, or aloof.

PATIENTS WITH SOCIAL ANXIETY

Another problem that often arises with lonely patients early in treatment is some form of social phobia, fear of being in the company of other people. They may hold the belief that they are going to be rejected or that they will look foolish and embarrass themselves. Sometimes anxiety symptoms intensify and patients interpret their symptoms as signs that they are going crazy, will lose control, or will do something that will be a tremendous embarrassment. Therefore, the patient may avoid other people completely.

Other socially phobic patients engage in "spectatoring" behavior, a term borrowed from the sex therapy literature (Kaplan, 1974). Spectatoring refers to the tendency of some lonely patients to observe themselves while they are engaged in social interactions. This morbid self-monitoring contributes to patients' discomfort and makes it even more difficult for them to engage other people or to derive pleasure from relationships. With lonely patients who are phobic in this manner, treatment would proceed as with other types of anxiety. Some of the most common techniques are teaching distraction procedures, helping them answer automatic thoughts, and role-playing. These procedures are illustrated in the case study at the end of this chapter.

SELF-DISCLOSURE IN NONINTIMATE RELATIONSHIPS

Once the patient is able to initiate social contact and obtain pleasure from casual friendships, the therapist encourages the patient to deepen one relationship (usually with a same-sex friend) by including the self-disclosure of private thoughts and feelings. This is a very important step in therapy since it serves as a prelude to an intimate opposite-sex relationship, but without the "threat" of permanence and commitment. The therapist instructs the patient to share a personal problem or feeling with a potential close friend, and to ask questions that encourage the friend to do the same.

Patients who are unable to carry out this assignment often believe that friends will reject them if they disclose weaknesses or shameful thoughts. The therapist can assist these patients to recognize that sharing thoughts about, for example, inadequacy, worthlessness, anger, and dependency, is an important aspect of intimacy, that most close friends will welcome an opportunity to hear and disclose private feelings. The therapist can play the part of the patient self-disclosing, while the patient plays the part of the listening friend. As patients listen to the "friend's" self-disclosure, they almost inevitably report feeling understanding and caring for the friend, instead of disgust. They often conclude from this role-playing that their "secrets" are not so terrible after all and that they can probably improve intimacy through self-disclosure.

The therapist must be especially alert at this point for abrupt terminations of, or feelings of dissatisfaction with, relationships. The lonely patient is often very sensitive to what other people would consider normal problems that arise in a relationship, and any disagreement, criticism, injustice, or slight may be exaggerated. The therapist can work with patients to identify thoughts that illustrate such logical errors in thinking as "arbitrary inference," in which the patient draws an unjustified conclusion from the evidence available. For example, a lonely patient whose boyfriend tells her she is gaining weight may inaccurately conclude from his statement that he no longer loves her and she may withdraw from him. Many lonely patients will have to be helped to work through problems instead of terminating relationships prematurely.

INITIATING INTIMATE RELATIONSHIPS

Once the patient has been able to develop a close friendship of a nonintimate nature, therapy is directed toward helping patients develop intimate relationships, usually with partners of the opposite sex. (The same procedures could, of course, be applied to homosexual patients.)

PATIENTS WHO DO NOT KNOW WHERE TO LOOK

The initial goal is to work with the patient to develop a list of possible ways of finding a suitable partner. The therapist must convey the belief that it may take a long time to meet a partner who shares interests, is enjoyable to be with, seems attractive, and meets all the other qualifications that make an intimate relationship possible. Nevertheless, it is generally not effective to wait around the house, or go alone to movies, expecting to meet someone. The therapist at this point can introduce the concept of the *probability* of meeting a desirable partner. For example, if the patient believes that about one out of every 30 members of the opposite sex would be a suitable partner, then the patient would be very likely to initiate a good relationship if he or she could meet 30 or more eligible people.

The therapist can suggest some of the common ways that men and women find partners:

1. Contact old acquaintances or friends.
2. Ask friends to arrange a date with someone who seems compatible.
3. Become involved in a club or organization with others who share the patient's interests (tennis, poker, theater, church, etc.).

4. Approach acquaintances in everyday situations (especially at work, but also on public transportation, in their apartment buildings or neighborhoods, at restaurants).
5. Join groups that are particularly oriented to the single person (e.g., singles dances, bars, vacations).

PATIENTS WHO RESIST INITIATING CONTACT

A significant proportion of lonely patients resist initiating contact with potentially intimate members of the opposite sex. Therefore, once again, the therapist can help the patient identify the automatic thoughts leading to this avoidance behavior. Many female patients believe that it is inappropriate for a woman to try to initiate a relationship. Here the therapist must alert patients to changing social mores.

Both men and women avoid initiating opposite-sex relationships as a result of what is commonly called "the fear of rejection," the belief that they are, in some respect, unattractive to the opposite sex and are likely to be ignored by desirable men or women. Sometimes this belief is based on evidence from previous relationships or attempts to establish relationships. Furthermore, patients who anticipate rejection usually identify particular personal shortcomings that they believe are responsible for their difficulties with the opposite sex. In addition to testing out hypotheses that they are "ugly," "stupid," or "boring," patients can be helped to question the myth that, for example, all women want men who are tall, dark, self-confident, athletic, and charming. Ideally, patients would reinterpret "rejection" as "incompatibility," rather than as evidence of general undesirability or rejectability.

PATIENTS WITH LOW TOLERANCE FOR DISCOMFORT

Another common problem among lonely patients is low tolerance for discomfort. Most people find the process of initiating an opposite-sex relationship somewhat uncomfortable; they feel it is safer to be with someone they know who accepts them. The "singles scene" therefore often involves situations and settings that create discomfort. In these instances, the therapist should try to focus the patient's attention on the positive benefits of increasing the chances of meeting someone who will care about them and whom they will care about. Often this discomfort can be reduced by helping the patient view the process more as playing a game than as putting him- or herself on the line. Having a friend along to share the trials and tribulations may also make it easier to initiate relationships.

PATIENTS WITH SOCIAL-SKILLS DEFICITS

Many lonely patients feel they do not know how to initiate opposite-sex relationships. One of the most effective procedures for this problem is role-playing. The therapist models an appropriate way of beginning a conversation; then they reverse roles and the patient tries to incorporate the therapist's strategies. The therapist can present alternative reactions from the potential partner, ranging from full acceptance to refusal. The patient can then rehearse the situation at home through imagery, by imagining both overt behavior and covert responses to dysfunctional automatic thoughts. Role-playing not only improves social skills, but reduces anxiety by challenging patients' beliefs that they will fail.

DEEPENING INTIMATE RELATIONSHIPS

Once the patient has located a desirable and interested partner, and they seem reasonably comfortable with each other, the final step is for the patient to deepen the relationship.

PATIENTS WITH DYSFUNCTIONAL BELIEFS ABOUT THE OPPOSITE SEX

It is not unusual for lonely patients to find it much easier to disclose to someone of the same sex than the opposite sex. Underlying this difficulty is often a distorted or exaggerated view of the differences between what males and females consider acceptable behavior. Some lonely men, for example, believe that women would not sympathize if they discussed fears of being rejected, and thus feel they have to present a more confident image to women than to other men. Women may believe that they cannot discuss feelings of dependency because men will either take advantage of or lose respect for them. The therapist must urge these patients to test the validity of their hypotheses directly. The therapist can also ask patients whether they would want to carry on a long-term relationship with partners who are unable to accept them as they are.

PATIENTS AFRAID OF ENTRAPMENT

Many lonely men and women fear entrapment; that if they become too intimate, they will lose their freedom and privacy. The partner will become too dependent on them and will come to love the patient more than the patient loves the partner. The patient anticipates feeling guilty about not being able to meet the partner's expectations. The therapist should convey the notion that freedom is a continuum, not an all-or-nothing proposition. Furthermore, the patient can exert control over the level of freedom in the relationship. Entrapment only exists when one partner or the other is afraid of expressing discomfort with the other person's demands; lovers are not obligated to meet all of each other's demands. The degrees of intimacy, dependency, and freedom are determined through a negotiation process.

PATIENTS WITH SEXUAL INTIMACY PROBLEMS

Sexual intimacy is often a problem for lonely patients. Some patients have difficulty initiating sexual intimacy, while others initiate it but report sexual dysfunction or low satisfaction. The discussion of sexual dysfunction extends beyond the boundaries of this paper. However, it will be instructive to identify some of the most common problems with lonely patients.

The first is related to the "spectatoring" discussed earlier in this paper. Just as lonely patients often feel that they may embarrass themselves or perform poorly in conversations, they often believe that they are awkward or unsatisfactory in bed. The therapist can first offer the view that sexual intimacy is a form of closeness and pleasure, rather than a performance with evaluative implications; then specific techniques to avoid spectatoring can be suggested.

Sometimes lonely patients feel psychologically isolated during physical intimacy. Frequently they have held back certain feelings (usually critical) about themselves, their partner, or the relationship that create distance. Once again, encouraging patients to challenge the perceived dangers in sharing these feelings should increase intimacy.

PATIENTS WITH DIFFICULTY MAKING DEMANDS OR ADJUSTING EXPECTATIONS

Lonely patients sometimes find it difficult to achieve a balance between making reasonable demands and expecting too much from a relationship. They sometimes feel that they are giving too much in a relationship and getting too little. Often this can be overcome by standard assertiveness training. At the other extreme, they may expect to have all desires met in one relationship. The solution here is for the therapist to reeducate the lonely person, to explain that even an excellent intimate relationship can rarely meet all needs for personal contact. Lonely patients should be encouraged to find additional sources of support and companionship.

PATIENTS WHO CONSISTENTLY SELECT UNSATISFACTORY PARTNERS

The final problem that one sometimes encounters with lonely patients is a tendency to choose unsatisfactory partners. Their relationships either end relatively quickly or are extremely painful to endure. For complex reasons, some patients are attracted consistently to partners who do not meet their needs. They are sometimes cruel, do not care for the patient, act in a rejecting manner, or seem exceedingly dependent or disturbed. If the therapist and patient identify such a pattern, they can work together to develop clues for recognizing undesirable partners in advance. The patient must also be convinced that the negative consequences of continuing a relationship with such partners will outweigh their initial attraction and appeal. The therapist can recommend spending time with partners who do not interest them as much at first, yet seem to have other qualities that will prove important in the long run.

THE CASE OF MIKE B.

The case of Mike B. illustrates the cognitive–behavioral approach to loneliness, focusing especially on the treatment of social anxiety and difficulties in initiating relationships.

DIAGNOSIS AND BASELINE DATA

Mike was a 19-year-old college student whose parents suggested that he come to the Mood Clinic because he seemed withdrawn. During the diagnostic stage, it became clear that Mike was severely depressed, had experienced a dramatic loss of self-esteem, and had completely isolated himself from all but minimal contact with his family. His loneliness score was very high (27) and he reported that he was nervous about communicating with people and did not know what to say or how to act. Mike also complained that he had not taken a girl out in a long time and that he often had the feeling other people did not like him. An examination of his ratings of past relationships suggested that Mike was experiencing transitional loneliness as a result of college, since his friendships seemed satisfying throughout high school (although he mentioned no intimate female relationship).

SCHEDULING ACTIVITIES

The therapist asked Mike to keep an hour-by-hour activity schedule during the week. Mike had just finished his freshman year at college and was spending the summer living at home. The schedule revealed that Mike was spending most of his day in his bedroom alone, watching television or listening to his stereo. The only time he spent in social contact was at meals with his parents, brother, and sister. Mike reported very little sense of mastery or pleasure during the week, and felt guilty because he was acting so irritable around his family. The therapist and Mike worked together to plan a schedule for the following week that would include activities to get him out of the house and into some activity, such as golfing or swimming.

INITIATING NONINTIMATE RELATIONSHIPS

These activities seemed to produce a marked positive change in Mike's affect. However, he was not willing to contact any of his old friends or have any conversation with his family. Mike's reasons were as follows: (1) "Other people think I'm strange." (2) "My family tries to control everything I do."

Mike felt the family problem was more urgent and wanted to work on that first. He said that his parents constantly criticized him for not having chosen a career yet, but he could not very well tell them to stop because they were right. The therapist proposed that he and Mike test the hypothesis that "a college student should choose a career by the end of his freshman year." After listing the advantages and disadvantages of an early decision, Mike concluded that he had plenty of time to explore alternatives. However, he did not think he could ever persuade his parents of this. Mike and the therapist rehearsed a conversation with his mother in which Mike was to explain his reasons for postponing a choice, thank her for her concern, and ask her to stop nagging him about it. His homework assignment was to "try out" this new approach at home. After a couple of weeks of role-playing and of actual encounters with his parents, Mike reported that he was now able to stand up to his parents and was spending more time just talking to them.

Despite this progress at home, Mike was still unwilling to call friends. He said he felt very nervous around them but did not know why. The therapist suggested that Mike close his eyes and picture calling a male friend to play golf. Mike did not feel any anxiety in imagining the scene until the golf match was over and he had to carry on a conversation with his friend. At this point, Mike said he felt very anxious and was having these thoughts: (1) "He thinks I'm strange." (2) "I'm not acting normally." (3) "I don't know what to say."

The therapist helped Mike test the validity of each of these thoughts. After careful analysis, both of them agreed that Mike was definitely *feeling* strange, that he felt removed from the conversation, and that he was "spectatoring," that is, observing his own behavior while in the situation. However, Mike also realized that, to the person he was talking with, he probably did not seem "weird" but merely quiet. He agreed that he had falsely assumed that other people could somehow "read" what he was thinking.

The therapist provided Mike with a strategy for stopping his "spectatoring" so that he would not feel so anxious. When he became aware that he was observing himself, he would intentionally focus on some innocuous aspect of the environment, such as furniture or scenery, and describe it in detail to himself. These thoughts would distract him from his maladaptive self-monitoring. Next he would begin to focus on the other person by repeating verbatim what his friend was saying. Finally, he would join the conversation by repeating or rephrasing what the other person had just said. Mike and the therapist practiced this procedure several times during the session by carrying on a casual conversation. Mike's assignments were to write rational responses to his automatic thoughts ("He thinks I'm strange," "I'm not acting normally") as he had in the session, and to call a friend, play golf, and practice the distraction procedure.

Mike returned for the next session feeling he had made considerable progress. Although he still felt quite anxious, he had "gotten up the nerve" to call a friend and play golf together. Mike said that he had to keep telling himself that he did not *look* strange and not to read too much into his friend's facial expressions and comments. Also, he had tried the distraction procedure and, although he was focusing better on the conversation, he still remembered thinking, "I don't know what to say next." The therapist then tried the "talk show host" technique to help Mike challenge the belief that he was incapable of carrying on a conversation. He pointed out to Mike that conversing was a skill, not an inherited trait. The therapist role-played a Johnny Carson interview, with the therapist playing Johnny, and Mike the famous guest. Mike observed that "Johnny" carried on a conversation primarily by asking the guest questions and by sharing personal experiences that confirmed the opinions the guest was offering. They then reversed roles and Mike practiced being the talk show host. Finally, Mike practiced applying the technique with the therapist playing the role of his golf partner. Mike's discomfort seemed to be considerably reduced, and his assignment was to practice the technique *in vivo* and to reevaluate the hypothesis that "I am incapable of carrying on a conversation."

During the next few weeks, Mike practiced the distraction and talk show host procedures, and used the Daily Record of Dysfunctional Thoughts (Beck *et al.*, 1979) to reevaluate his self-criticisms about his social skills, career uncertainty, and relationships with his parents. He gradually increased the frequency of his social contacts, and his loneliness, anxiety, and depression were considerably reduced.

INITIATING OPPOSITE-SEX RELATIONSHIPS

In the eighth session, Mike mentioned a recurring thought, that he could not ask a woman out. After eliciting in detail Mike's previous experiences with women, the therapist recognized a pattern in which Mike would go out with women who were very aggressive about approaching him, even though he was not attracted to them. When these women initiated a sexual encounter, Mike felt he had to prove himself or they would think he was strange. He was unable to "perform." Mike had never gone out with women he considered attractive because he became too anxious to ask them for a date. When he imagined calling one of them, he had the automatic thought, "They won't want to go out with me; they'll think I'm dull and boring." The therapist worked with Mike to examine the evidence he had to validate his assessment. He recognized that, in fact, he had had no experiences of rejection before. On the other hand, he had never pursued a relationship with a woman he wanted, so he did not know how they would react. Mike believed that women were only attracted to outgoing, charming guys and would not appreciate his qualities. The therapist asked him what qualities he looked for in women. Mike eventually concluded that different women were probably attracted to different qualities in men, and he guessed that many would prefer a more subdued style (just as he preferred in women). He also examined some of his friends' relationships and recognized that many of his quieter male friends seemed quite attractive to women he admired. Mike's assignment was to think of someone he would like to ask out and to answer his dysfunctional thoughts during the week.

In the next session Mike and the therapist role-played asking a woman friend out for a date and carrying on a conversation. His assignment was to rehearse this phone call and first date in his mind repeatedly during the week until he felt comfortable doing it. The following week, a woman who worked at the clinic was enlisted to help Mike practice in a more realistic situation. The "trial run" was very successful and Mike volunteered the belief that he might be more interesting to women than he had thought.

DEEPENING INTIMATE RELATIONSHIPS

During the next week, Mike called and went out to dinner with a girl he liked. He reported feeling a little nervous because he was afraid she would try to pressure him about sex more quickly than he wanted. The therapist explained the need for honest self-disclosure in a close relationship, and they rehearsed a conversation in which Mike explained his feelings of attraction but also expressed his desire to wait until they got to know each other a little better before becoming physically intimate. During the next few weeks, Mike disclosed his private feelings to his girl friend and reported being surprised at how much control he felt he had just because he could ''open up'' to her and say what he wanted.

By the 15th session, Mike and the therapist agreed to terminate therapy. He no longer felt lonely (his loneliness score was 3) and had made plans to spend the next year abroad working in England.

CONCLUDING COMMENTS

Mike's case was unusual in the speed with which he was able to challenge many of his automatic thoughts. He rapidly grasped the concept of viewing negative thoughts as hypotheses to be tested, and was extremely good at identifying these thoughts in real-life situations. Perhaps his habit of spectatoring was helpful in allowing him to ''distance'' himself from his thoughts long enough to challenge them. Once he was able to challenge his thoughts, Mike had little difficulty in carrying out the behavioral assignments that would increase the quantity and quality of his social contact. Without the cognitive changes, it is unlikely that Mike would have been willing or able to engage in adaptive but anxiety-producing behaviors. The specific skills he learned in the sessions, and the related homework assignments, increased his belief that he could succeed in social situations. The changes in thinking and behaving worked together to reduce his loneliness.

Mike was also exceptional among lonely patients in the easy availability of desirable partners. Many older patients (e.g., those who are not in college) have far fewer opportunities to meet potential friends. In these cases, much more time would be spent in therapy on developing ways of meeting new people and in overcoming resistance to following through under less-than-ideal circumstances (e.g., singles groups).

Finally, Mike's case did not illustrate the anger, bitterness, and mistrust that often accompany loneliness. With more cynical patients, especially those who have been recently divorced or separated, considerably more effort has to be devoted to dealing with overgeneralizations about why *no* relationships can work, *no one* of the opposite sex can be trusted, or *no one* will ever want them.

Nevertheless, Mike's treatment illustrates many of the themes that do arise with lonely patients and the variety of techniques available to the cognitive therapist. Our experience with lonely patients offers considerable encouragement regarding the treatment of this difficult, and increasingly prevalent, problem.

REFERENCES

Beck, A. T., Rush, A. J., Shaw, B. F., & Emery, G. *Cognitive therapy of depression*. New York: Guilford Press, 1979.

Bradburn, N. *The structure of psychological well-being*. Chicago: Aldine, 1969.

Kaplan, H. S. *The new sex therapy*. New York: Brunner/Mazel, 1974.

Lynch, J. *The broken heart: The medical consequences of loneliness*. New York: Basic Books, 1977.

Ortega, M. J. Depression, loneliness and unhappiness. In E. S. Schneidman & M. J. Ortega (Eds.), *Aspects of depression*. Boston: Little, Brown, 1969.

Rosenbaum, J., & Rosenbaum, V. *Conquering loneliness*. New York: Hawthorn Books, 1973.

Shaver, P., & Freedman, J. Your pursuit of happiness. *Psychology Today*, 1976, *10*(3), 26–32.

Wenz, F. V. Seasonal suicide attempts and forms of loneliness. *Psychological Reports*, 1977, *40*, 807–810.

Young, J. E. *Loneliness in college students: A cognitive approach* (Doctoral dissertation, University of Pennsylvania, 1978). *Dissertation Abstracts*, 1979, *40B*, 1392. (a)

Young, J. E. *An instrument for measuring loneliness*. Paper presented at the Annual Convention of the American Psychological Association, September 4, 1979. (b)

COGNITIVE THERAPY
OF SEXUAL DYSFUNCTIONS:
A CASE STUDY

Sonja Fox
Gary Emery

INTRODUCTION

New treatments for sexual dysfunctions have recently been developed
and tested (Masters & Johnson, 1970; Kaplan, 1974). These new short-
term treatments, despite different terminologies, use similar techniques. The techniques consist mainly of *in vivo* behavioral tasks and
skills training: The person learns to overcome sexual deficits by approaching the arousing behavior in a gradual way.

These new treatments have high rates of success (Annon, 1974;
Masters & Johnson, 1970). The question becomes: Can cognitive therapy improve on them? And if so, how? Jeffrey Steger (1978), in a review
of the treatment of sexual problems, provides some useful guidelines.
He concludes cognitive intervention can improve behavioral procedures in a number of situations: when the client's anxiety or fear stops
the person from engaging in the *in vivo* procedures; when the client
doesn't have a partner to engage in *in vivo* procedures; when the client
has ruminating thinking that interferes with *in vivo* procedures or
has attitudes ("sex is bad and immoral") that block the *in vivo* treatment.

This chapter illustrates how cognitive therapy was used with one
case of sexual dysfunction. The client, a 39-year-old woman, had some

Sonja Fox. Center for Cognitive Therapy, University of Pennsylvania, Philadelphia,
Pennsylvania.
Gary Emery. Department of Psychiatry, University of Southern California Medical
School, Los Angeles, California.

indicators for cognitive intervention that Steger outlined. She hadn't had sex with her husband for seven years and her thoughts were crucial in stopping her from trying *in vivo* procedures. The husband initially didn't want to engage in therapy, and she had some basic beliefs about sex that blocked *in vivo* procedures.

The chapter follows the case through completion and draws mainly from verbatim transcripts of therapy and the therapist's notes. The client was seen by the first author for eight sessions.

FIRST SESSION

THERAPIST: Okay, you wanted to tell me basically why you're here. I didn't read your folder because I prefer first to hear from you.

PATIENT: Okay. I have a sexual problem that has gone on for an awfully long time. I suppose really it started when we got married. I mean it really wasn't evident at that point but became evident within a couple of years after we got married. It was hard for me to be involved in any kind of sexual activity with my husband.

THERAPIST: Was this right from the very beginning?

PATIENT: Well, in my head it was. I don't think he realized it—at that point.

THERAPIST: But you realized it or you didn't realize it?

PATIENT: I realized it even then.

THERAPIST: Even then?

PATIENT: I didn't deal with it at that point but within a couple of years it . . . well, it got to be a problem. Let me see when the problem really began. It was really quick actually. . . . It must have been about the end of the first year. I went to Mexico on an extended buying trip. I was gone for four weeks. When I got back was the first time he realized there was a problem.

THERAPIST: How did he realize the problem?

PATIENT: Well, because it was hard for me to be positive about sex. It was one of those classic TV jokes . . . you know, "I'm too tired," "I have a headache," and all the other excuses that I worked up.

Then we went through a really long period of a year or so when I went along with it but it wasn't easy for me. He sensed that and was put off by the fact it wasn't a positive thing—as far as I was concerned. We went from that to just absolutely not talking about it for a year or so.

THERAPIST: During the time when you weren't talking about it was there any sexual activity going on?

PATIENT: No. At that point there was nothing. He was really bitter. Threw things and said there was something wrong with me . . . and something was wrong with our relationship . . . and I think there was a change in our relationship that I'm sure made the whole thing worse.

THERAPIST: Worse?

PATIENT: Worse than it otherwise would have been. I was in a situation where I was extremely successful. Top-level executive men were all the things that I thought have some extrinsic value. And I probably was evaluating him by those terms. It was one of those situations where I was seeing he wasn't ideal. We have both now faced the fact that we are what we are and he's him and I'm me and it's probably well that we balance one another.

THERAPIST: Well, it sounds like you've done a lot of learning in the meantime.

PATIENT: Then after that I became involved with an older man who was unhappily married. At the point when we were really about to become seriously involved I admitted to myself that I really liked my husband a whole bunch even if I wasn't in love with him.

THERAPIST: Let me interrupt you just for a minute. When you were considering your relationship with this man, what would the sexual relationship have been?

PATIENT: It was definitely a sexual relationship. I mean that was a part of it. But you know what was funny? I realized it was exactly the same kind of thing as it would have been with my husband.

THERAPIST: You weren't enjoying the sexual relationship?

PATIENT: No, I do enjoy sexual relationships. There's something about marriage or seriousness. I don't exactly understand what it is. But that's where it changes.

THERAPIST: So it's not that you don't enjoy sex, but you don't enjoy sex within your marriage?

PATIENT: In a restricted environment, I think is what it is. I don't think it was exactly marriage. I have a feeling that it might be long-term. I don't even know how to put it into words. I've thought about it an awful, awful lot. My husband and I have talked about it an awful lot since. He can't understand any of it. He really can't even understand why there's a problem. Because we had a very good sexual relationship before we got married.

THERAPIST: Before you got married. And it deteriorated almost the minute you got married?

PATIENT: Almost the minute we got married. It wasn't quite that bad, but I'll tell you it was close. Now, that sounds really pathetic except that it's true. Even knowing this, I still can't change it. That's the worst of it. It's hard to talk about. It was hard for me to come here. We have all the outside trappings of an extremely successful marriage plus all the inside trappings of an extremely successful marriage.

I mean, my husband says, "If you can get better, great. And if you can't, it's a good marriage the way it is. And I don't like it this way but I'm willing to let you have your problems the same as you're willing to let me have my problems."

At this point the therapist is trying to make sense of the woman's problem. The therapist's intent is to identify the problem. Through careful questioning she's trying to obtain essential information. We find there is usually no need to go through a formal structured assessment interview. By focusing on the problem area the essential information will come out. The therapist feels free to interpret the patient in an attempt to identify the problem.

THERAPIST: You never looked for help before?

PATIENT: I went to the family doctor. He knows how happy we are, and I think he didn't realize the seriousness of it. Plus, it's hard for me to express the fact that we really have a problem. . . . He suggested that instead of spending money on a psychiatrist we should try to work it out ourselves.

He wanted us to try touching, being close to each other, but that's really not a problem. It's really just sex—sexual intercourse or anything to do with it—that's where I cut out.

I just can't. . . . I think I might be able to make myself do it. But I wasn't happy when I was doing it. I had to shut myself off—in the

back of my head somewhere—even to go through with it. I don't
want to have to do that. I really don't.

THERAPIST: When you're feeling loving and affectionate and then arrive
at a point where you're aware you're feeling very uncomfortable,
do you have any idea what you say to yourself?

PATIENT: I never thought about it.

THERAPIST: You see, feelings don't come first. There's an event. Let's
call that A—a situation. And then the next thing we're aware of is
C—which are feelings. But something happens. There's a missing
part to the puzzle. You can call it a three-piece puzzle. Before a
feeling is generated you say something to yourself. Most thinking
is in the form of self-talk. Now, if you sit down and think about it
you'll probably realize that's true.

I want you to try to sensitize yourself to that this week and really
grasp the idea that feelings don't come out of the blue: They're
the result not of a situation but how we are interpreting the situation. And it can't be the sex situation because you have been in
sexual situations before and you enjoy them. So it's not sex itself.
It has to be what you're saying to yourself, about a particular sexual situation, at a particular time, that generates the feeling.
That's what we have to try to track down.

PATIENT: Is that where the problem is?

THERAPIST: Exactly. And it's true in almost any problem that you have.
It's the self-talk, not the situation that's the problem. It's what
you're saying about the situation. Human beings interpret situations. I don't care what they are.

Take this therapy situation. Four people could come in—the situation would be the same, the office, me and everybody knowing
they are going into therapy—but each person would be responding and generating different feelings.

One person might come in very anxious because she's saying to
herself, "I'm going to be embarrassed. I'm never going to make
it. I've never been able to talk to people." Another person might
come in and feel at ease because she's saying to herself, "I've
always made out well when I talk to people, so this will solve my
problem." Do you understand what I mean?

PATIENT: Yeah, I see what you mean.

THERAPIST: So it's not the situation, it's the self-talk. And this is true about the slightest thing. We are continually making statements to ourselves. Asking questions. Maybe just using a word. But at any rate we have some thought process going on that's interpreting the situation. And from that feelings are generated. The woman who's coming in and saying, "I never could talk to people," is going to feel anxious. She may not be aware that's what she's saying.

Now, we're not talking about unawareness or unconsciousness in Freudian terms. We're talking about thoughts that are there but we're not always aware of them because they become automatic. We have a lot of automatic thinking and it works well for us most of the time. If we had to think about everything we do we would never learn to drive a car, for example.

That has to become automatic. Our emotional responses finally become automatic because we're saying the same things to ourselves all the time. And that's basically what we are going to try to get at.

As you're talking it may come into your head, "What kind of self-talk am I engaging in that makes sex enjoyable in one circumstance but not in the other with the same person?" Because you're saying that you enjoyed sex with your husband for a certain period of time. He wasn't your husband then. Now you have to be saying something differently about the situation in order for your feelings to suddenly become different. And this is what we have to get at.

If you go through any exercises to get closer to your husband, try to find the first statement you're making that is making the situation go downhill.

Do you ever get any visual imagery? Some people think in terms of images really.

PATIENT: I'm very verbal.

THERAPIST: I'm not an imagery person myself either. But for some people they have a definite visual image of something unpleasant.

Okay. Go on with your story. I just wanted to interrupt at that
point so you'll see what we're doing.

The best time to introduce the cognitive model for emotional
problems is when it relates directly to material the patient has brought
up. The therapist can introduce the model in many ways. Here the
therapist used the ABC method borrowed from rational–emotive therapy (RET). Nearly always the therapist has to present this rationale a
number of times and in different ways. The more specific the material,
the better.

PATIENT: That's interesting because it's almost any situation where I
    might get into a sexual situation with him. It really doesn't have to
    be the classic sexual getting into bed. . . . It's almost any time that
    I might be forced to interrelate that way. And yet I really can't
    think of what it is.
THERAPIST: Can you think up an example now?
PATIENT: Well, the thing is I know exactly what my example is. The
    thing that goes through my head is—I guess you don't really ver-
    balize quite this much when you really think of things.
THERAPIST: It's done in shorthand.
PATIENT: But basically what I'm thinking is "This is going to be a sexual
    situation, therefore I will avoid it." I've gotten that far into it.
THERAPIST: Now we have to go to a level a little below that and see what
    you're thinking or saying to yourself that makes you want to avoid
    it.
PATIENT: That's where I don't really know. It's obvious that the next
    thing is "Oh, my God, you know . . . here I am in this situation.
    What am I going to do to avoid it?" And that's really where I stop.
    I can't go any further back to that.
THERAPIST: That's what we've got to try to get at—some of the self-
    statements. Now that you've become aware of what your task is
    going to be, you'll find yourself being able to get more in tune
    with this.
PATIENT: I see what you're saying. All the other doctor suggested was
    that we try to touch and try to be close to each other. That part
    really doesn't bother me as long as it doesn't become sexual in any
    overt kind of way. I still come to the same point. It's the last thing
    that really hits my head. . . .
THERAPIST: "I must avoid it"?

PATIENT: I must avoid this form of touching.

THERAPIST: So then the next question we have to ask is what are you saying to yourself that makes it imperative to avoid it.

PATIENT: I really don't know.

THERAPIST: There are some basic beliefs that we have about life that cause the self-talk and I'm wondering what your basic belief is. What's your basic hypothesis or attitude that underlies this?

At times the patient doesn't have automatic thoughts or is unaware of them. Here the therapist can inquire about meanings and basic beliefs. These beliefs are historical and the therapist has to talk about the past to uncover them. The therapist often asks about underlying beliefs while mapping out the territory in the first interview; not necessarily to modify them immediately but to make psychological sense of the situation.

PATIENT: Well, there again we go back again. . . . I'm sure it's my mother's fault. The worst of it is I'm conscious of all my mother's problems. Most of them I have managed to overcome. But I think this is one that she got me on and I don't know where she got me and I don't know why it is.

THERAPIST: How was her relationship with your father?

PATIENT: Very sick.

THERAPIST: Could you describe that relationship to me? You may have picked up some beliefs or attitudes from this.

PATIENT: I have but I don't know how to get away from them. My mother married my father to get away from home, not because she loved my father. My father, on the other hand, loves my mother, I think, a great deal. But they have a real bad marriage. My mother slept with my father or at least had sexual relationships with my father only in the sense that she felt there was a responsibility to produce children. And I assume that the moment that responsibility ended the whole thing ended. She had a nervous breakdown after my sister was born. And I wonder now . . . looking back on it . . . if maybe that didn't stem from fear of sex.

My father got a heart disease and that was the final straw because then Mother at 35 had to go back to college. So she, with two kids and just really not that far away from having electric-shock therapy and the whole deal, went back to college. Went through four years of college in two-and-one-half years. Became a teacher and then paid for my sister and me both to go to college.

THERAPIST: Your mother seemed to bloom?

PATIENT: She was able to move out of the bedroom. That was the very first thing she did.

THERAPIST: So then she was able to live with this fear of sex gone?

PATIENT: Exactly. That's right. That was one fear out of the way. And it was a big one obviously because she moved the whole way across the house to the other end.

THERAPIST: Do you think anywhere in your head is rattling around the belief that if you have sex with your husband you're going to be destroyed by it?

PATIENT: I don't know. You know I have thought about all of this.

Oh, I have other things. My father and I really did a whole dredge session. The other thing that Daddy thinks might have affected me is it's hard for me to expose my sexual parts. I cover myself constantly. My mother was that way, she decided when I was 13 that my bust was getting too big and bound me up for a whole year . . . in hopes that I wouldn't be busty and therefore sexually appealing. Oh, she really . . . she had it all. The whole deal.

THERAPIST: Your body shouldn't be exposed or looked at, and you saw your mother suddenly blossom forth when the sex was totally out?

PATIENT: You're right, that's true. I never connected all that, but you're right, it's true.

THERAPIST: Well, as we go on we might find a lot more that never consciously added up. But little by little they began to accumulate in your head until it's a belief system—maybe one that you're not even aware of.

PATIENT: I never thought of it that way. Mother was always kind of a lumpy mother until Daddy's illness.

THERAPIST: That appears to be to be a striking happening.

PATIENT: That's right, it was. She went to school. She did well. And she lost a lot of her craziness at that time. I really didn't want to get married. To me marriage was an unhappy rather than a happy experience.

THERAPIST: Perhaps this sex problem is tied right into some strong marriage beliefs . . . like "marriage isn't for fun". . ."marriage can't bring you anything"?

PATIENT: You're right. It's funny but my view of marriage is very unhappy.

You have to understand that the first guy that I had sexual experience with slit his wrists and almost died when I told him I wouldn't marry him.

THERAPIST: These things are all adding up. Sex and the connection with marriage turned out to be extremely disastrous. The sex was okay until the marriage came into it and then he tried to destroy himself?

PATIENT: We were going to get married and then I decided that I didn't want to do it. And when I called him and told him he tried to commit suicide.

THERAPIST: The sex was really good until marriage came into it and then it almost destroyed him. You got another connection there.

PATIENT: I didn't see him again for a couple of years. And the next time I saw him . . . that's funny, it really is. I never put all these things together. It was so awful. That is another one I can remember. He came to the house and I didn't know he was coming. He had severe acne as a child and had really bad pockmarks. He had had sandpaper surgery and he was like one of those ghost things with just eyes and a nose and he came to the house and we went out to the car together. . . .

THERAPIST: Perhaps sex in marriage represents such a destructive situation to you that you have some basic beliefs there that you're not aware of, and that's what's bothering you, because it's not your lack of sexual response. And it's not a lack of sexual response with your husband. So you have to be saying something really serious to yourself that either scares the heck out of you or is terribly repulsive. And I believe we can find it sooner or later.

PATIENT: I see what you're saying. It does all kind of go together. I guess I knew all of the things individually.

THERAPIST: But couldn't add them up?

SUMMARY OF FIRST SESSION

The therapist explored the hypothesis that the patient's dysfunctional belief revolved around the theme that sex within marriage leads to destruction. The patient had never been able to put these details together before.

Our experience is that insight by itself is not sufficient. We find there is often much insight in the first session, but then the real work of changing beliefs and behaviors starts.

The therapist asked the patient if it was possible to get her husband involved in therapy. Her homework for the next week was to be more affectionate with her husband to the point where she was beginning to be anxious and to catch her thoughts at that time.

SECOND SESSION

The patient said that her husband didn't want to try experiments again, although he wanted her to get better. He didn't want to open up a problem area again. The patient said they still slept in the same bed and were affectionate with each other. She also said her husband no longer showed sexual arousal. (The therapist formed the tentative hypothesis to herself that perhaps the husband now feared impotence.)

The patient and her husband discussed their wedding night. He became angry because his recollections were quite different from hers. She recalled that she thought *his* sex behavior changed after marriage. The therapist discussed the possibility that his change was in response to hers—*not* in response to marriage.

During the session the therapist discussed alternate ways to view resuming sex with him. This was an attempt to change the cognitive set about sex. The following is an example:

THERAPIST: What's the big deal about letting him put his penis in you—if you love him and realize that it would give him much pleasure?

PATIENT: *(Laughs.)* I hadn't thought of it that way. What if I can't get any physical pleasure?

THERAPIST: Maybe your body will respond in time—women get sexier as they get older. Maybe you could get rid of the ideas of "duty" and "obligation." Do you think you could replace them with "gift-giving expression of love" whether it is physically satisfying or not?

PATIENT: Maybe, I haven't thought of it like that.

Part of the patient's homework was to write out her belief/value system about sex after nine years of marriage. The therapist explained they might eventually use systematic desensitization and introduced relaxation training. During the next week the client was to practice this twice a day.

The client was positive toward therapy and quite motivated during the sessions. Often in early sessions therapy goes very smoothly. Honeymoon periods such as these often come to an end when the clients realize the difficulty in changing behavior. This is what happened in this case.

THIRD SESSION

At the beginning, the patient said that she hadn't done her homework and that she didn't have time to deal with the problem now because of work and other demands. She said perhaps she should stop treatment until she had time to give it the attention it deserved.

The therapist decided to devote this session exclusively to work on her avoidance behavior and her thoughts that kept her unaware and unconcerned that she was doing it. This can be quite confrontative, but if a good relationship exists and the client has faith in the competence of the therapist it can be quite effective.

THERAPIST: We have to get in touch with what you're saying to yourself that makes you believe that avoiding the problem is better than solving it. Would you do this in your work?

PATIENT: Well, no.

THERAPIST: You might not have a job if you spent all your time figuring out avoidance strategies. It makes me wonder what you're thinking about your marriage. Well, let's try to straighten that out today.

PATIENT: I did think about it on the train and I think about it when I'm going someplace, but for whatever the reasons, I really never . . . I just haven't stopped to deal with it and I keep thinking I'm avoiding it but I haven't figured it out.

THERAPIST: Well, it's a matter of priorities. You came here and you stated you had a problem and you know what you have to do basically. You have to work on it to get rid of it.

PATIENT: But for whatever reasons, my husband and I have ended up with more than we can possibly do. But it's like Sunday . . . we picked fruit. It took all day. In other words we have expanded our activities from 5:00 A.M. to midnight. . . .

THERAPIST: The last time you were in, you indicated your husband made it clear he was disappointed that you weren't working on this problem.

PATIENT: True.

THERAPIST: Now, how about then and now?

PATIENT: We haven't talked about it at all.

THERAPIST: Do you pick up any signs from him? How do you perceive him as feeling about your coming here and not doing anything?

PATIENT: I guess it's another one of those things we just shut off—or don't pay attention to.

THERAPIST: Do you ever solve problems at work—big problems, important problems—by shutting them off and saying, "I'm going to pretend that it doesn't exist and maybe it will go away."

PATIENT: No. It's true. We don't see that much of each other so I'm not really forced to face it an awful lot of the time. We don't really spend enough time together—unless I go into one of those phases where I'm not gone a lot and I see him regularly. Then I begin to realize it again. But then I'll not be there again.

You're right. I'm sure one of the reasons why I finally did come here was because I happened to be around an awful lot in November, December, and January. We went back to having a day-in, day-out relationship. I began to realize that it's strained; but then I don't have to face it when I'm not around a lot. I guess what I really thought was maybe I should put it off until there is more time, but you're right.

THERAPIST: Do you think there's going to be more time?

PATIENT: Yeah, that's true. You make time for the things that are important to you.

Many, if not most, clients have some blocks to changing behavior. These can be beliefs that lead to anxiety and guilt that in turn lead to avoidance. One of the ways to overcome the blocks is for the therapist to confront the client. The confrontation has to be done in a supportive way. One of the best strategies is to ask questions that lead to the client confronting him- or herself. To be effective the therapist often has to confront the client many times and in many different ways.

Another way to overcome the client's avoidance is to increase his or her motivation. In this session the therapist did this by having the client list the advantages versus the disadvantages of working on the sex problem. During this exercise it became apparent the client had trouble with the word "marriage." Semantics can play an important role in cognitive therapy so the therapist focused in on this.

THERAPIST: I think the word "marriage" is making you block.

PATIENT: It really does.

THERAPIST: Okay. Let's pretend the word "marriage" doesn't exist. I wish you would put it totally out of your vocabulary because it seems to cue you into a lot of thoughts that flit by your head so fast you don't even try to grasp them . . . that word seems to block everything. And you suddenly become slowed down.

PATIENT: Yes. That's true . . . as soon as you say things that I do with him. But I don't think of those as marital functions.

THERAPIST: I don't think there are marital functions. Marriage is a ceremony. A legal ceremony. A legal ceremony for the disposition of property and to give your children a name. That's really all that marriage is specifically. A relationship that might exist in the marriage could also exist whether or not that ceremony were ever performed. So we're not talking about that legal aspect. That's really all that word marriage means—that you have legalized a relationship. Now, what does this particular relationship mean to you. Now we're cooking.

PATIENT: Because when you say that . . . that's what always throws me off because as soon as you say marriage it becomes this giant amorphous problem.

SUMMARY OF THIRD SESSION

The client tried to justify her avoidance by referring to her "total lack of discipline." The therapist asked if it didn't require discipline to do her job properly—didn't she have to keep appointments, records? The therapist then asked if she was responsible with her pets.

The client concluded, "I guess there are certain areas of my life where I choose to be disciplined and other areas in which I choose not to be."

The therapist stressed the negative effects of avoidance behavior: "Each avoidance powerfully reinforces further avoidance. The consequence is that the problem becomes progressively more difficult to resolve as a result."

The client appeared to be considerably shaken by having to be really serious during this session. She agreed to come in for two sessions the next week. The therapist suggested that since her husband was so orderly, she could work out how to do her homework (collecting her thoughts) with his help. The rationale was this would involve him in therapy before tackling the sex issue directly and perhaps desensitize his fears about becoming involved.

FOURTH SESSION

The client brought in some homework, although it was poorly done. She and her husband had not cooperated on the problem. She had again avoided thinking about it except in a minimal way. She admitted that she and her husband arranged such hectic schedules on weekends that they were "too tired to even think about the problem." He had refused to cooperate with her on homework, although he was relieved she decided to continue in treatment. She again spent a great deal of excess time on material relating to work, parents, etc.

She discussed with her husband the possibility of resolving problems by thinking about one at a time rather than trying to think of many at once. During their discussion, they agreed that in the past her husband had supported her on everything she did until he ended up taking it over. He had decided in this instance that since she created the problem, it was definitely her responsibility to work it through by herself and he was determined that in no way would he take it over.

During therapy the therapist and client discussed details of the sexual problem. The following points about the client were elicited: (1) Does not like to touch or be touched ("It's wrong"); (2) probably could tolerate coitus but *not* affectionate foreplay or resolution (again, this is accompanied by the thought, "It is wrong"); and (3) no exposure of body.

The therapist asked if she could replay a successful sexual experience with the husband before marriage and get a clear image of the whole experience in her mind—step by step. The client said she could remember time, place, situation, but not the feelings and that even talking about it elicited anxiety. The therapist asked her to continue to try this for the coming week.

The therapist and client started working up a hierarchy for systematic desensitization that the client was to complete during the week. The therapist encouraged her to walk around the house wearing bikini underwear. The client said she would be uncomfortable but could do it.

FIFTH SESSION

Often in therapy chance events play a role in how therapy evolves. The therapist has to be prepared to use these events if possible to advantage. This happened in this case.

The client reported her husband read her desensitization hierarchy without her knowledge. He started to put into *practice* the items he had read.

She stopped him when he put her hand on his penis. She was not really anxious and the only thought she could catch was "I must avoid this." He was very cooperative and good-natured and she was not unduly upset.

The therapist worked on the possibility of the client changing her thought from "I must avoid" to "I want to avoid, but I'm not going to." The therapist explained how powerfully reinforcing it is each time a behavior is avoided and stressed the necessity of the client being able to force herself in small steps to do the formerly avoided behavior, *even though she might feel some anxiety.* The therapist repeatedly stressed the fact that despite the morning's happenings, nothing catastrophic had happened as a result of the sexual behavior of the husband.

The therapist also stressed that this was a new ball game. She pointed out when the client's avoidance behavior started: (1) she did not want to be married, (2) she did not love or respect her husband, and (3) she wanted to change him. Now, all of the conditions were reversed, but she was still practicing the same behavior.

The client discovered as she was carrying out her task of gradually exposing her body that she did not have any discomfort at the nudity but recognized that she feared arousing a sexual response in her husband.

THERAPIST: Had you run around in your birthday suit last night in front of your husband?

PATIENT: No. It was Friday. I guess I was just wandering around getting something out of the laundry room, which is through the house and around. I just decided that instead of wrapping a towel around me I would go with nothing on.

THERAPIST: With no clothes on at all?

PATIENT: Yeah, well, see, the thing is that's when I really realized that it is not nakedness per se that upset me.

THERAPIST: But you thought that it was?

PATIENT: Yeah, I did.

THERAPIST: What does upset you?

PATIENT: It's down to the point where it's just plain . . . I was afraid I would arouse a sexual response in my husband.

THERAPIST: Okay, so you did arouse him. And you went fairly far in a sexual activity. Have you suffered for it?

PATIENT: It's true. After seven years I guess that's pretty far.

THERAPIST: It's interesting to me because you started out saying, "This is hopeless."

PATIENT: Well, I was really upset because I had a feeling it would work.

THERAPIST: I hope that I didn't give you the impression that it would work that fast. That's why I kept saying, "Easy does it, easy does it." Now, if we take longer and you desensitize yourself with relaxation through every one of these steps, it might take us two months or so. But if you went through this this morning, it can be totally speeded up. You are able to laugh and see how cute your husband was.

PATIENT: Oh, yeah.

THERAPIST: So I don't think we're stepping on dangerous ground here. And I'm not suggesting that you let him do this again tomorrow or encourage him if you don't feel like it; but I'd like you to do some thinking about this terrible catastrophic thing you must avoid that in fact you didn't avoid. You're still in one piece and you're laughing. Did your husband get some pleasure out of seeing you?

PATIENT: Oh, yeah. He really did.

THERAPIST: Did it occur to you at any time, "Hey, I would really like to give him this pleasure"?

PATIENT: What bothers me is that when I isolate it and think about it reasonably in an isolated situation, it's very reasonable. You're right. But in the actual situation when I'm faced with it, I fall back on the same response. And for whatever the reason I can't seem to eliminate it.

THERAPIST: It's got to be there somewhere. And if we can't find the reason, let's try to get some new reasoning in, anyway, namely, that you went that far this morning and nothing terrible happened. Did you in fact learn that you could stand it?

PATIENT: Well, I avoided it.

THERAPIST: You were subjected to all this, though. Let's put it that way.

PATIENT: And I survived.

THERAPIST: And you survived. And nothing terrible happened. And you love you husband as much as ever. Or, do you suddenly love him less?

PATIENT: No. It's true.

THERAPIST: Now, if you could replay that scene to yourself enough times with him acting in such a cute . . . I can't think of any other word . . .

I'm getting a mental picture of this. You know how few men would be like that. And it shows that he must be terribly healthy because for most men after seven years of that kind of avoidance he would have built up such a neurotic block he would have been impotent, and we would have had to work with him for months. But obviously he's a well-put-together person. It was a leap into faith this morning for him to do that. It showed tremendous desire on his part to have a full relationship with you. And if you could play this scene over and over in your head you may begin to dislodge some of the thoughts that block you. Maybe we'll never find out what you were saying. I don't know. But we certainly have to assume it's not in your best interests, whatever it is.

You may never be the world's hottest lover, but I don't think that's anything you have to tell another person about.

SUMMARY OF FIFTH SESSION

The therapist suggested that the client try to defocus her thoughts from herself and find pleasure in giving her husband pleasure by giving him a gift only she could give. She also advised the client that she would surely feel anxious and uncomfortable during these early episodes, but that the anxiety would not harm her and could eventually be overcome if she distracted herself by the thought of giving to a loved one.

The therapist asked her to try to replay a positive sexual experience with her husband from before marriage and encouraged her to practice relaxation and to discourage her husband from pressuring her, but not to back away from all that she had accomplished. The therapist lavishly reinforced her response (joking and laughing) at the morning's episode, rather than being angry, repulsed, or discouraged.

SIXTH SESSION

The client continued with exposure in front of her husband. She reinforced her husband for his behavior on Friday. Her husband did not initiate any new advances.

The therapist gave her more relaxation training and explained how this could be used for desensitization.

The client said that her behavior had changed a greal deal from reading and discussing recommended books. Even her coworkers had noticed this. She had sent books to her mother. She realized that *she* must take the initiative in the sex problem.

SEVENTH SESSION

The client reported she was identifying her thoughts and replacing them with more realistic ones. She said she realized the situation was ludicrous. She reported she was no longer anxious about nudity and no longer avoided touching her husband. She even enjoyed it. She said she now realized that it did not make her anxious or repulsed and that she was simply wanting to avoid it because avoidance had been more comfortable.

She felt she'd been using hierarchy items to delay. She said she was now able to face the fact that she was only developing a more elaborate avoidance system. She now realized that the only way was to simply go ahead and do it and try to become sensitive to the direct feedback.

The client at this point seemed to have what Mahoney (1974) calls a cognitive click. Many clinicians have reported that patients often have an all-or-none belief change. There is often a critical stage in the hierarchy of any shaping procedure: Once this stage is successfully passed, the remaining steps are easily attended. It appears that this cognitive click is not an "ah-hah" insight phenomenon; rather it is the result of accumulating evidence against previously held belief.

EIGHTH SESSION

The client reported she arrived home from a camping trip last Sunday cold, tired, and dirty but remembered her commitment to take the plunge. She asked her husband if he wanted intercourse. She was not at all upset with the sex even though she received no particular pleasure. The second time she found pleasurable. She waited three days after the first time and realized that she was avoiding it again and initiated sex, knowing that for a long time he would probably not make the first move.

The therapist and client discussed the possibility of some changes occurring in the relationship but both agreed the relationship was much stronger than most *because* of the lack of sex. The client said she now realized how much she used avoidance behavior. She said she now knew the value of doing rather than thinking about "why."

The couple planned to have a real honeymoon in California. The therapist and client agreed that there was no further need for treatment at that time but that the client should contact the therapist at the first sign of difficulty.

A month later the client called and said that she was pregnant. She said their sex life was fine; both were overjoyed and her husband was "ridiculously happy about the baby and everything."

SUMMARY

This client had both cognitive and behavioral avoidance. She not only didn't engage in sex but tried to put it out of her mind as well. The major focus of therapy was to help the client overcome this avoidance. The cognitive avoidance was targeted for change first. This had to be addressed before the behavioral avoidance could be worked on.

In order to get the client to face and confront her dysfunctional thoughts and beliefs about sex, the therapist went through three steps. First, the therapist presented the rationale that the client's thoughts and beliefs were crucial in maintaining the problem. Second, the therapist got the message across that these faulty thoughts and beliefs were under the client's control so they could be changed. The first two steps were geared to increase the client's motivation to work on the cognitive avoidance. The third step was to keep the client focused on the avoided material during the session and outside of the therapy. This last step required a directive and repetitive approach. In doing this the therapist had to use good clinical skills and judgment because it is easy to lose the client at this point.

A number of the new therapists have talked about the importance of restructuring the client's attitudes about sex (Masters & Johnson, 1970). Other writers have discussed the importance of the therapist's identifying and overcoming the client's resistance in carrying out the behavioral treatment (Munjack & Oziel, 1978). Cognitive therapy is a modality that seems to be tailor-made to handle these two concerns.

REFERENCES

Annon, J. *The behavioral treatment of sexual problems* (Vol. 1): *Brief therapy*. Honolulu: Enabling Systems, 1974.

Kaplan, H. S. *The new sex therapy*. New York: Brunner/Mazel, 1974.

Mahoney, M. J. *Cognition and behavior modification*. Cambridge, Mass.: Ballinger, 1974.

Masters, W., & Johnson, V. *Human sexual inadequacy*. Boston: Little, Brown, 1970.

Munjack, D., & Oziel, J. Resistance in the behavioral treatment of sexual dysfunctions. *Journal of Sex and Marital Therapy, 4* (2), 1978, 122–138.

Steger, J. Cognitive behavioral strategies in the treatment of sexual problems. In J. Foreyt & D. Rathjen (Eds.), *Cognitive behavior therapy: Research and application*. New York: Plenum, 1978.

COGNITIVE THERAPY
OF ALCOHOL DEPENDENCY

Gary Emery
Sonja Fox

INTRODUCTION

Alcohol dependency has been a focus of both clinical and national concern for some time. In terms of social disruption and financial loss, the cost of alcoholism is enormous. Over 80 million people in the United States consume alcohol, and according to some definitions, 9 million are judged to be alcoholic (NIAAA, 1974).

A number of behavioral-therapy programs for treatment of alcoholism have recently been developed. They have met with some success in teaching the alcohol-dependent person how to limit exposure to problem-drinking situations and how to control the frequency and amount of alcohol intake. There usually is no attempt to modify the client's internal motivation or change the significance of drinking as a part of the behavior pattern (Pattison, 1976). The focus is on helping the patient to develop control over drinking behavior, not on resolving the basic psychological problems that may have led to dysfunctional drinking in the first place.

Pattison (1976) believes that since neither the controlled drinker nor the controlled abstainer in behavioral programs has learned to change the symbolic significance of alcohol the person remains at risk of returning to dysfunctional drinking; failure to treat maladaptive drinking as a symptom of psychological problems undermines the suc-

Gary Emery. Department of Psychiatry, University of Southern California Medical School, Los Angeles, California.
Sonja Fox. Center for Cognitive Therapy, University of Pennsylvania, Philadelphia, Pennsylvania.

cess of the behavioral approach and prevents the patient from deriving total benefit from the treatment.

Cognitive therapy, on the other hand, lends itself to expanding the goals of alcohol-treatment programs. In addition to teaching clients to modify drinking behaviors, cognitive therapy teaches patients how to modify the psychological states that underlie problem drinking.

In cognitive therapy, a person's cognitions ("automatic thoughts," "self-statements," "underlying beliefs") and specific behaviors that precede alcohol abuse are central in determining treatment intervention. Specific targets of treatment need to be established by the therapist and client within a collaborative framework. Both cognitive and behavioral means are used to focus on these targets and achieve specific goals.

ETIOLOGY

Despite abundant research on alcoholism, the etiology of alcoholism remains unclear. Rather than look for a single cause, it is perhaps more fruitful to look at the multiple determinants of the problem: genetic, biological, cultural, social, psychological, cognitive, and situational factors, as well as the nature of alcohol itself. Certain individuals may have a genetic predisposition to the problem that will surface under particular circumstances. Once the individual becomes dependent on alcohol, he or she becomes subject to a biological tendency to drink to excess. Our society is ambivalent about drinking but, overall, drinking is approved and encouraged. There are numerous social pressures from family and friends to drink. Some individuals drink to cope with anxiety, boredom, or depression. The time, the place, and interpersonal environment may all become triggering mechanisms for alcohol consumption.

One of the determinants of the problem is alcohol itself: its specific properties and their physiological effects. Alcohol has two significant effects. The immediate effect is a pleasant "high"; the secondary, or rebound effect, is the "low that follows the high." A person's excessive drinking is often the result of an attempt to keep the "high" going in order to ward off the inevitable "low."

The interaction of these determinants varies with each individual.

In light of these considerations, the most promising method of intervention would be one that deals with determinants that an individual can most readily control, namely, how the person thinks and acts.

THERAPIST MALAISE

A good therapist–patient relationship is crucial to the success of alcohol-dependency treatment. The therapist has to show interest, concern, and some appropriate enthusiasm. The therapist is asking a patient to give up what is a significant part of his or her life when he or she asks the patient to change his or her drinking habits. Many individuals believe their alcohol problem is hopeless. For this reason, the therapist's role is particularly important with respect to "revolving-door" alcohol problems. We have found that many apparently hopeless cases of alcohol dependency respond if the therapist can get involved.

Because of the psychological difficulties of working with this group, many therapists become discouraged. They lose interest in their patients and often transmit this sense of hopelessness to their patients. This situation is often complicated by a lack of administrative support. To fight off the malaise, you can follow these procedures:

1. Ask yourself where your distortions are. Are you looking at your effectiveness in all-or-none terms? Are you focusing on the failures and ignoring the rest?
2. Try to spend more time on those that have a good chance of getting better. Most therapists spend 80% of their energy and time on 20% of the patients, often those who don't derive as much benefit from this amount of attention as the others would.
3. Ignore fellow workers who spread discouragement.
4. Form a group (formal or informal) of task-oriented counselors or therapists who meet to discuss cases and to reinforce one another's successes and offer help and suggestions for problems.

DISTORTIONS

There appear to be some common cognitive distortions consistently occurring in staff (as well as clients) and corrections of such distortions might significantly affect treatment outcome. These common cognitive distortions are as follows:

1. *Distortion*—Alcoholics are manipulative and manipulative behavior is totally "bad" and must be extirpated. *Correction*—Manipulative behavior can be viewed as shrewd, innovative, problem-solving activity when channeled in a socially adaptive way, and in fact, is practiced intensively and ubiquitously by "successful" people in our society.

2. *Distortion*—Alcoholics are not goal-oriented. *Correction*—The lifestyle of the alcoholic demonstrates goal-directed activity rarely achieved by the average individual. Approximately 80% of the activities of the alcoholic are directed toward the goals of obtaining and drinking alcohol. The task of therapy is to change goals, not to convince the individual that he or she never had any and therefore has no skill or experience in this area.

3. *Distortion*—Alcoholics are weak, dependent individuals. *Correction*—The activities in which an alcoholic must engage to satisfy his or her drinking and the sacrifices and hardships he or she must endure to maintain his or her drinking demonstrate amazing strength, initiative, and perserverance.

4. *Distortion*—One must always confront an alcoholic, and preferably in the group situation. *Correction*—Most of the alcoholic's interpersonal interactions with peers and authorities (police, treatment personnel, etc.) are confrontative; he or she has become an expert at this because his or her lifestyle has demanded defensiveness. The average therapist is not even in the same league with him or her in terms of this skill.

In other words, therapists see the alcoholic as totally lacking in resources that are, in fact, well developed, but because these resources are misdirected, they are not recognized as existing. The immediate consequences of the therapist's distortion is to convince the alcoholic that he or she has nothing going; that all present coping behaviors are without value, that he or she has learned nothing that can be useful in sober life, and consequently, rehabilitation must start from zero. It's no wonder many alcoholics get depressed during treatment.

Clearance of these distortions would enable the therapist to approach the alcoholic with a positive feeling (and a consistently more accurate assessment of his or her strengths and potentials); this in turn would lead to more hopeful feelings in the client, thus working to lift depression early in the treatment process rather than adding to it.

One-to-one therapeutic relationships that are supportive, unprejudiced, and *rational* are rarely within the experience of the alcoholic; these represent an area of deficient skills for the alcoholic as well as a novel treatment strategy against which he or she has prepared few defenses except avoidance.

PROBLEM IDENTIFICATION

The first step in treating someone with alcohol problems is to translate vague problems and difficulties into treatment targets. Targets are relevant to the patient's alcohol problem. They may include the patient's nonassertiveness, apathy, anxiety and depression, hopelessness, and specifically, his or her excessive, habitual use of alcohol.

DEPRESSION AND DRINKING:
CASE HISTORY 1

One theory views alcoholism as a form of self-medication when faced with negative affect. For example, Mendels (1970) discussed the hypothesis that the alcoholic's excessive drinking serves as a defense against underlying endogenous depression. A number of empirical investigations have documented the prevalence of depression among alcoholics. Curlee (1972) found that in an alcoholism treatment unit, 69% of the patients scored in the pathological range on the MMPI Depression Scale shortly after admission. Conversely, anxiety and/or depression may develop as a consequence of alcoholism and of the client's view of him- or herself as an alcoholic. The precise causal relationship between affective states and alcoholism has not been clarified.

Depression is often one of the targets of treatment. The patient's depression may be secondary to the alcohol, or it may be primary, with the alcohol problem coming after the onset of depression. The following is a case in which depression was the target for change.

The patient, Mr. A., was a black 43-year-old male employed as a car polisher. He was referred by the probation department for treatment for drunk driving. He said that he had been a moderate drinker until two years before when his father had died. At that point his drinking escalated, and he was now drinking throughout his working day. He was seen for seven sessions over a period of two months.

An analysis of this drinking behavior (he kept drinking records that tracked mood and situational variables) indicated his major problem was drinking to excess to alleviate dysphoric moods. He explained his depression as being perpetuated by obsessive thoughts centering on his father's death. The most prominent thoughts were: (1) His mother was responsible for his father's death because, believing in faith healing, she had refused to send him to the hospital when he first became ill and had asked to go. (The client had finally called police emergency and had his father taken to the hospital against his mother's wishes, but it was too late.) (2) He blamed himself for not acting sooner. (3) He couldn't forget his father's suffering. The following is how the therapist helped the client construe this experience in a different way:

> THERAPIST: Did your father believe in faith healing?
> CLIENT: Yes.
> THERAPIST: Did your father believe that God takes a person when He is ready—in spite of anything one does?
> CLIENT: Yes.
> THERAPIST: Did your father believe suffering is necessary and redemptive?
> CLIENT: Yes. He'd never suffered any pain before.
> THERAPIST: Are you aware that Jesus had a moment of weakness on the Cross? Wasn't your father entitled to a moment of weakness, without changing the basic philosophies by which he had lived a lifetime?
> CLIENT: I never looked at it this way!
> THERAPIST: Is it possible for you to look at what happened from your father's (and mother's) point of view?

The therapist then proceeded to outline that his father had died the way he had lived, and she discussed with him the difference between "quantity" and "quality" of life. The therapist suggested that at age 75 the father did not have much time left to him; and that if the patient had managed to "save" his life by getting medical treatment that was against his father's belief, he might have added a couple of years of quantity to his life but might have robbed him of the quality his father had been trying to achieve for 75 years.

The therapist suggested that by virtue of age alone (that included the notion of being nearer death), his mother might have been more in tune with what his father really wished despite a moment of weakness when he was in pain. The therapist again stressed that Jesus had experienced a similar moment of wavering belief but that—if it had been possible—taking him down from the Cross during that moment of weakness would have nullified the purpose of his existence.

It was evident that the patient had never considered the situation from this perspective. His subsequent relief was clearly visible.

The patient reported at the next session that he had gone home after the last session and thought over what had been discussed. After making a serious effort to view the situation from his father's perspective, he came to the same conclusions that had been reached in the session. He went to his brother, told him what had taken place, and described the change in his thinking and feeling. His brother felt that his new interpretation and understanding of the situation was more valid than his previous attitude. Together they went to the mother and discussed it. Her response was to smile at him and say, ''Son, I was sure that someday you would understand it.'' From then on, his relationship with his mother improved greatly.

DRINKING BEHAVIOR

Mr. A., in addition to depression, had developed maladaptive drinking patterns. These were the next target for change. As a result of the relief from depression, he was now motivated to work on his drinking problems. When he went to work, he moved his bottle from the refrigerator in his work area into a file cabinet in his boss's office. His reasoning was: (1) He would have been embarrassed to go to his boss's office when he wanted a drink, since either his boss or a customer was usually there. (2) The three-minute walk from his working area to the filing cabinets interrupted the behavioral chain and gave him a chance to make a choice rather than simply respond to habit. As a result of this behavioral engineering, he was able to finish a car in two-and-one-half hours instead of four. His boss noticed this improvement the first day and commented, ''I'm glad to see that you're your old self again.''

SIX-MONTH FOLLOW-UP

This patient stated that clearing his depression had changed his behavior and attitudes in many areas of his life. At the follow-up visit, he reported that he no longer was bothered by depressive thoughts, that he didn't even keep a bottle at work anymore.

About twice a day he goes to a nearby bar if he wants a drink and he never drinks at home, since drinking alcoholic beverages is against his mother's religion. He has not become intoxicated since coming for treatment and has no desire or need to. His drinking habits have returned to what they had been for most of his life before the death of his father started the problem drinking. This change in drinking behavior was confirmed by both his mother and his probation officer.

ANGER, ANXIETY, TENSION, AND DRINKING: CASE HISTORY 2

Other emotional disorders related to the central problem can be targeted for change, as the following case illustrates.

Mr. B., 51, was referred to legal authorities for drunken driving. He had a 15-year-history of alcohol abuse. He complained of intense anxiety, as well as headaches, confusion, and aggressive behavior during drinking episodes. He was employed in an executive position and had a stable but emotionally charged common-law relationship with a woman.

He attributed his drinking to "anxiety, frustration, and confused feelings." Having received no previous treatment, he attended the first session at the order of the court. He was seen for a total of 17 one-hour sessions of cognitive therapy in a period of 18 weeks, with several booster sessions over a two-year period.

The initial treatment phase involved an investigation of how his drinking urges were related to the situations in which the urge occurred, and his cognitions and emotions preceding the urges. He kept detailed records of his urges. The urge to consume alcohol occurred when he had intense feelings of anger, anxiety over losing control, or severe headaches. These physiopsychological states became targets for treatment.

ANGER AND ANXIETY

The patient expressed a fear he might lose control, particularly in situations involving his common-law wife. He had developed a series of rules about anger, such as "I should always be in control of my emotions," and "I shouldn't get angry or I will lose respect." His basic notion was that a person could only have respect (which he valued highly) if he was always in control. As mentioned, he was also concerned that any expression of his emotions would lead to uncontrollable behavior. These cognitions were reinforced by an incident in his teen years when his father had attacked him physically and the patient had picked up a knife and threatened to kill his father.

The initial therapeutic intervention involved assertiveness training that included behavior rehearsal and the modification of dysfunctional cognitions. For example, the client listed a series of situations in which his wife would demonstrate a "lack of respect." These situations ranged from demands from her that he do most of the housework to times when she would tease him in front of her girl friends. It was explained that there was little evidence as to whether his wife did or did not respect him, since she was unaware of his feelings and thus had no reason to change her behavior. Once the patient understood that his interpretation of her "rejection" was his own idea and not necessarily a fact, he agreed to "test" his idea.

The testing necessitated his acquisition of specific behavioral assertive skills. A hierarchy of situations was developed with respect to degree of stress he perceived—that is, his estimate of the degree of probability that he would lose control; and he and the therapist discussed appropriate responses to the various situations. Eventually, the patient demonstrated that he was able to assert himself without losing control.

TENSION HEADACHES

The tension headaches experienced by this patient were understandable, given his imposition of severe control over any expressions of emotions. In later sessions, he was trained in relaxation techniques to control his headaches. (He had reported undesirable side effects from medication.) Since the most severe headaches occurred in the morning, he was also instructed to record his "automatic thoughts" immediately upon arising. These thoughts were typically related to problems with which he expected to be confronted during the day—for example, "What if Mr. Jones doesn't pay his bill?" "If I don't finish all of my work today, I'll have to go back tonight." The successful strategy for altering the pattern of early-morning headaches involved making a list at night of jobs to be done on the following day and using relaxation methods in the morning.

Two-Year Follow-Up

The patient reported he had not been intoxicated once since starting treatment, although he had drunk a small quantity of beer on a few occasions. This report was confirmed by his wife and by his probation officer.

His relationship with his wife improved and he expanded his business activities. He believes he has learned how to solve problems, particularly as they related to anger and anxiety, and he is no longer bothered by tension headaches. His wife recently described him to the therapist as a "new man."

PAIN, SLEEP DISORDERS, AND DRINKING: CASE HISTORY 3

In a number of cases, the person's drinking problem is related to his or her effort to alleviate pain or cope with sleep problems. One such case was Mrs. C., 34. A registered nurse, she came to the clinic suffering from polydrug abuse (including alcohol dependency) and undiagnosed physical symptoms of slurred speech, ataxia, loss of equilibrium, numbness, and tingling sensations in her extremities, and incapacitating headaches. No physiological reasons could be found for her symptoms, although she had received extensive physical and neurological workups. She was so incapacitated that she had been given an involuntary leave of absence of three months.

Her history indicated continuous attempts at treatment for the past five years, including three inpatient admissions for alcoholism and one as a psychiatric patient. She had been dismissed from her last three jobs as a registered nurse for stealing medication from her patients. Her self-respect was at low ebb, and she was overcome by feelings of anger and hopelessness about her lack of success in finding effective treatment.

Insomnia and pain were two problems related to her drinking.

INSOMNIA

The patient's insomnia was partly maintained by her belief that she had to have a great deal of sleep. The following was her answer to this belief:

> I thought all day, why do I want to sleep? I have told myself many times in the past that if I sleep, I don't have to think. I used to think depressing thoughts . . . until it became a habit with me. Anyway, I can choose what I want to think about . . . I don't have to think, "What if this would happen?" I am a human being with a good sensible brain. Why not use it for constructive thoughts, instead of depressing ones?

Through relaxation and cognitive restructuring, she was able to solve her sleep problem.

HEADACHES

The patient was taught to monitor her headaches and the thoughts associated with them. This monitoring helped to decrease their occurrence and provided data showing her that the headaches were not constant as she believed, but time-limited. The patient was taught relaxation exercises to lessen the pain and cognitive techniques to decatastrophize the headaches. She was also taught that she could learn to tolerate a certain amount of pain.

ALCOHOL AND DRUG ABUSE

As the above conditions were worked on and modified, her desire for alcohol and drugs decreased. In the first part of therapy, she abstained from alcohol and attended AA meetings. Later, she was able to engage in controlled drinking. During treatment, the patient went on one drinking binge that lasted two days and ended when the therapist intervened with a home visit.

ONE-YEAR FOLLOW-UP

At one year the patient had not abused alcohol or drugs for six months, and her employer reported that she was working at a high level of competence. She had enrolled in a graduate school where she was receiving excellent grades. For the first time in five years she had begun dating and her physiological symptoms had disappeared completely.

She wrote the following evaluation of her progress:

I have been in and out of therapy since 1971—mostly *in*. Never had I made such progress as I did in the last year. With this therapy, besides the sessions, I read the suggested books, practiced relaxation, kept a diary, had homework to do, and practiced new ways of thinking and doing. I was made to feel that I was helping myself, and I really was! I don't know how therapy was tapered off without my realizing it. I honestly don't know if my alcohol and drug problems are gone forever, but I sure do have a better chance in life. And I do feel good about life and myself.

UNPLEASANT SOCIAL INTERACTIONS AND DRINKING: CASE HISTORY 4

At times the drinking behavior is related to social interactions, as was the case with a 47-year-old bus driver. He was treated for depression, but he also had a drinking problem, which was worked on at the same time the depression was targeted for change.

He drank to excess in two social situations: (1) when he was angry with his wife, and (2) when he was socially anxious amidst a group of people.

ANGER

His thoughts proceeding from anger with his wife were concerned with what he considered to be lack of respect from her. His distortion was that his wife's disagreements with him and refusal to wait on him were signs of her lack of love. As a result, he believed he could get even with his wife by getting drunk. Both sets of distortions were worked on, and assertiveness training was initiated to improve his communication with his wife, who did not realize that he interpreted her behavior as disrespectful.

SOCIAL ANXIETY

The client drank to control his social anxiety at work and at gatherings with friends and relatives. In social situations, he believed everyone had to like him. He related this need for approval to his early upbringing in foster homes, where he believed that if the foster parents did not like him they would send him back to an institution.

He was able to overcome social anxiety at work by telling himself,

"This is a commercial relationship. These people don't have to like me." The problem in social situations outside of work was more complex. One distortion was that people were always "putting him down" or about to do so. Consequently, in the interests of what he construed to be self-defense, he would often subtly criticize others while talking to them. This problem was worked on through cognitive restructuring and social-skills training.

ENHANCEMENT OF POSITIVE MOODS

Interestingly, when he finally started to have good times with others, he frequently drank to excess. His distortion in this area was that if he felt good, he could maintain and expand this mood by drinking. To challenge this belief, he was asked to run experiments to see if alcohol did indeed enhance his mood. For example, at a party he rated his moods on the hour. He discovered instead that alcohol actually led to disintegration of positive mood.

DRINKING BEHAVIOR

In addition to modifying the above, the patient was taught a variety of controlled-drinking strategies. These included: drinking more slowly, buying beer by the six-pack instead of the case, and not getting drinks for others at parties.

ONE-YEAR FOLLOW-UP

The client had overcome depression and was functioning at a much higher level at the follow-up. He believed he had acquired the ability to control his drinking. He was no longer drinking before beginning work and had only been intoxicated one weekend since treatment was terminated.

MODIFYING DRINKING BEHAVIOR

We use a wide range of cognitive and behavioral procedures to directly modify maladaptive drinking behavior. These interventions are adapted to the needs of a particular patient.

GOAL SETTING

Setting realistic treatment goals is a crucial part of treatment. The client
has the choice of whether to try controlled drinking or to abstain entirely. Initially, however, we strongly suggest that the person refrain from
drinking for a period of time. Some patients need to go through a de-
toxification program that requires their being hospitalized.

Even if we believe that a particular patient will have trouble with
controlled drinking, we work with him or her toward this goal if it is the
direction in which the patient wishes to move. Some clients will stay in
treatment only if they have the option of achieving the ability to control their drinking. If a patient has a severe liver problem or other
health-related problems, however, we discourage a controlled-drinking
program.

After the person has failed to benefit from a controlled-drinking
program, he or she is more amenable to trying an abstinence program.
When the treatment goal is determined by the patient, the collaborative nature of the therapist–patient relationship is strengthened.

CONTROLLED DRINKING

In a controlled-drinking program, the overall goal is to reduce the patient's consumption of alcohol. The following are general strategies to
be used, in the form of suggestions to the patient.

1. Sip your drinks. Don't drink more than an ounce of alcohol an
   hour (one beer, one mixed drink, or one glass of wine); this will
   keep you from becoming intoxicated.
2. If you finish before the hour is up, add mix or ice to your present drink.
3. Tell those offering a refill, "Thanks, but I haven't finished this
   one yet."
4. Plan how much you want to drink before you start and stick to
   the plan.
5. Don't offer to get drinks for others.
6. Stay away from the bar or the area where drinks are being served.
7. Dilute drinks; add an extra amount of ice and tinkle it frequently. The sound becomes a substitute for substance.

EXPERIMENTATION AS A THERAPEUTIC INTERVENTION: CASE HISTORY 5

There are variations on this set of strategies. One patient, Mr. E., alternated days of drinking (wet days) with days of not drinking (dry days). After the patient was able to master these, his program included a "damp day," a controlled-drinking day.

His program consisted of a three-day sequence: (1) dry days (no drinks), (2) damp days (not over 4 ounces of alcohol), and (3) wet days (not over blood level of 0 on breath analyzer). The damp days presented the most challenges.

DEVELOPMENT OF PLAN

After Mr. E.'s treatment goal had been established, the next step was to develop a plan for implementing this goal and a way of dealing with the problems that would also arise. A potential pitfall of developing self-control plans is that they may be too complicated. An overabundance of techniques quickly reaches the point of diminishing returns.

Novice therapists often try a new technique when the first doesn't appear to work, often before the first one has been given a fair trial. You should keep your eyes on the goals of therapy, and not on how many techniques can be used. The fewer techniques effectively used, the better. With Mr. E., the therapist started off with standard procedures and didn't go on to others until it was clear that the initial ones weren't working.

SELF-MONITORING

The first part of his plan involved self-monitoring. This provided a basis for a behavioral assessment. The patient wrote down the times when he took a drink or the times when he had the urge to drink. This procedure is simple and can be done on a tablet. From this record, problems will become evident so that procedures to control future deviations can be developed. The plan may dictate that the patient drink moderately or not at all.

One of the purposes of self-monitoring is to discover the functions alcohol serves for the patient. One way to discover these functions is to construct with the patient a diagram of the various uses of alcohol. His therapist and Mr. E. drew up such a diagram (see Figure 1).

About half of the time alcohol was used to increase positive feelings and the other half to control negative feelings and situations. For Mr. E., alcohol served three general functions:

1. *Alcohol as fun.* At these times he drank socially with business associates, at home with his wife and close friends, and special pleasant times such as trips.
2. *Alcohol as social facilitator.* The second function of alcohol was to help Mr. E. in handling social situations. These were both negative and positive situations where he believed alcohol increased his social skills.
3. *Alcohol as self-treatment.* The third general function of alcohol was to control negative feelings and to handle difficulties.

After the patient and therapist delineated these patterns specific plans for breaking up the patterns could be made.

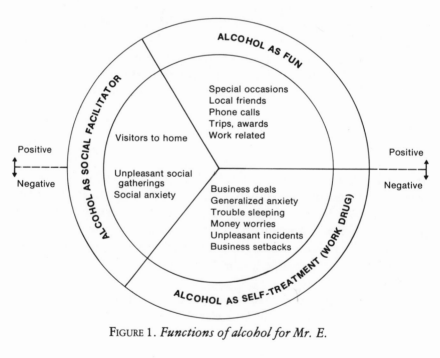

FIGURE 1. *Functions of alcohol for Mr. E.*

When Mr. E. deviated from the plan, he recorded what he was thinking, doing, and what his environment was at that time. Once these days were known, future plans could be made that represented a correction of the first plans. This corrected version is called an after-action report, and it is essential to the designing of future strategies.

DISTORTED AND DYSFUNCTIONAL THOUGHTS

When Mr. E. broke his plan, he tuned into what he'd been thinking. Most of Mr. E's thoughts were some form of rationalization or excuses.

Excuses appear to be the most common type of dysfunctional thought found with those with alcohol problems. These are reasons people give for breaking restraint. Human creativity has few bounds when applied to the development of excuses. Almost any occurrence can be used as an excuse, from "It's Sunday" to "I'm tired." *Excuse* is a somewhat pejorative term, but nevertheless they are *excuses,* not logical explanations or actual causes for disregarding a plan.

One of Mr. E.'s common themes was on the difficulty of following the plan. He often thought: "I can't do it," "It's too hard," "Nothing works," "I have no control." Hopelessness is a major element in failure to follow a program. Once Mr. E. made his hopelessness explicit, he could begin to challenge it.

His general answer was "How do I know unless I try? I have no evidence that I can't do it in the future."

Another common mistake of Mr. E. was to brood about having drinks. There are a number of ways in which such ruminations can be controlled: He walled them off by telling himself, "I'm not going to think about this now. I'll think about it at another time," and practiced thought stoppage through diversion or involvement in an engrossing activity.

ASSUMPTIONS

Usually patients have underlying assumptions based on myths about alcohol and their interpretations of these myths. These assumptions can be identified and changed. Examples of assumptions are: "I have no control," "It is unfair that I should be deprived of a good time," "I have to really be concerned about others' opinions, so I have to accept food or drinks when I'm offered them."

Patients seem to harbor various myths about alcohol. They can bring up any of these myths in order to justify their drinking. Some of Mr. E.'s beliefs were: "I need to drink to keep my business going . . . to be creative . . . to be sociable . . . to give me energy." It was necessary to get Mr. E. to become aware of these subversive myths so they could be analyzed, challenged, and tested.

After uneven progress in the beginning, Mr. E. was able to moderate his drinking. At a year follow-up this was most readily evident in improved health and social functioning.

CONTROLLING ENVIRONMENT

While self-control is important, it's also important for the patient to learn how to control his environment. One person broke his plan when he was trying to go to sleep after only two drinks and his wife brought up a problem involving one of the children. He then became excited, tried to calm down without success, and finally began to drink.

He changed his environment by planning specific times more appropriate to discussion of issues of this sort, times when he was unlikely to become excited enough to start drinking excessively.

One way of teaching the patient to control his or her environment is for the therapist to go out with the client and have a drink. Once on the street the patient can decide which bar to go to. The therapist can find out what the person is thinking and ask if one type of bar is more likely than another to lead to maladaptive drinking. The therapist can use the same procedure in the bar with respect to what is ordered, where to sit, how fast the patient drinks. Moreover, the therapist can serve as a powerful model of adaptive drinking.

CRITICAL INCIDENTS

A person's way of handling critical incidents, that is, difficult situations, is extremely important to the development of self-control procedures. Mishandling critical incidents is a major cause of breakdowns in self-control regimes. A critical incident leads to (1) deviation from the plan, and (2) abandoning the plan when the person says to himself, "I blew the whole thing."

The following are suggestions you can give patients to help them handle critical incidents:

1. What you tell yourself immediately after the critical incident is *crucial*.

2. Instead of filling your mind with short-circuiting ideas such as: "This shouldn't happen," "I wish it had not happened," or "I want to get out of here," tell yourself something along these lines: "I am going to choose to handle this situation rather than let it handle me. I am being offered an opportunity to handle a situation that has been a problem in the past. I'm being given another chance to handle it rationally and effectively."

3. Take charge of the situation. One way we've found helpful is to react in a way that is the opposite of how you feel like reacting to that incident. For example, if you feel like panicking, force yourself to be (or at least to *act*) calm and rational. If you feel like avoiding the situation and running away, make yourself move toward it. If you are ashamed or embarrassed, force yourself to disclose even more potentially "shameful" or embarrassing material. If you're angry and want to tell someone off, be empathetic and listen to what he or she has to say.

4. Most important, believe you have taken some control and that you have some choice in the situation.

You should adapt these guidelines to each particular patient.

DECISION POINTS

Part of using the critical incident technique is to teach patients to recognize points in time where they can *choose* to control the situation or let the situation control them. Marlatt (1976) writes on the importance of teaching patients to become aware of subtle decisions that don't appear to be related to loss of control—but are. We use a similar method and teach patients to make their decisions explicit. This is done by having them write out two scripts, one maladaptive that leads to breaking restraint and another that is adaptive. You can point out that at these decision points the decision is relatively easy but once one chooses a road, it becomes difficult to backtrack.

Initially there are a number of decision points but later they become fewer and harder to spot and use. Bill Hoffman, in his autobiography as a compulsive gambler (1968), describes this clearly.

> The idea of giving Jake the worthless check troubled me. We had been close through grade school, high school, and college. I knew the check

would end all that, would make friendship impossible. It seemed unfair that a lifetime of building a relationship could be destroyed by one act. But I knew it could and did not stop myself, for I had embarked upon a journey I had not wanted to take, fancying myself rather more an interested observer of the trip and its outcome than the sole traveler, and there was no turning back.

Three weeks before I had written the first check to bet the horses. I'd bounced more than 30 others since. (p. 11)

If Mr. Hoffman had been a patient we would have taught him to become aware of choice points before he started his journey.

We use these during treatment and as a tool to maintain gain. For example, one patient would start getting dressed in a special way before he went on drinking binges. He had a "drinking hat" he would put on as a sign of the binge to come. He was taught to see putting on his hat as a decision point that he could control.

Another woman who had had no drinks for two months decided to pack a bottle of whiskey for a camping trip, "in case someone else might want a drink." Once she reflected on her behavior, she recognized this as a choice point and didn't pack it.

CONCLUSIONS

Many therapists have given up on being able to help people with alcohol and other substance-abuse problems. We believe this is premature; there are many new and promising ways of helping this group of individuals. Cognitive therapy is one of these new approaches.

REFERENCES

Curlee, J. Depression and alcoholism. *Bulletin of the Menninger Clinic,* 1972, *36,* 451–455.

Hoffman, W. S. *The loser.* New York: Funk & Wagnalls, 1968.

Mendels, J. *Concepts of depression.* New York: Wiley, 1970.

National Institute of Alcoholism and Alcohol Abuse. From *Program to people: Toward a national policy on alcoholism services and prevention.* (DHEW Publication No. [ADM] 75-155). Washington, D.C.: U.S. Government Printing Office, 1975.

Pattison, E. M. New abstinent drinking goals in treatment of alcoholism. *Archives of General Psychiatry,* 1976, *33,* 923–930.

SPECIAL TECHNIQUES

As many of the contributors to this volume have emphasized, very few of the cases we encounter in clinical practice are simple or straightforward. The treatment of disturbed individuals often demands a great deal of creativity, perserverance, and personal maturity from the therapist. No matter how routine or mechanized the procedures associated with a particular form of therapy may appear to be, the success of the treatment with a given patient will depend, ultimately, on the personal resources of the therapist. Through the course of treatment, the typical therapist will make innumerable decisions and emit scores of responses without the benefit of an all-encompassing therapeutic model. All of us, then, even the most "orthodox" adherents to one school or another, are innovators and integrators in our day-to-day clinical work.

This final section reflects the efforts of five authors to extend the conceptual and strategic boundaries of cognitive therapy by devising new techniques and by incorporating tools and ideas from other treatment approaches. Diane B. Arnkoff argues convincingly for flexibility on the part of the cognitive therapist, but perhaps more importantly, she acts as a powerful role model for all of us. At times, she confronts her clients in a highly personal way, and uses her "self" fearlessly as a therapeutic instrument. Readers will be surprised, and it is hoped inspired, by the way she blends Gestalt techniques with a cognitive viewpoint.

As Arthur Freeman points out, cognitive therapists are generally not trained to use dream material in treatment. Freeman illustrated how the dream can be viewed from a cognitive perspective, without recourse to psychodynamic constructs. He shows how dreams and images, like other cognitions, are amenable to restructuring. His chapter should help to stimulate further interest among cognitive therapists in dream phenomena.

Though some systems theorists might disagree, Richard C. Bedrosian contends that family therapy and individual therapy are by no means incompatible with one another. In his chapter on the use of significant others, he suggests ways in which the cognitive therapist, who works primarily from an indidivual viewpoint, can utilize family members in treatment. Even the practitioner who has no intention of restructuring the family needs to be aware of the connection between the patient's interactions with significant others and his or her psychological symptoms. Therapists with more ambitious (or grandiose) goals can interweave cognitive and relationship interventions.

How does a therapist determine whether a client's response to a stressful life event is pathological or within normal limits? Janis Lieff Abrahms suggests that the difference between depressive reaction and the natural process of mourning lies in the individual's cognitions. She describes a number of creative interventions that she employed with two women who had sustained recent losses. In both of the cases, the scope of therapy went considerably beyond the meaning of the precipitating event. Abrahms's vivid descriptions being the cases alive for the reader.

William B. Sacco advises us to take therapy out of our offices, into the situations where the client actually experiences distress. While he details the advantages of *in vivo* treatment, he also cautions us regarding its potential contraindications. Sacco describes an interesting series of interventions designed to produce a direct and immediate challenge to the individual's dysfunctional cognitions. His narration reveals his sensitivity to the relationship issues in cognitive therapy.

Ideally, this section of the book should stimulate controversy and creativity. Readers who view themselves as "purists" of one form or another may look askance at some of the strategies recommended. So be it. As cognitive therapists, we know that growth and change can occur only if we challenge our most cherished assumptions.

FLEXIBILITY IN PRACTICING COGNITIVE THERAPY

Diane B. Arnkoff

INTRODUCTION

The popularity of cognitive therapy is attributable in part to its broad base. The relationship of cognitive therapy to behavior therapy is evident in such aspects as the use of homework assignments, the interest in assessing change outside of the therapy hour, and the concern with the communicability of techniques. Cognitive therapy is also related to psychodynamic therapy in its emphasis on mental events. In fact, the stated goal of cognitive therapy is to modify distorted patterns of thinking. In a time when clinicians prefer to think of themselves as eclectic rather than as belonging to one school (Garfield & Kurtz, 1976), cognitive therapy is appealingly broad.

In keeping with the wide scope of cognitive therapy, one purpose of this chapter is to discuss the blending of cognitive procedures with those more commonly associated with other forms of therapy. Cognitive procedures are defined here as actions by the therapist that focus directly on modification of the client's distorted conceptualizations (Beck, Rush, Shaw, & Emery, 1979). These procedures may be differentiated from therapeutic techniques that are aimed, for example, at intensifying affect or modifying motor behavior. However, orthodoxy in restricting cognitive therapy to "cognitive" techniques will serve no useful clinical purpose. Furthermore, flexibility in marrying procedures need not imply the practice of atheoretical, trial-and-error therapy. The cognitive viewpoint, that maladaptive ideas underlie distress, is, in fact, more characteristic of cognitive therapy than is any one technique. In discussing the blending of procedures, I will endeav-

Diane B. Arnkoff. Department of Psychology, The Catholic University of America, Washington, D.C.

or to show how the therapy remains consistent with this cognitive viewpoint.

One theme of this chapter, then, is that flexibility in using techniques is both possible and desirable. A second theme is the importance of flexibility on the part of the therapist as a participant in therapy. In doing cognitive therapy, it is important for therapists to shift approaches as evidence regarding the particular client becomes available, and to be aware of the distortions that they themselves bring to therapy. Conclusions regarding the client's personality and needs are necessary, but such conclusions can become a liability if not subject to revision in light of new evidence. And just as the client has beliefs that are maladaptive, the therapist's ideas and resulting actions are fallible as well. A willingness to revise tactics in the light of new understandings of the client, the therapist, or the relationship, is central to effective therapy. In the second part of this chapter, I will discuss some of the pitfalls I have discovered in my own fallible practice of cognitive therapy.

FLEXIBILITY IN TECHNIQUES

As a therapist, I make use of cognitive techniques with most of the clients I see. But like most therapists, I rarely restrict myself to those techniques that are considered cognitive. Two approaches that I attempt to unite with my cognitive procedures are a deliberate use of my relationship with the client, and various Gestalt therapy techniques.

THE RELATIONSHIP BETWEEN CLIENT AND THERAPIST

The use of the relationship is, of course, a time-honored therapeutic procedure. Certain of the client's interpersonal difficulties are bound to manifest themselves in the interaction between therapist and client. By using the "here-and-now" relationship as a focus of therapy, the therapist capitalizes on the affect that the client has invested in therapy.

The use of the relationship as a therapeutic tool may be interpreted in cognitive terms. The therapist marshals immediately available behavioral evidence of the client's difficulties, and uses it to persuade the client to modify distorted beliefs. In the case I will discuss here, I used aspects of the client's interaction with me as evidence of how he conceptualized our relationship, and more importantly, other relationships, in maladaptive ways.

Paul was a 25-year-old white-collar worker who came to therapy because of growing interpersonal conflicts at work and at home. His immigrant parents had taught him that he must follow a strict path of hard work in order to survive in a hostile environment. He was determined to succeed and pushed both himself and his coworkers to an extreme.

The most serious stress, however, was in his marriage. Paul had never paid much attention to Sarah in the three years of their marriage, but it had never occurred to him that his neglect of her could cause a problem. He had assumed that, like his mother, she would always be there. Sarah was growing increasingly restless, particularly since Paul refused to have children until his success in his work was assured. In desperation over what she saw as their growing rift, Sarah had had a brief affair.

Paul was shocked when he found out about the affair. Sarah had violated her role in a way he never thought possible. If she meant to gain his attention, she succeeded. In fact, Paul began to obsessively ruminate about the affair. He constantly thought about it, and even his dreams were reenactments of Sarah's shocking transgression. He was alternately angry and extremely anxious. His health and work were suffering. He went to his doctor for tranquilizers, but to his surprise the doctor referred him instead to therapy.

Paul and Sarah's initial request was for marital therapy, which was provided later, but I will discuss here only the work that I did with Paul alone. Little progress could be made initially with Paul and Sarah as a couple, primarily because Paul attributed responsibility for their problems solely to Sarah. In fact, Paul did not feel that he played any part in any of his conflicts. Everyone else should be in therapy; he was the only reasonable person around. As might be expected, he continually contemplated leaving therapy in its early stages. He stayed only because he assumed that his doctor must be right that he had a problem, though he certainly could not see it. He agreed to my proposal for individual sessions before we moved into marital therapy, but he was surprised that I thought it necessary.

Paul was not a therapist's ideal of the verbal, introspective client. My initial attempts to challenge the distortion that he was completely right and others completely misguided merely left him puzzled. In his rigid scheme, it was entirely possible for him to have all the answers!

Paul frequently let me know when I did and when I did not meet his expectations of a therapist, giving me an evaluation of my work after every session and often during the session. He rendered his judgments in a friendly way, without overt hostility or anger. He just thought I ought to know how I was doing. I saw his comparison with his standards as a possible opening for reaching him.

Many things about me surprised Paul. No doubt he was not expecting a female therapist when he applied to the clinic for therapy. After the first session, he remarked that I was too short to be a therapist! When I asked him what he was looking for, he answered that he just thought that all therapists looked like a male pastoral counselor he had seen briefly a few years before. He was surprised that I did not offer advice, and amazed that I laughed at his jokes (again in contrast to the previous counselor). Most importantly, he was surprised at my human faults and inconsistencies.

In an early session, Paul began by complaining about my manner of leading him from the waiting room into my office. I walked authoritatively in front of him rather than with him, and he disliked my distant manner. He felt that this behavior was inconsistent with my friendly demeanor during the session itself. In this case I decided not to deflect attention from myself by asking Paul what he wanted from our relationship. Instead I looked at what he might be telling me about myself. I realized that he was right in that there *was* an unusual contrast between my behavior at the beginning of a session and later on. When I reflected on it, I saw that my stiffness as the hour began was evidence of my discomfort with him because of our difficult relationship. When I told this to Paul, he blinked in astonishment. He had not expected an admission of fallibility.

A couple of sessions later, he said he couldn't figure me out, since I was so different from week to week. Sometimes I was active, apparently with a goal in mind, sometimes I leaned back and was observant, and sometimes I was plainly uncomfortable. Why was I so inconsistent? Again, I could have made an observation about what he was asking for, sending the ball back into his court. Alternatively, I could have told him that I was reacting to how difficult it was to work with him. But since he was trying to understand me, I decided to keep the focus on myself. I admitted that, like him, I had moods. Sometimes I felt like being one way, sometimes another. Once more he was astonished. He had expected neither my inconsistency, nor my admission of it.

The content of therapy through most of these early sessions was Paul's feelings about his wife. He had always assumed her to be one kind of person—his perfect image of a wife. Recent events had shaken up his feelings for her. Instead of being his ideal of purity, she had had a brief affair; instead of being simple, she was complicated; and instead of being serious, she took much of life lightly. He could not understand the "change" in her. Actually, he was probably just getting to know her after three years of marriage. Since she was turning out to be a different person from the woman he thought he married, it was obvious to him that they should end their relationship. Yet, so far he was staying with her. His own ambivalence puzzled him.

I was struck by the correspondence between his distortions about his wife and those about me. He had rigid expectations of a wife and of a therapist. He could not imagine either role being played differently. In fact, it took a gross violation of his wife's role, namely, her affair, to make him see her any differently from his ideal image. With me he was aware from the first session that I was not what he expected, and I decided to use that anomaly.

Just after I had admitted to Paul that my moods affected how I acted with him, I reminded him of all the other ways in which I did not match his expectations. Yet, he returned every week. What did he think of how I actually was as a therapist? Paul looked interested, and pensively replied that I wasn't bad. He didn't understand why, but he kind of liked what we were doing in therapy. I said it seemed similar with Sarah. He was learning that she wasn't the person he thought, yet he was still with her and even liked some of what he saw in her. He was uncharacteristically silent.

From that session on, the discrepancy between his image and the apparent reality became a frequent theme for us. The complexities of his feelings about his wife made progress difficult, but the change in our own relationship remained a solid touchstone. We spent several months in individual therapy, first eliciting Paul's concept of how the world should operate, and then comparing his expectations with real events. Paul still had a lot of painful learning ahead when we decided that we had done as much as we could in individual therapy. Yet, he had also come a long way, as exemplified by his beginning a later session with "You know, I think I'm finally beginning to live in the real world."

While Paul and I were doing individual work, I occasionally saw Paul and Sarah together or Sarah alone to assess the current status of their relationship. Sarah decided after some early uncertainty that she wanted to continue the marriage if at all possible. She realized that her former acquiescence to Paul's conception of her role was not adaptive. Part of the reason that Paul could continue in his distortions was that she had tried to mold herself into the quiet wife he was looking for. While I was working with Paul alone, and later when we moved into marital therapy, Sarah began to clarify her own wishes. My work with the two of them mainly involved facilitating their communication, to strengthen Sarah's assertion of herself as a separate person, and to help Paul to see her as she really was.

Paul came to therapy with rigid rules and expectations of himself and others, which led him to his controlling behavior. He was ready for change because his model of the world no longer worked for him. But he could not see his distortions when we dealt only with his relationship with his wife. He had too much at stake in being right about her, and was too accustomed to his beliefs about her to change them easily. By using my relationship with him, I not only dealt with the immediate "here and now," but I also allowed him to be different in a relationship that was less crucial to him than his marriage.

Paul's relentless judgments of my performance initially disconcerted me. Yet, in paying so much attention to what I was like, he allowed me first to see, and then to challenge, his maladaptive expectations. Unlike his wife, I did not accept his expectations of me as being reasonable. Unlike his coworkers, I did not reject him when I rejected his expectations. Since I accepted my own idiosyncrasies, he had to learn to accept them as well. In time, he began to accept that Sarah was also different from his expectations, and, eventually and painfully, how he himself did not have to measure up to his own unreachable standards.

My use of my relationship with Paul is functionally similar to what a psychodynamic therapist would do; the aim of using the relationship to modify a distorted pattern is the same. However, there are some differences worth noting. First, I did not make extensive use of the past with Paul. As might be expected, he could not initially see the relevance of his childhood to what he thought of as mainly his wife's problem. Once the groundwork had been laid in exploring his feelings about his wife, however, we did examine the roots of his rigid views. With a great deal of relief, he realized the misery of his overly controlled childhood. Yet, in this case, the work on the past was more of a useful side trip than the primary journey.

More importantly, my role as a therapist differed greatly from dynamically oriented therapy. In no way did I attempt to be a blank screen. We uncovered Paul's projections, but not through my neutrality. Our relationship was powerful evidence to Paul that his image of people was distorted—precisely because I shared with him my own inconsistency and fallibility. He learned that he valued our relationship even though I did not match his expectations. In this case it was important that I vigorously insert myself into the therapeutic relationship.

One final note about Paul. Although I let him know that I did not share his world view, I never claimed to have a perfect hold on reality myself. What was truly new to him was that there could be no one, correct way to see the world (Arnkoff, 1980). Had I offered him another rigid world view to replace his own, he might have accepted it easily but made little real progress. Learning about uncertainty took a lot more work for him.

Gestalt Techniques

In addition to using my relationship with a client, I frequently use Gestalt techniques in therapy. These techniques can facilitate cognitive changes, as the following case illustrates. The procedures are especially useful when it is important to disrupt the client's usual pattern. The repetitious pattern to be broken could either be an internal one of automatic thoughts, or a pattern between client and therapist in which the work is no longer moving forward.

With a client I saw in a university counseling center, I used the Gestalt techniques of a focus on sensory awareness, and the empty-chair technique. Jerry, a college sophomore, came to the counseling center because he realized that the goals he had set out to pursue in college were more his parents' than his own. His parents had not gone beyond high school, but his older brothers had both done well in college and were settling into stable careers. Jerry's parents hoped he would get a business degree and be a credit to the family. He threw himself into his work as a freshman and did fairly well. He had not been very interested in his courses but assumed that would come with time. Now in his sophomore year and taking courses in his major, he realized that he was truly not interested in business. He was becoming increasingly unable to study, but because he believed that his being in school was essential to his parents, he felt he should continue to try. He was telling his parents in every letter that he was studying very hard, but he knew that his grades for the semester would show that to be untrue. When he came into therapy, Jerry believed that he was at a crucial turning point in his life. He thought that he had to decide either to follow his parents' wishes and advice and stay in school until he finished, or to leave school and strike out on his own with an uncertain future.

Initially Jerry was caught in his ruminations over this problem. When he described his situation to me, he kept using the same phrases, such as "I don't know what I'm going to do," and "I just know I can't go on like this." When I asked him how he felt about various aspects of the problem, trying to understand if he felt anxiety at his uncertain future, anger at his parents, and so on, he could only answer with the same ruminative litany. His ruminations over his dilemma were interfering with his academic and social life. Similarly, his implicit rule that acknowledging his emotions would be dangerous was impeding his work in therapy. Early sessions of therapy, like the rest of his life, were like a broken record of ruminations.

Clearly something had to be done to break the pattern. In an effort to bring him into the present, I suggested a simple awareness exercise. (For discussions of awareness in Gestalt therapy, see Fagan & Shepherd, 1970; Perls, 1973; and Polster & Polster, 1973.) I proposed it with the rationale of helping him to control his ruminations, which had been increasing. First I asked him to close his eyes and focus for 30 seconds on all the sounds he could hear. The second exercise was to focus for another 30 seconds on any visual stimuli in the room that he chose. He was to concentrate his awareness in each exercise, striving not to let his attention be divided.

Jerry was embarrassed to do something so contrived, but he tried it out. To his surprise, he enjoyed the exercises immensely. He said he experienced sounds and sights more richly than he ever had before. When ruminations intruded, he labored to get back to the task because he "didn't want to miss anything." He was eager to try the exercises on his own, and so we discussed how he could use them when ruminations interfered in his studying. As Jerry was already beginning to experience a reduction in anxiety, he was an eager participant in therapy from then on.

The awareness exercises were an experiment that falsified some of Jerry's long-standing, maladaptive beliefs. He had demonstrated to himself that he could break his ruminations, which he had despaired of before. Further, he had learned that disaster did not befall him when he paid more attention to his senses than to striving toward some long-term goal.

Jerry's plight clearly had two sides: to stay in school, or to leave and get a job. Initially he saw it as a conflict between what he wanted, to set out on his own, and what his parents wanted, for him to get a degree. He saw it as an all-or-nothing choice. He knew he did not like school, but he could not bear to hurt his parents. When he entered therapy, neither side was winning. He was still in school, but his worry and preoccupation were draining all of his energy from studying. He was frozen.

Once we had agreed that he was caught between two sides, I proposed the empty-chair or two-chair technique (Greenberg, 1979; Perls, 1969), as an experiment designed to help Jerry clarify his conflict. I moved two chairs near us and designated one for each side. I told him that when he was sitting in one chair, he was to throw himself into being only that part of the conflict. The two sides were going to talk to each other. He would be free to switch from chair to chair, and at times I would ask him to switch.

I chose to ask Jerry to separate the two sides of himself artificially with the intent that it would be an improvement over his habit of coming to a stalemate each time he thought about both aspects of the problem at once. I chose an "experiential," emotional procedure rather than a more intellectual technique (such as listing the pros and cons of each decision) precisely because Jerry had difficulty acknowledging his contradictory and intense emotions. He would have been more comfortable with an intellectual approach, but in this particular case, it would have led to more of the same ruminations rather than a shift toward resolution.

Jerry was eager to try the experiment. I asked him to stand between the two chairs and choose where he would like to begin. He readily chose the side that wanted to leave school. The following is an abbreviated transcript of the experiment. "L" stands for the part of him that wanted to leave school, "S" for the part that wanted to stay in school, and "T" for therapist.

L *(matter-of-fact tone of voice)*: The reason why I don't want to stay in school is that I'm turned off by it. I feel that I want to get out and really do something. I feel that life is passing me by in college—I feel cooped up. I want to be outside in the real, living world.

T *(attempting to stir up the emotion behind his statement)*: Tell that side, "You're cooping me up."

L *(with more feeling)*: Yeah, you are, you're cooping me up. You're holding me back from getting out and trying something different, even if it's a mistake. I'd like to find out for myself without taking somebody's word for it. If it was up to me, I feel it would be worth a try. You may be right, that I'd have to come back to school, but there's no harm in trying, and I may even like it. But at this point, you're cooping me up, and I don't exactly like it.

The part of Jerry that wanted to leave school had now made a forthright statement of its position, so it was time to hear from the other side.

T: Switch chairs. *(Client switches.)* Now tell that other part how you feel.

L *(sing-song, warning voice)*: Well, when you talk about getting out of school, you gotta remember, what exactly are you gonna do in the future? You don't exactly know what you're gonna do if you get out. A lot of people will be disappointed in you. Everybody says you're not wasting your time here, and maybe you're not. *(Sounding unconvinced, automatic.)* You have to think about what you really want to do and what you need a degree for. Even though it may seem pointless at times, maybe it's one of those things you have to do.

Jerry's tone of voice and his words here reflect what he believed was his parents' point of view. He had not yet acknowledged or perhaps even recognized that his investment in this side went beyond a mechanical repetition of "shoulds." I realized that his beliefs about the dangers of leaving school were important, but I did not yet see an opening to develop this side's agruments. I decided to return to the side that wanted to leave school.

T: Switch. *(Client switches.)* Tell that part how you react to that.

L *(more assured)*: Well, I think the only way you're going to find out about things is if you look into them yourself. Maybe I'm trying to find out if college is worth it this way.

T: Say, "I'm tired of being here because that's what other people are telling me to do."

L *(weary):* Yeah, I'm tired of being here because other people say and I don't know for myself. To me, the right thing to do would be doing something that's important.

T *(attending to the desire for independence and looking for the fear accompanying the desire):* Say, "I want the chance to make my own mistakes."

L *(sad):* Yeah, I want the chance to make my own mistakes. . . .

T *(softly):* And I feel. . . .

L *(beginning to cry):* I feel that I should do what I want to do and not be held back by what everybody thinks I should do, and I should not be held back by you, I think, the scared part of me. You keep me from doing what I want to do, because I'll be out on my own, and what I do will be up to me, and I'll have to support myself. You make me think the safer place to be is here, 'cause it'll be hard out there.

For the first time, Jerry clearly identified his fears. The affect was an essential aspect of the beliefs behind his wanting to stay in school, and was a key to uncovering those beliefs. I seized the opening he gave me.

T: You're scared, and that makes me feel. . . .

L: You're scared, and that makes me feel that it's more comfortable to stay in school, but I don't really know—even if you make me scared, I feel that I should find out. I think the main problem with your and my attitude with trying to handle school is that you're rushing it, while at the same time, I don't like it.

Jerry decided himself to switch chairs at this point, perhaps to experience the fear and to see where it would lead.

S: Well, if you say I'm the scared part of you. [To therapist: I don't know if I'm exactly on this side yet.] I guess the only way my side could be effective would be to pound in the facts that in this world, that's what you've got to do. [To therapist: I don't know if I can get any farther.]

Jerry was on the verge of experiencing his fear but retreated into his familiar authority position. I decided to help him to experience his fear by having him state it.

T: Try this—say to that side, "O.K., I am scared."

S: Yeah, I guess I am scared, because what if you get out, you're gonna be at home, and your folks won't be especially pleased. You'll have a low-payin' job, and it'll be day-to-day living. Why can't you figure out what you want to do while you're in school?

Jerry's beliefs about his fate once he left school may well have been pessimistically distorted. But there would be time later to work on the reality of his fear; I decided for now to continue to encourage his recognition of the affect and the reasons behind it.

> T: I'm scared because I don't know what's going to happen.
> S *(energetically):* I'm scared, yeah, because—well, you'll probably end up back in school again, and there goes some time wasted, and people are gonna look down on you. *(Switches.)*
> L: For some reason, I want to stay on this side. *(Getting sad.)* I really don't think I'm going to find the reason for staying in school. *(Beginning to cry.)* It's been almost a year now that I've been thinkin' about this, and all through this time I've been feeling of little importance.
> T: I gave you a year, and I feel. . . .
> L *(louder):* Yeah, I tried a year, and I feel that it's important to find out what you want to do. Together, in this place, we're not really finding out what we want to do. You're just keepin' me in here by makin' me scared but at the same time, you're not looking to figure out what we're going to do while we're in here. I think I'm looking harder than you are. I've gotta be myself, even if I foul things up. I feel I've gotta do this. *(Softly pounding chair with his fist.)*

Jerry was reacting to the change in the side that wanted to stay in school. When that side had merely repeated introjected norms, the side wanting to leave school had become ritualized as well. Now that he recognized his fear, he could also develop his desire for independence. Jerry was angry at being held back by his fear. It was always difficult for him to express anger, so I decided to encourage it here in an action rather than in words.

> T: You're hitting the chair. Do that harder, and tell that side how you feel.
> L *(hitting chair, speaking loudly):* You think about time a lot, and I'm sort of pissed off at you, 'cause I already felt this way last year, and now we've gone through a whole 'nother year, and we still haven't found a purpose. If I'd left school then, who knows what would have happened? Maybe I'd be back in school already! At least we would know—I would know—it wouldn't be other people telling me, but I would know myself.

I was pleased that Jerry was able to express his anger, especially since it was followed by the beginning of a possible resolution: to leave school as an experiment, with the possibility of returning later. I was still concerned about his coming to this resolution without sufficient understanding of his fears, so I turned again to the dangers in leaving school.

T: I need you to switch. *(Switches.)* What you said makes me feel. . . .

S: That makes me feel. . . . *(Pauses.)* I don't know if I can say anything here.

T: Just sit there for a minute—it's really important.

S: OK. *(Pause.)* O.K. I don't know if I'll try and persuade that side. . . .

T: Just say how you feel.

S: O.K. *(Subdued.)* I'm scared because I would like to persuade you. I'm scared of being left behind. If I get out of school, people will be mad at me for takin' time out for myself, and I'll be in the same classification as a bum. But I gotta admit that I really don't think I'm gonna get anywhere if I just accept things as they are. You're gonna keep me from trying to change my attitude to liking school.

T: You're interfering with me, too.

S: Yeah, I'd like to try something. I'd like to figure things out, not waste time, learn what you want to do here, but there are two sides of me —us, or whatever, and the attitude is not going to change from one to the other, just like that.

T *(attempting to strengthen the feelings and beliefs that had been discovered):* I want you to know that I exist, too.

S: Yeah, I'm here, and this is the part of me that's concerned about other people's feelings. I'd like to make other people feel I'm being productive, and you say, "Who cares what people say?" I'm disappointed—I'd like to see our attitude become one attitude and really like school, but you won't seem to let me. It's time you satisfied yourself, but I'm disappointed because I don't think I've done enough here.

T: I'm disappointed in you because you won't let me do what I need to do.

S: Yeah, I'm disappointed.

We ended the experiment here. Though no clear resolution had emerged, it was clear that we had made progress in clarifying and developing the meaning of his conflict. The previous stalemate between inflexible positions was broken, with the emergence of new affect and its associated beliefs. His wish to stay in school had been expressed previously only as a ritualized rendition of what he believed were his parents' arguments. During the experiment he uncovered an internalized network of beliefs about the disasters that would befall him if he struck out on his own. He feared that he would fall on his face, and thereby hurt not only himself, but also the people he loved. At the same time, his desire for independence and anger at being held back were also developed more fully. Since he was no longer frozen in a stalemate, the possibility emerged of an integration of both sides into "what *we* want."

My work with Jerry was hardly finished at the end of this exercise. He came into therapy believing that he needed either to stay in school with unwavering motivation, or to leave school and strike out on his own with perfect confidence. At this point in therapy, he had decided to leave school but was still hopeful of destroying any doubts about that course of action. We needed to work on whether that was possible. The work was made easier by our having discovered his fearful side. First, we examined the distortions that emerged in his beliefs about leaving school. For example, we worked on whether he would really be "in the same classification as a bum." He began to see that if he did not like working and decided to return to school, his decision to leave school still would not be a mistake. Further, and much to his surprise, when he told his parents of his decision, they were understanding even though they were disappointed. His intense fear turned out to be based on distorted ideas of how destructive the decision would be, yet he still was realistically apprehensive about the uncertainty of his future when he left school. He even began to value his cautious, careful side. Close to the end of therapy, he said, "I guess the most important thing about this decision is that I make a decision and carry it out even though I'm scared."

The process of the empty-chair technique may be interpreted cognitively. The artificial separation of each side set the stage for an uncovering of a complex network of beliefs and assumptions. Jerry recognized his dichotomous pattern of believing he had to choose one side and eliminate the other. His experience told him that he needed to work toward a complex integration rather than a simplistic choice. The empty-chair technique may appear on the surface to promote dichotomous thinking by separating sides so concretely, but it can actually serve as a demonstration of the untenability of dichotomous thinking. The technique can help clients accept their varying and conflicting experiences.

The importance of affect in the empty-chair procedure may also be interpreted cognitively, since affect is an inseparable part of cognition (Arnkoff, 1980). The immediacy of the empty-chair experiment facilitates the intensification of affect. I repeatedly encouraged Jerry to express his emotions, and as he voiced and acted out feelings, the beliefs and assumptions tied to his affect emerged as well. Using affect as a route to beliefs would not be the appropriate direction with all clients, but it was useful with this client since he was at an intellectual stalemate.

FLEXIBILITY AS THERAPY UNFOLDS

One aspect of being flexible is to integrate various styles of therapy. Another aspect of flexibility requires the therapist to remain open to new information. Just as the goal for the client is to abandon maladaptive patterns, so the goal for the therapist must be to struggle against rigidity. This struggle may take many forms. For example, I have sometimes found that I was impeding therapy because I had too great a stake in the client changing in a certain fashion. Similarly, it is important for therapists to allow new information about the client to persuade them to change course, and to be aware of their own maladaptive cognitive patterns as they may affect therapy.

The goal of appropriate flexibility, like all meaningful goals, cannot be attained to perfection. Just like the client, the therapist is fallible in understanding the "real" world. Nevertheless, flexibility rather than perfection is worth striving for.

I will offer two cases from my experience as examples in which I managed to realize that a shift in direction was necessary and therapeutic. In the first case, I saw with little difficulty the value in shifting gears, and was amply rewarded for my foresight. In the second case, I probably could have seen the difficulty early on but only changed my approach when it became painfully obvious that the therapy was not producing results. In this case, I waited for the whole iceberg to appear when the tip of it could have alerted me.

Both illustrations I will give deal with my misperception, or incomplete perception, of what the client needed to gain from therapy. In the first case, I believed that therapy was proceeding very well, but the client helped me to broaden my concept of the work we needed to do together. Leslie was a young woman who felt aimless and wished to use therapy for self-discovery and self-acceptance. She had left college after two years because she "wasn't motivated enough to do as well as she could." She had been working as a secretary for six months in a job that bored her. Her parents were both very successful in their careers and were pressuring her to go back to school; she herself was not certain what she wanted to do. Leslie was bright and motivated, and we were both excited by the progress we were making in our fast-moving sessions.

When she came for her sixth session, Leslie looked tentative and pale. As usual, I began by asking her what she wanted to work on. She said she was tired today. As we worked, she developed the theme that she was tired of the demands of others to which she was easy prey. She spoke of her boyfriend, friends, and parents as demanding a great deal from her.

My role in this theme began to dawn on me. The following is an abbreviated version of our exchange:

> THERAPIST: You've listed a lot of people who make demands on you. Am I one of those?
>
> LESLIE *(quickly):* Oh, no, no, no. You're different from the others—you're really interested in me, and besides, you're not demanding.
>
> THERAPIST [This was just what I wanted to hear, but I felt dishonest.]: Oh, really? But I do make demands, like videotaping you, asking you to try this and that, asking you what you want to work on. . . .
>
> LESLIE *(pause; with surprise):* Yes, maybe so. Well, maybe a little. I mean, it's different, but. . . .
>
> THERAPIST: But I do make demands.
>
> LESLIE *(laughing, relieved):* Yes, I guess so.
>
> THERAPIST: Do you want a rest?
>
> LESLIE *(laughing):* Yes. I *need* a rest.
>
> THERAPIST: OK, we can go at your pace. I guess I'm not promising to stop asking you to do things. But we can always talk about my demands.
>
> LESLIE *(sigh):* No one else has ever been honest with me about their demands.

We spent most of the balance of the session chatting about her hobby of photography. Ordinarily I try to spend little time in therapy chatting. But here it became clear that it would be therapeutic for both of us to violate my own implicit rule against "wasting time." For Leslie, it was important to feel that she merited my attention even when she was not earnestly striving toward some goal. Paradoxically, to accept not working was, in fact, work for her. The session was therapeutic for me in helping me to abandon a rigid notion of what constitutes progress in therapy.

Later, we continued the theme of demand by examining how she encouraged other people to demand a lot from her and how she believed that she should be capable of handling everything. When we worked on termination, Leslie pointed to the session I have just described as pivotal. She recalled that I tried to be honest about my demands and encouraged her candid feedback. She saw this session as helping her to gain distance from her own self-expectations.

With Leslie, the shift in my conception of progress was fairly smooth. But such was hardly the case with Bill, a student I saw in a university counseling center. In this case, being flexible meant changing my approach as a last resort, when I could no longer deny that what I planned for the client was not working.

Bill was a junior in college who had never been on a date. His stated goals for therapy were to start dating and to be more relaxed about women. Bill was not verbally sophisticated, which may have helped convince me that his situation was not complex. I could easily detect distorted cognitions regarding his worth and how women were likely to react to him. He was also clearly deficient in dating skills and practice. Since the case seemed straightforward, I readily decided on a plan that coupled cognitive therapy techniques with behavioral heterosocial skills training.

As therapy proceeded, Bill always had a semireasonable excuse for only semicompleting his assignments. He was certain he was not trying to avoid doing them; it just didn't work out somehow. For example, he always went to at least one fraternity party every weekend. In an early session, we decided together that during the coming weekend, he would initiate a conversation with a woman at a party and sustain it for at least ten minutes. Since he had managed to do this on occasion in the past, Bill was certain that he would have no trouble completing the assignment successfully. Yet, when he came the next week, he said that he had not gone to any parties on the weekend because he had too much studying to do. (Ordinarily, even final exams did not deter him from going to parties.) We agreed on the same assignment for the following week, and this time he went to a party, but he did not see any unattached women he could talk to. He had talked to a woman in one of his classes for five minutes about an assignment, and that went "O.K."

When I tried to elicit Bill's beliefs about women or about his self-worth, he had very little to say. He answered most questions in as few words as possible. When I made an observation, he routinely said only that I may be right. If I chose to be silent, he would break the silence by asking what he should do next. Most of the time he just looked at me, waiting for my next move. He did consistently come to sessions, in spite of complaining that he was getting very little from them.

I was angry with Bill. I alternated between seeing him as a poor candidate for therapy, and myself as a poor candidate for therapist. Usually I can bring myself to confront a resistant client, but I was cautious with Bill. I knew he would turn the tables back on me. I predicted that he would say that I should just tell him what to do and he'd do it. I had the feeling that I'd end up believing that I was still doing something wrong.

Many clients would simply stop coming to therapy at this point. If Bill had stopped coming, I doubt if I would have ever understood what happened. But he kept coming, out of desperation. He was afraid he would graduate from college without ever having a date. I slowly began to see how I was misperceiving him. He gave me little to go on at the beginning, so my therapeutic plan was largely forged out of ignorance. Now his behavior with me gave me more knowledge of him. The contract that we had implicitly agreed on was one in which I would do most of the work, and he would passively reject or undermine my efforts. We had never established the collaboration that is a hallmark of cognitive therapy (Beck *et al.*, 1979). Because I had no choice—he was still there, staring at me expectantly—I changed my tactics. We needed to deal with his passivity before any other work could be done.

Our unproductive sessions were not many in number; they just seemed like an eternity to me. At the beginning of the fifth session, I told Bill that I was frustrated with my having to carry the sessions. He seemed surprised, and he let me know that he thought it was my job to direct the work. (In fact, I had certainly given him that impression by falling into the pattern of running the previous sessions!) But he did agree that whatever we were doing was not working.

I went on to tell him how I felt in the sessions. In reaction to his passivity, I felt inadequate and uncomfortable. I wondered if other people, especially women, reacted similarly to him. This time he seemed even more surprised. It had never occurred to him that anyone would feel inadequate because of his passivity. *He* was the one who felt inadequate in relationships with women. He assumed that women were perfectly self-confident and only wrote him off because he was dull. I had worked on this idea with Bill in previous sessions to no avail. Suddenly, he was discovering the nature of *his* impact on women.

When we had explored the possibility that the women he met also lacked confidence, I continued to describe for Bill how I reacted to his passivity. Just as I was frustrated with him, I felt his frustration at me. While he seemed to be giving up control to me, he was actually retaining it by being passive. By not working with me as an active participant in therapy, he was ensuring that he need not change his familiar habits.

Again, he was surprised. But he listened and worked on what I was saying. He could see that sometimes he controlled his parents when they asked him to change an annoying habit by ignoring their request or by finding a reason why change was out of his control. He could also see that he might be controlling our relationship by refusing to be drawn into dialogue. But when I suggested that he might be angry with the people he controlled passively, he denied it. He was angry only with himself. I said that anger with oneself was sometimes a safe cover for anger at other people.

To my surprise, he began the next session by telling me that he had thought about anger and realized that he was angry at a lot of people. He included me in his list: He had been angry with me in a previous session for asking him to do something he had not wanted to do. However, he was no longer angry at me about that, nor about anything else. We spent a long time talking about the incident in which he had been angry at me. I reasoned that talking about even past anger directly was a sign of progress. I did my best not to be defensive in order to give him evidence against his unspoken fears of retaliation or loss if he expressed anger. We still wavered in our ability to break the habits we had developed with each other. But since we had a common experience of futility to draw on, we were both aware of our traps. We continued to discuss the issue of passivity and control in later sessions. We explored how his ''I can't'' usually meant ''I won't.'' In turn, I tried to control my own tendency to become more active in response to his passivity and then feel angry when he remained inactive. I looked at him more as a complex person about whom I was learning, and less as a straightforward ''case.''

We made only moderate progress toward Bill's goal of dating frequently. He had not yet gone on a date when we terminated therapy at the end of the semester, but he had initiated several extended conversations at parties. He said it was helpful when he did talk to women to remember that they, as well as he, could be anxious. When he realized he was chastising himself, he had started to ask himself at whom he might be angry. If he realized that he was angry at someone else, his self-blame usually subsided. He saw his growing self-acceptance as a prelude to being comfortable with women.

Bill and I made the progress that we did only because he stayed through the early, rocky part of therapy. He continued to come, not because of my expertise, but because he was too desperate (and too passive!) to break appointments. I do not know how many other clients

I have lost because I assumed too easily that I understood, and because I embarked on a course that did not match the client's needs. When a client is as passive as Bill was, an active therapist is in danger of leaving the client behind. In retrospect, I was uncomfortable from the beginning when I tried to envision my work with Bill as a collaboration. Perhaps a therapist should be cautious if a therapeutic plan comes too easily. It may be that only the therapist has been involved in drawing up the contract.

I certainly cannot say that I have mastered this problem. But whenever I find myself being very certain of how to proceed at the outset of therapy, I remember Bill. A new picture is always emerging of the client if only the therapist looks for it. It is clear that hanging on to a treatment plan as if it is chiseled in rock is maladaptive for the therapist.

Flexibility in therapy involves tailoring interventions to the therapist's current understanding of the client. To be therapeutic, some aspect of what the therapist and client do must be different from what the client does with other people. But what that difference is varies from client to client, and even from session to session with the same client. Therapy is a fast-moving process of subtle exploration and persuasion. It requires flexibility by the therapist, first in choosing the means, and then in being willing to change them when new evidence becomes available.

ACKNOWLEDGMENT

The author is grateful to Guy Pilato, Annette Ranck, and Bill Ray for helpful discussion of some of the issues raised in this chapter.

REFERENCES

Arnkoff, D. B. Psychotherapy from the perspective of cognitive theory. In M. J. Mahoney (Ed.). *Psychotherapy process: Current issues and future directions.* New York: Plenum, 1980.

Beck, A. T., Rush, A. J., Shaw, B. F., & Emery, G. *Cognitive therapy of depression.* New York: Guilford Press, 1979.

Fagan, J., & Shepherd, I. L. (Eds.). *Gestalt therapy now: Theory, techniques, applications.* New York: Harper & Row, 1970.

Garfield, S. L., & Kurtz, R. Clinical psychologists in the 1970's. *American Psychologist*, 1976, *31*, 1–9.

Greenberg, L. Resolving splits: The two-chair technique. *Psychotherapy: Theory, Research and Practice*, 1979, *16*, 310–318.

Perls, F. S. *Gestalt therapy verbatim*. Lafayette, Calif.: Real People Press, 1969.

Perls, F. S. *The Gestalt approach and eye witness to therapy*. New York: Bantam, 1973.

Polster, E., & Polster, M. *Gestalt therapy integrated: Contours of theory and practice*. New York: Random House, 1973.

DREAMS AND IMAGES IN COGNITIVE THERAPY

Arthur Freeman

> She further confounded me by reporting a dream one day. As a client-centered therapist I'd had little experience with dreams. . . . When my patient told me her dream I felt handcuffed; my limited armamentarium gave me no way to deal with it meaningfully, apart from a comment on the mood or feeling of the dream. I felt as if something valuable had been brought into the room and just shoved aside into a corner—or, more properly, that it lay between us untouched, thus depriving her of its potential value.
>
> ROSALEA SHONBAR (1968)

INTRODUCTION

The early pioneers in the development of psychotherapy, Freud, Adler, Jung and others, despite major disagreements on the foci of treatment, all agreed on the importance of the dream as an important, if not essential, psychotherapeutic tool.

For Freud, dreams were the royal road that led to the unconscious and were an essential part of the psychoanalytic treatment. For Jung, the dream symbol was important, as it reflected not only the personal but also the collective unconscious of the individual. For Adler, however, the individual's dream life corresponded directly and entirely to the dreamer's world picture. There is, however, little argument over the affective implications of dreams. The disagreements come from considerations of the source of dreams. Adler (1927) states: "The purpose of dreams must be in the feelings they arouse. The dream is only the means, the instrument to stir up feelings" (p. 127). The dream, for

Arthur Freeman. Center for Cognitive Therapy, University of Pennsylvania, Philadelphia, Pennsylvania.

Adler, then, becomes the equivalent of an automatic thought, which seems to arouse particular emotions, based on the person's belief system.

The cognitive–behavioral (C-B) therapist, however, is often at the disadvantage described by Shonbar, in that he or she is generally not oriented or trained to use the dream as grist for the therapeutic mill. The dream has not been a central part of cognitive-behavior therapy, up to the present point, for a number of reasons. A cognitive therapist whose early training was behavioral might have had little or no training in the use of dreams in the therapeutic encounter and in fact may have learned that since dreams have no direct behavioral component, they ought to be avoided. Cognitive-behavior therapists with psychoanalytic training may refrain from using dreams as a way of further distancing themselves from their early psychodynamic influences. Some cognitive therapists avoid using dreams in therapy as a result of their belief that dream work is of no value (Ellis & Harper, 1975). Regardless of the underlying reason, the avoidance of dream work as part of therapy causes the loss of extremely valuable cognitive and affective data regarding the patient. Mahoney (1974) views the dream as a fruitful area for exploration in cognitive therapy.

Beck (1971) outlined a cognitive model of dreams. He regarded dreams as ''a kind of biopsy of the patient's psychological process.'' The patient's dreams are idiosyncratic and dramatize his or her view of the self, the world, and the future. It follows that the dream would also embody the patient's cognitive distortions. The dream would not then necessarily be the royal road to the unconscious, but rather the more commonly traveled route toward the individual's conscious personal interpretations.

MANIFEST AND LATENT CONTENT

Since the major source of information on the utilization of dream work as part of the therapeutic process comes from the psychoanalytic schools, it is important for the cognitive therapist to understand some of the frequently used psychodynamic language in order to reconceptualize it in cognitive terms. A major issue is the use of manifest and latent content of dreams. Freud differentiated between the two types of dream content as follows: The manifest content is the way the dream appears to the dreamer, while the latent content consists of the associated thoughts, attitudes, and memories. The latent content, according to dynamic theory, contains the repressed or hidden meaning that is available only on interpretation. From the Freudian point of view, the manifest content can be discarded.

It is necessary to view dreams, though, as reflecting the cognitions and affective responses of waking experience. Beck (1967) points out that concentrating on the manifest content of dreams is far more satisfactory than attempting to infer underlying processes. Since the manifest content is readily available to the dreamer and can be reported to the therapist, it is available for immediate use in the therapy session. Utilizing material that is readily available, the patient can obtain a sense of mastery and self-knowledge without depending on the therapist to somehow magically interpret the symbolism of the dream. Beck states: "If the patient has a dream in which he perceives other people as frustrating him, it would be more economical to simply consider this conception of people as being frustrating rather than to read into the dream an underlying 'masochistic wish' " (p. 180). Further, Beck (1967) found that "dream themes are relevant to observable patterns of behavior" (p. 181), and that "dreams were analogous to the kind of suffering the depressed patient experienced in his waking life" (p. 208). These findings are in full accord with Adler's contention that the dream themes are directly relevant to the patient's waking behavioral experience.

Dreams differ from the waking cognitions by the relative absence of external input. They are the product of the dreamer's internal world, but maintain an essential continuity with the waking thought processes. In studying typical dreams of psychiatric patients, Ward, Beck, and Roscoe (1961) and Beck and Ward (1961) found dream themes characteristic of the particular disorder manifest in the waking experience.

Beck (1967) states: "In the course of the psychotherapy of patients with neurotic–depressive reactions, it was noted that there was a high incidence of dreams with unpleasant content" (p. 170). As treatment progresses, and the individual is better able to meet and overcome the day-to-day problems of life, the dream content will change to reflect the waking changes.

As patients who previously may have had dreams of helplessness or failure progress in treatment, their dreams begin to reflect their mastery. This process can be seen quite clearly in the case of a 27-year-old graduate student who had been procrastinating over completion of his dissertation for over a year. The material to be written was laid out on his desk. He had conducted the research and analyzed the results but was unable to complete the appropriate charts, tables, and interpretive prose, perhaps the easiest part of the entire project. His waking cognitions concerned questions of his ability to successfully complete the dissertation and earn the doctorate, the relative value of the dissertation to the literature of the field, flaws in the design, etc. His underlying assumption was one of personal worthlessness. He believed that any product of his must be tainted and similarly worthless. As the days grew to weeks, the weeks to months, the individual had numerous anxiety dreams that would cause him to wake several times during the night, feeling a sense of dread. The thought that accompanied the dream, though the exact content of each dream was not always clear, was "I've got to get going, the material is sitting there waiting to be worked on." The most common dream theme was of work uncompleted. Several dreams were sexual in nature, but the sexual relationship was never consummated. The cognition associated with the dream was "I can't finish anything." As the student actively challenged the various dysfunctional cognitions and began working on the dissertation in small bits, the frequency of the anxiety dreams diminished. As he experienced a growing sense of mastery, by understanding that the dissertation needed only to be appropriate and acceptable, the amount of work produced increased, until the individual, toward the completion of the dissertation, experienced no more anxiety dreams. On follow-up at six-month intervals over the next three years, the individual reported that anxiety dreams were experienced only in those situations where he had procrastinated and not completed required work, and that the anxiety dream became a signal for him to increase his efforts. In a three-year follow-up, the individual reported that when he was awakened by a fearful dream in the middle of the night, rather than lying awake and ruminating, he would resolve to take concrete and positive action in the morning to resolve whatever issue existed as a source of anxiety. The anxiety dream in this case became an aversive stimulus to complete work, and alerted the individual to his own dysfunctional cognitions.

While the cognitive view of dreams is that the dream material is idiosyncratic to the dreamer, certain dream themes are fairly common.

Adler (1927), a major proponent of the use of dreams, and the earliest
of the cognitive therapists, outlines several common dream themes that
he viewed as extensions of the individual's waking cognitions, behavior, and lifestyle. Consequently, dreams of falling might represent a
loss of status or prestige, while dreams of flying might represent activity, ambition, or a sense of looking forward. Dreams about dead people
might reflect the fact that the dreamer has not yet "buried" the person
and is still under his or her influence. For a fuller description of the
various and more common dream themes, the reader is referred to Adler (1927). A caveat should be noted: While common dream themes
exist, they should be viewed only as *assumptions* of meaning and
should be validated with the dreamer. If we, as cognitive therapists,
begin to assign meaning on a point-by-point basis to various dream
symbols, then we fall into the trap of losing the richness of the individual's idiosyncratic world view.

Since the dream is not fettered by the constraints of the waking
state, the dreamer is freer to express ideas that may in fact presage activities. The dream may then have a predictive value. The dream, while
not being a prophetic occurrence, allows a tapping of a less restrained
cognitive stream. The use of this less restrained cognitive stream can
also be a value to the therapist. Green (1971) reported using his own
dream to help him in understanding a patient's present difficulty in
therapy. By tapping into the dream images, the resultant affect and the
understanding he derived from the sleeping cognitions, the therapist
could utilize another part of his experience in assisting the therapeutic
collaboration.

COGNITIVE DREAM WORK

Based on the work of Beck and Adler, the following guidelines for
cognitive dream interpretation are offered:

1. The dream needs to be understood in thematic rather than symbolic terms. *Comment:* The particular cognitive transformations in the
dream are viewed not as representations of something else, but within
the context of the dream theme. The search for symbols may, in fact,
distract from the dream work. As the therapist might continue to
search for the "true meaning" expressed in the dream symbols, he or
she may begin to stray from a basic understanding of the individual.

Even Freud would probably have agreed that at times a cigar *might* be a cigar and nothing more.

2. The thematic content of the dream is idiosyncratic to the dreamer and must be viewed within the context of the dreamer's life. *Comment:* In maintaining the cognitive continuum from waking to sleep, we are able to view the dream as part of the overall life experience. Dreams are not isolated phenomena and need to be connected to the patient's current concerns. No "universal symbols."

3. The specific language and imagery are important to the meaning. *Comment:* The words, voice tone, images, and quality of language very much influence the affect being expressed. By using the dreamer's words and symbols, we can better understand his or her dream intent. For example, a dream image of being alone in a large stadium conveys a very different sense from being alone in a small room.

4. The affective responses to the dreams can be seen as similar to the dreamer's affective responses in waking situations. *Comment:* Happiness, anxiety, depression, or any of the host of emotional responses would be the same in dreaming or waking situations.

A patient reported a dream of being in court. His lawyer informed him that the judge trying his case was a Judge Klause. He could clearly see the name Klause spelled K L A U S E on the judge's bench. He knew without being told that Judge Klause was a harsh and severe critic. The emotional response both within the dream and upon awakening was a sense of fear and foreboding about imminent punishment, a typical affective reaction to authority figures for the patient.

5. The particular length of the dream is of lesser import than the content. *Comment:* Since we dream in images and pictures, a dream image or fragment may be exceptionally brief but yet have tremendous emotional impact. For example, a fragment or image where the dreamer sees her child lying dead on the street in front of a car can produce a sense of terror that persists well into the following day.

6. The dream is a product of, and the responsibility, of the dreamer. *Comment:* The particular material that the dreamer chooses to include in the dream, while possibly being a product of the previous day's experience, still becomes a function of, and idiosyncratic to the dreamer. For example, a patient reported a dream of his boss being cruel to him. The affective experience was first fear, and then anger that the boss had intruded on his sleep. As the patient spoke about the

boss, he became angry that even his time at home was not safe. The therapist reminded the patient that the *boss* did not intrude on his dream or his leisure time. Instead, it was the patient who carried a mental representation of the boss with him wherever he went. While there may have been reality issues related to the boss, his intrusion on the dream needed to be identified clearly as a product of the dreamer.

7. Dream material is amenable to the same cognitive restructuring as are any automatic thoughts. *Comment:* Dreams can be reworked to arrange affect shifts, alternative outcomes, or new solutions. By utilizing the Dysfunctional Thought Record (Beck, Rush, Shaw, & Emery, 1979) dreams can be restructured with appropriate disputation and rational challenges to the depressogenic and dysfunctional dream material. The dream can be written down as the incident, with an assessment of the nature and degree of the emotional response, followed by the dysfunctional thinking expressed in the dream, and degree of belief in the dysfunctional dream material. The patient can then learn to dispute the dysfunctional themes embodied in the dream, and to change his or her affective response to the dream as a result.

8. Dreams can be used when the patient appears "stuck" in therapy. *Comment:* The dream can assist the patient in building further skills to deal rationally with dysfunctional thinking. When the particular direction or momentum of therapy seems lost, the dream material can be a valuable adjunctive tool, particularly in outlining new areas for exploration. Patients often readily accept the use of dreams because they are so personal and such a familiar part of their experiences.

9. Dreams cannot become the sole focus of the session and need to be dealt with as part of the agenda setting. *Comment:* An active dreamer may wish to use the entire therapy hour to discuss several dreams. The therapist needs to be judicious in using dreams in the session, so that the exclusion of other important material does not occur.

Using the above-mentioned guidelines, the following cases demonstrate the cognitive use of dreams.

CASE 1

A 31-year-old psychologist (who was analytically oriented) reported the following dream: "I was sitting on the couch when out from the opposite wall came this huge snake. It struck at me with incredible speed, not allowing me to move away. It sank its fangs into my arm. All I could

do was look at it and comment on the pain and the fact that it was biting
me. I woke up feeling anxious and frightened. It was a scary dream.''

The basic cognitive elements involved were her helplessness and
inability to react, her passiveness in response to being attacked, and her
feelings of anxiety when placed in a position that required direct action. These cognitions paralleled her dysfunctional cognitions in the
waking state. She was extremely effective on the job but often felt anxious when called upon to be assertive.

The therapist tried to restructure the experience by asking the patient what she might have done differently in the dream. Her initial
response was that she could do very little, that she was at the mercy of
her dream content (cognitions). The therapist emphasized that since
she was the sole producer, director, stage manager, and casting director
(she recruited the snake), she could recast or restructure the scene as she
wished.

At first, she restructured the dream tentatively, by visualizing
herself trying to hold something over the snake hole in the wall (a
''finger-in-the-dike'' response). With further encouragement and
some modeling on the therapist's part, she restructured the scene so
that she immediately severed the snake's head. (When she protested
that she did not have a knife, it was pointed out that the knife could
come from the same source as the snake, her imagination.) As she
restructured the dream scene to one of greater control, and assertion,
there was a rapid affect shift from anxiety to relief.

Comment: Leurner (1969) has the patient revisualize the dream
but for the primary purpose of altering the negative elements. The
snake could become a Sesame Street character, or the patient could offer the snake a treat or erect a transparent shield. In restructuring the
dream, a positive outcome can always be effected.

CASE 2

A 32-year-old male professor of history had the following dreams: "I
was in a house—it seemed to be a house on a farm. My two kids were
with me. There were Nazi soldiers searching for us and I knew we
couldn't get away. I was upstairs with the kids when they came into the
house. I felt so terribly helpless—I had no weapons—no way of protecting us. They would get us and I couldn't do a damn thing about it! They
would kill my kids, and I woke up feeling anxious and scared. There was
a real knot in my stomach. I looked at the clock and it was 1:30 A.M. I

didn't know if I could get back to sleep. I did fall back to sleep and had
another dream. I was in a school building, one of the college buildings, I
think. It was pretty empty. There were, I knew, intruders in the building. I didn't know who they were or why they were there. I had a gun, a
pistol, but I knew it was loaded with blanks. A group of them suddenly
appeared and I told them to put their hands up. They saw the gun and
did. Then one of them made a break for it and I fired. When they didn't
hear a ricochet, they all scattered, knowing I only had blanks. But I had
the last laugh because I suddenly had bullets and quickly loaded the
pistol. I hid in a room that looked to be a cross between a biology lab and
a home economics lab. In there I saw a woman who was a student of
mine, one whom I think is rather attractive. I told her to keep quiet, that
I had a gun and could protect us. I really felt good and powerful. I then
kissed her and that really felt good. I remember feeling that I was not
only going to beat the 'bad guys,' but I had this woman, too. I woke up
right before the alarm, about 7:00 A.M., and really felt good. I felt 'up'
all day."

Comment: The helplessness of the first dream was carried through
to the point of waking in a distressed state. The sense of not having
power to protect one's children was clearly quite depressing. The second dream is significant not only because of the success experiences of
seduction and self-defense but also because the area of success was the
school. The sequence from helplessness to competency seems to say, "I
can be successful. Failure won't keep me down." The second dream
challenged the dysfunctional thoughts in the first. The sequence of the
dreams (like the sequence of Rorschach responses) is important. The
"up" feeling of success followed him through the day, even though it
had its roots in imagination.

CASE 3

A 24-year-old female graduate student reported the following dream:
"I woke up early one morning. I was at my parent's home. I went
downstairs and saw my boyfriend's car parked in *my* garage. I felt an-
noyed because he didn't tell me."

The affect associated with the dream was sadness and helplessness.
The associated information elicited involved an ongoing conflict over
her sexual relationship with her boyfriend. She felt that he would often
be unaware of her needs or insensitive to her feelings. His demands
took precedence, which she allowed, and she experienced anger and
depression as a result.

In this brief dream fragment, the basic themes are the patient's loss of control and her subsequent anger. In restructuring the dream during the therapy session, the patient attempted a number of strategies in dealing with the unwanted car. She first tried locking the garage doors, thus forcing the boyfriend to park out in the cold. This strategy set up a situation where he had to ask to be allowed to park in the garage. Further strategies included demanding that she be informed of his desire to park, discussing his parking as part of a mutual decision and even having him park on her demand. As she discussed the various strategies that she might have used in the dream, there was a rather rapid affect shift, resulting from the dream restructuring. She experienced a sense of pleasure and satisfaction that helped her to resolve that she would not allow herself to be used any longer. Utilizing the restructured images in her dream, she was able to begin asserting herself in the relationship with her boyfriend.

THE USE OF IMAGERY

Beck, Laude, and Bohnert (1974) observed that with the onset or exacerbation of anxiety, many patients have thoughts or visual fantasies revolving around the theme of danger. The anxiety, they conclude, was a direct result of the visualization of the danger-laden image. Their observations have direct implications for the treatment of anxiety.

The use of imagery, like the use of dreams, can add immeasurably to the therapy. Since few patients can describe symptoms without describing accompanying images, the image is a ready, accessible entry point for cognitive intervention. Images may be visual, auditory, gustatory, or olfactory. Images may utilize an economy of words, but they provide a directness of meaning and a vivid affective experience for the patient. The affect-laden image can often penetrate the depression and isolation of the lonely patient. The image-maker does not always have to be the patient, since the therapist can suggest images and imaging techniques to effectively break through a number of symptom clusters. Images can be made evocative through the inclusion of multisensory elements. For example, a young psychiatrist harrassed his wife by interpreting nearly all her actions at home. A colleague confronted him, saying, "It's important not to get so used to tearing away peoples' masks that you no longer hear the rip." The use of the auditory and visual image, combined with the kinesthetic "rip," is exceedingly powerful.

The therapist does not have to be the image-maker, but can call upon the patient to produce the images. The imaging can become part of the homework assignment arrived at between the patient and the therapist. The patient can be asked to develop a number of images that help focus on the particular symptoms currently being addressed in treatment.

CASE 4

A patient who voiced a constant concern about public speaking was asked to develop at least six images where she would speak in front of a group in a number of different capacities, that is, teacher, lawyer, and actress. The homework assignment was quite difficult for her because she was to picture herself performing effectively in front of a group. As she was able to feel more at ease with the image, she was then able to lessen her public-speaking anxiety and did eventually speak in front of a group with a minimal amount of comfort. (It should be noted that the difficulty in imaging was then recorded on Dysfunctional Thought Records and dealt with as part of the homework.)

CASE 5

Literature can be used by the therapist as a source of imaging, since many writers are particularly skilled in creating highly evocative images. The case of a young married woman who sought treatment for perceived sexual dysfunction illustrates the use of literature to stimulate imaging. The woman reported that she needed artificial lubricants in order to engage in intercourse, a requirement that she viewed as proof of her failure as a woman. A gynecological examination revealed no organic problems.

During the second session she raised the sexual problem as an agenda item. When asked to describe her sexual fantasies, she had great difficulty, because she claimed she wasn't sure of what a fantasy entailed. When asked to construct a sexual fantasy during the session, her production was limited: "I am having sex with a guy, against my will." When asked to elaborate, she added a partner—"I'm having sex with two guys." The lack of creativity was striking in that she was by training a creative artist.

She agreed to read *My Secret Garden* (Friday, 1973), a collection of women's sexual fantasies, as a homework assignment. At the third session she reported that she and her husband had had intercourse three times that weekend, with no difficulty at all. She was able to model her fantasies after several in the book, and could lubricate easily. She practiced her fantasy behavior on buses, at work, and at parties. She enjoyed her fantasies, and maintained an active sexual relationship with her husband. At a three-month follow-up, she reported no sexual problems.

Comment: The patient reported that since her fantasy life was rather limited, she had never used the images as a means of becoming sexually excited. After the "aha" experience of the book, she could reproduce her own images at will. She experienced an increased sense of her own sexuality, greater control of her body, and a general lifting of her depression. While this did not ameliorate all the problems in the marital relationship, it did allow a major success experience to occur.

CASE 6

A 32-year-old male graduate student feared "going crazy." He was asked to visualize the scenes of his "craziness" and to write them down. The images and behaviors were vague, but always accompanied by dread and fear. He had great difficulty dealing with the unspecific images. As part of his homework, he read *I Never Promised You a Rose Garden* (Green, 1964), the story of a schizophrenic girl. He had read about one-half of the book when he came in for his next session. He asked the therapist if the book typified what "going crazy" meant.

He was not, he said, afraid of "going crazy" in the manner of the Hannah Green character. His fears were more focused on being publicly embarrassed by a possible loss of control. In imaging done during the session he was asked to visualize a series of public embarrassments, with an accompanying decrease in anxiety.

Comment: The use of the main character in *Rose Garden* was intended to offer the patient the most extreme image of insanity. He was able to recognize quickly how little he resembled a schizophrenic and began to change his self-image accordingly.

CASE 7

A 34-year-old woman who had been through a course of cognitive therapy aimed at reducing depression and anxiety relative to her work situation and her sense of competence therein returned for therapy specific to an ongoing sexual problem. The problem had been a secondary item on the agenda of the earlier course of treatment. The patient was well socialized to cognitive therapy and to use of the various techniques. Among the first interventions of the session were attempts at imaging. The patient reported that she had great difficulty in imaging and would often find herself distracted by any one of a number of work- or home-related issues. This was especially true in sexual situations, where she found herself very quickly and easily distracted. Due to the distractability, she and her husband had fewer and fewer sexual contacts, which had the consequence of marital conflict. She reported that she would often reject certain dreams, because as a feminist, she could not accept the males in a superior position. Any dreams that involved sadism or masochism were likewise rejected because she was by nature and belief nonviolent. And if the fantasy involved a man or men other than her husband, she would reject that, too, because she believed in monogamous relationships. As we discussed the dismissal of images and the resultant distracting effect she commented, "My God, I only allow myself politically correct fantasies." Indeed, she severely limited the range of her fantasies and her sexual responses as well. As she could accept and challenge the dysfunctional notion that her fantasies must be politically correct, she was able to gain a greater freedom and sense of control over her fantasies, her body, and her sexual relationships.

   Comment: Here the patient severely limited herself to only the "right kinds of fantasies," rejecting other themes as inappropriate or wrong. As the patient began to realize that her fantasies and images did not have to be acted out, she could then indulge her fantasies and enjoy them more fully.

SUMMARY

The present chapter deals with the use of dreams and images in the context of cognitive behavioral therapy. Dreams have historically been an important part of the psychotherapeutic process. The therapist trained in cognitive behavioral therapy is frequently not trained or prepared to work with dreams in psychotherapy and may lose valuable opportunities to tap the richness of imagery offered in dreams.

   The cognitive model sees the dreamer as idiosyncratic and the dream as a dramatization of the patient's view of self, world, and future, subject to the same cognitive distortions as the waking state.

The following guidelines can be set for C-B dream work:

1. The dream needs to be understood in thematic rather than symbolic terms.
2. The thematic content of the dream is idiosyncratic to the dreamer and must be viewed within the context of the dreamer's life.
3. The specific language and images of the dream are important.
4. The affective responses to the dreams can be seen as similar to the dreamer's affective response in waking situations.
5. The particular length of the dream is of lesser import than the content.
6. The dream is a product of, and the responsibility of the dreamer.
7. Dream material is amenable to the same cognitive restructuring as any automatic thoughts.
8. Dreams can be used when the patient appears "stuck" in therapy.
9. Dreams cannot become the sole focus of the session and need to be dealt with as part of the agenda.

The cognitive therapist can enrich his or her armamentarium by including dreams and imagery as part of the psychotherapeutic collaborative process. They offer an opportunity for the patient to understand his or her cognitions as played out on the stage of the imagination and to challenge or dispute those depressogenic thoughts, with a resultant positive affect shift.

REFERENCES

Adler, A. *The practice and theory of individual psychology*. New York: Harcourt, Brace & Co., 1927.

Beck, A. T. Cognition, affect and psychopathology. *Archives of General Psychiatry*, 1971, *24*, 495–500.

Beck, A. T. *Depression: Clinical, experimental, and theoretical aspects*. New York: Harper & Row, 1967. (Republished as *Depression: Causes and treatment*. Philadelphia: University of Pennsylvania Press, 1972.)

Beck, A. T., Laude, R., & Bohnert, M. Ideational components of anxiety neurosis. *Archives of General Psychiatry*, 1974, *31*, 319–325.

Beck, A. T., Rush, A. J., Shaw, B. F., & Emery, G. *Cognitive therapy of depression*. New York: Guilford Press, 1979.

Beck, A. T., & Ward, C. H. Dreams of depressed patients: Characteristic themes in manifest content. *Archives of General Psychiatry*, 1961, *5*, 462–467.

Ellis, A., & Harper, R. A. *A new guide to rational living*. Englewood Cliffs, N.J.: Prentice Hall, 1975.

Friday, N. *My secret garden*. New York: Trident Press, 1973.

Green, H. *I never promised you a rose garden*. New York: Holt, Rinehart, & Winston, 1964.

Green, M. R. The case for flexibility in using psychiatrist's dreams of patient. *Roche Report: Frontiers of Psychiatry*, 1971, *1*(7), 6–8.

Leurner, H. Guided affective imagery (GAI): A method of intensive psychotherapy. *American Journal of Psychotherapy*, 1969, *23*, 4–22.

Mahoney, M. *Cognitive behavior therapy*. Cambridge, Mass.: Ballinger, 1974.

Shonbar, R. Confessions of an ex-nondirectivist. In E. Hammer (Ed.), *Use of interpretation in treatment*. New York: Grove & Stratton, 1968.

Ward, C. H., Beck, A. T., & Roscoe, E. Typical dreams: Incidence among psychiatric patients. *Archives of General Psychiatry*, 1961, *5*, 606–615.

ECOLOGICAL FACTORS IN COGNITIVE THERAPY: THE USE OF SIGNIFICANT OTHERS

Richard C. Bedrosian

INTRODUCTION

Cognitive therapy is a well-structured approach to the treatment of personal problems. Typically, treatment is offered to the patient in individual and group sessions. To date, no author has discussed when and how the important people in the patient's life can be included in cognitive treatment. Nonetheless, clinical experience indicates that even when the major therapeutic goal is to change the patient's dysfunctional cognitions, interventions with spouses or other family members can be vital to the outcome of treatment.

THE INTERPERSONAL CONTEXT OF INDIVIDUAL SYMPTOMS

An assumption that is implicit in the conduct of individual therapy is that the "problem" resides in the person who has appeared for treatment. That is, we generally assume that if we successfully modify a patient's cognitions, then he or she will experience more positive interactions with the environment as a result. Unfortunately, many patients, particularly those with chronic problems, bring dysfunctional cognitions and a dysfunctional environment into the consulting room with them. There is evidence, however, that environments tend to "resonate" with disordered behavior. Patterson (1976) reported that coercive parental behaviors were more likely to occur in the families of non-

Richard C. Bedrosian. Leominster Mental Health Clinic, Leominster, Massachusetts.

compliant, aggressive boys than in the families of normals. Similarly, Coyne (1976) found that normals responded to depressed outpatients with unrealistic reassurances and useless advice. Normals were more likely to experience depression, anxiety, and hostility as a result of speaking on the phone with depressed individuals.

Imagine how your life would change if your spouse were severely depressed for the next two years. You might begin by assuming some of his or her immediate household duties, such as washing or cooking, temporarily until the situation improved. As the months passed, and your partner remained regressed and inactive, your role would begin to change more drastically. For example, you might decide not to "bother" your spouse with decisions that have to be made about finances or child rearing. You may take over the social and recreational planning in the household. Gradually, you become the head of the household as your spouse assumes an increasingly passive, peripheral role. By the time two or three years have passed, it is likely that your entire family life would have been reorganized around your spouse's symptoms! You may well have become bitter, detached, and depressed in the process.

After two years of medications and various psychological treatments, your spouse starts working with a new therapist and seems to feel noticeably better. Your first reaction is skepticism; you've seen these false beginnings before. Nonetheless, your spouse forges ahead and becomes more active than he or she has been for years. The fact that things are happening so quickly worries you. One thing that you can be certain of, though, is that you, and only you, will have to be there to pick up the pieces if the treatment fails. You begin to wonder, sometimes aloud, if your partner's therapist really understands how serious the problems are.

Despite your misgivings and your occasional objections, your spouse remains in treatment and continues to show signs of stable progress. As your partner improves, he or she begins to assume once more some of the household responsibilities that have been your exclusive burden for so long. Naturally you welcome your spouse's recovery, but at times the positive changes seem to be a mixed blessing. You became accustomed to making many of the major household decisions unilaterally; now you must take another point of view into account. Arguments seem to flare up with increasing regularity, as the two of you renegotiate the division of household labor and the allocation of power in the family. Somehow the two of you pass through this unstable period to achieve a state of relative equilibrium in the marriage.

The preceding anecdote is actually a relatively benign representation of dysfunctional family situations encountered in clinical practice. A more serious set of circumstances involved a middle-aged craftsman who sought treatment from a psychology intern for his second depressive episode. The patient had tried a number of medications, with no success, prior to seeking psychotherapy at his wife's request. He experienced apathy, fatigue, and hopelessness, and had not shown up for his job for several weeks. The intern began treatment by asking the patient to record his daily activities, a standard assignment in cognitive therapy. Unfortunately, the man's wife did the recording for him. When the task was reassigned, the wife again completed the activity schedule for her husband. If the patient wanted to reschedule or cancel an appointment, his wife would call the clinic for him. At one point, she became quite indignant when the therapist telephoned their house and asked to speak directly to the patient, rather than relay a message to him through her. Although she said she wanted to see her husband improve as rapidly as possible, she repeatedly counseled him to be cautious in attempting new behaviors. Perhaps not surprisingly, the patient failed to show up for his fourth appointment. Thereafter, he could not be coaxed into returning to the clinic.

The case of a businessman in his late 50s reflects a family problem that became salient after successful individual treatment. The man had been a "workaholic" throughout his adult life. Although he was the head of a large, highly lucrative business, he worked long hours and delegated responsibility poorly. The man rarely if ever took time off from his business, and worked frantically around the house during the few free hours that he allowed himself. After he suffered a mild myocardial infarction, the businessman entered therapy. As a result of treatment, he began to modify his hectic lifestyle. He began working shorter hours and fewer days per week. He took not one, but several extended trips per year, and bought a resort home for his family. The patient had never felt better, but there were negative repercussions for his wife and their two daughters. Because her husband had always worked long hours for the previous 25 years, the wife had long been accustomed to running the household her own way. Now that the businessman was spending more time at home, he began to second-guess his wife's decisions, much to her displeasure. The daughters also began to resent their father, whom they regarded as intrusive and hypercritical. During the petty bickering that grew to characterize his home life, the businessman often found himself isolated and outnumbered. Subsequent treatment centered on the marital dyad. Fortunately, the spouses were able to reconstruct their relationship to accommodate to the husband's changing lifestyle.

The preceding vignettes illustrate several key points:

1. Family systems can reorganize very quickly in response to a member's psychopathology.
2. The family organization that accompanies individual psychopathology may not necessarily support increased adaptive behavior on the part of the patient, despite the good intentions of all the parties involved.
3. At times, dysfunctional family interactions can exacerbate the identified patient's symptoms, including his or her cognitive distortions.
4. Symptom relief in the individual patient may increase stress, at least temporarily, on other family members.

GATHERING DATA ON THE PATIENT'S INTERPERSONAL RELATIONSHIPS

Given that an individual seeks treatment for his or her symptoms, how does the therapist decide whether to make contact with family members? A thorough diagnostic interview can aid in the decision-making process. If the patient reports a history of family discord and/or treatment for such problems, contact with significant others may be indicated. Similarly, if the patient's symptoms are chronic and severely restrict his or her lifestyle, the therapist should obtain more data on the family system. In the absence of such global indications of family difficulties, however, the use of specific questions can be useful. Open-ended inquiries by the therapist such as "How are you and your husband getting along?" may well elicit bland, uninformative responses from the patient. On the other hand, the therapist can obtain valuable data by centering his or her questions around the interpersonal ramifications of specific symptoms. Some examples include: "How does your husband react when you say you're not interested in sex anymore?";

"What does your wife do when you stay in bed instead of going to work?"; "Can you talk to your husband about your suicidal thoughts?"; or "Who does the housework when you feel too tired to accomplish anything?"

During the initial interview, the therapist should inquire about relationships with relatives outside the patient's household, in order to obtain a more detailed description of the patient's psychological environment. Suppose the patient is a middle-aged woman. Where are her children, parents, and siblings, and what is the nature of her relationship with each of them? Similar information should be obtained for her husband and his relatives. How does he get along with her family? How does she get along with his? Whose side of the family exerts the most influence over the patient's household? Are there any significant differences in religion, ethnic background, education, or social class between the spouses? In what kind of a community does the patient live?

MAKING CONTACT WITH SIGNIFICANT OTHERS

To achieve maximum flexibility, the therapist should interview spouses or other family members as early as possible during the course of therapy. Early contact with significant others offers the therapist several advantages. First of all, he or she can then use a broader data base from which to generate a treatment plan. Without contact with significant others, the therapist may be misled regarding the nature of the family interactions, due to the patient's idiosyncratic cognitive distortions.

A woman in her late 30s, who sought treatment for depression and excessive anger expressed the belief during her initial interview that if she could control her symptoms she could have an idyllic life with her husband. She explained that her husband was a lay preacher at their fundamentalist church and described him as a highly devout, extremely supportive man. Fortunately, he had accompanied the patient to the initial interview, so the therapist spoke to the man alone. It turned out that the husband was a gregarious, thoroughly worldly-wise traveling salesman. His involvement with religious principles had a sociopathic quality, as illustrated by his frequent use of biblical quotations to enforce more submissive behavior from his wife. Since he claimed that he could no longer tolerate his wife's symptoms, he planned to leave her as soon as their youngest child, who was seventeen, left home for college. As a result of his interview with the husband, the therapist realized that the patient's assumptions about her marriage were extremely unrealistic, and decided to devote a good portion of his therapeutic efforts to increasing her sense of independence, so that she could still function effectively if the marriage collapsed.

Second, if the therapist makes contact with family members at the beginning of treatment, then they are more likely to view him or her as an ally rather than a potential competitor. For a variety of reasons, individuals are frequently apprehensive when their spouses or relatives enter treatment. The assumptions of significant others about what occurs in treatment, particularly when they blame themselves inappropriately for the patient's condition, can be quite distorted and unrealistic. Similarly, the patient's relatives may have dysfunctional cognitions about the therapist, especially if he or she has qualities that are attractive to the patient. Many family members consequently find it reassuring to come in and speak with the therapist, if only to discover that he or she is just a regular person who has no particular ax to grind.

Finally, early contact with family members means that they (and the patient) will be more amenable to conjoint treatment later on. Clinical experience indicates that it can be quite difficult to bring a spouse into the office for the first time after the patient has participated in individual therapy for some time. In such instances, the spouses may believe that the therapist and the patient will team up against them in some way if they attend a session. On the other hand, the patient may feel rejected by the therapist who asks to bring in the spouse for the first time during the middle of treatment. If the therapist sees family members early in treatment, however, then he or she can communicate to all the parties involved, through word *and* deed, that contacts with the patient's relatives are a typical part of the therapeutic process. Even when the therapist decides to treat the patient on an individual basis, he or she can ask the family members to remain ''on call,'' ready to come back into treatment if the need arises.

Any time the therapist wants to meet with the patient's spouse or family members, he or she should approach the individuals directly to request that they come in. The therapist's natural tendency is to ask the patient to speak to the relevant family members, but such a procedure can backfire in a number of ways. The patient may say to the therapist, ''I'm sure my wife doesn't want to come in,'' or ''My husband is too busy with his work,'' and avoid making the request or make it an unassertive, ineffectual manner. In some cases, the patient may not actually approach the spouse, but will assure the therapist that his or her partner has refused to come in. If there is an ongoing pattern of overt conflict in the family, then the patient's request will be colored by the friction in the household. Thus, a patient might approach his or her spouse with statements such as ''My therapist wants to meet the person who's driving me crazy,'' or ''The doctor thinks you're the one with the problem.'' A patient may then report that a family member has refused to come into treatment, but the therapist will have no idea why (or if) the refusal was made. Consequently, the therapist should call the family member(s) and ask for their help in the treatment of the identified patient. The overwhelming majority of family members will respond favorably to such a direct request. On those rare occasions when family members absolutely refuse to help, the therapist can make inferences about the quality of the patient's home life with much greater certainty if he or she has actually made the request.

BLOCKING DYSFUNCTIONAL FAMILY INTERACTIONS THAT EXACERBATE SYMPTOMS

In some cases, ongoing family interactions will create such high levels of discomfort for the patient so as to prevent therapeutic work on other important life problems. Two instances will be discussed below in which the therapist briefly intervened in the relationship difficulties before proceeding to focus on the patient's dysfunctional cognitions.

Leon was a 24-year-old who had lived with his parents for two years after he graduated from college. His presenting complaints involved a mixture of depression and anxiety, including insomnia, panic attacks, low self-esteem, overeating, and social isolation. Although he was dissatisfied with the menial job that he held, he was unable to take the necessary steps to seek other employment. He considered himself a failure with women, and had been impotent during his few sexual encounters. During the first two months of therapy, he was treated with a number of the standard cognitive techniques, activity scheduling, distraction techniques for the panic attacks, and the use of rational responses to counter his self-denigrating cognitions. Both he and his parents, who were paying for his treatment, were quite satisfied with his progress. The issue of his vocational adjustment was still a long way from being resolved, however. As Leon's mood began to improve, he entered an intimate relationship with April, a woman nearly 20 years his senior.

At first, Leon's relationship was extremely gratifying for him. Never before had he felt so confident and uninhibited in the presence of a female. After some initial difficulties, he developed a satisfying sexual relationship with April, which greatly improved his morale. Unfortunately, April was a chronically neurotic woman (she had been a patient herself at our clinic for a brief period) who had problems of her own sustaining intimacy. She repeatedly terminated their relationship in capricious fashion, only to take Leon back with open arms a week or two later. He would experience great distress during his periods of alienation from April, and during his more lucid moments would vow to avoid becoming reinvolved with her. He had a number of irrational beliefs, however, that seemed to prevent him from taking definitive action on the relationship. Among his dysfunctional cognitions were "I'll never find anyone else like April"; "I hunger for love"; and "No other woman would want me." Without pressuring the young man to break off with April, the therapist tried to chip away at the dysfunctional beliefs that kept Leon in the destructive relationship.

In the meantime, Leon's parents were aware of the discomfort he experienced as a result of the relationship with April. They became increasingly irritated as they watched him go back to her time after time. Although they forbade him to see her, Leon continued to do so. Soon even Leon's younger sister joined the parents in commenting on the relationship whenever he was in the house. While Leon ruminated over the problems with his family, his relationship with April remained unsatisfactory, as did his vocational situation. The more his parents complained, the more he defended his love for her. Finally, they told Leon that they would stop paying for his psychotherapy if he continued to see her.

The therapist, who had foolishly assumed all along that Leon had been paying for his treatment, invited the parents to attend a session with their son. The mother was unable to attend the session due to illness, but the therapist met alone with the father. After allowing the man to ventilate his anger and frustration, the therapist asked the father to specify concretely what he feared would happen to his son if the affair with April continued. While he did not foresee any possibility of the two of them marrying or having children, he did fear that Leon would lose valuable time by remaining involved with April. He acknowledged that neither his remarks nor those of his wife had any effect upon Leon, other than to antagonize him. The therapist pointed out that although Leon had grave doubts about April, the conflicts with his parents diverted his attention away from the real issues in his life, and forced him to defend a relationship that he really found to be unsatisfactory. The therapist stated that while he could empathize with the anguish and frustration being experienced by the parents, he did not believe that Leon could be pressured into making a decision. In fact, further coercion by the parents would probably result in more time being lost, which was exactly what the father had feared to begin with. Both the father and the therapist agreed that in the furor over April, Leon's vocational adjustment was being neglected. It was regrettable that communications between father and son were so strained, said the therapist, since the father could serve as a major resource to the young man in his quest for a career.

The therapist brought Leon into the office and again expressed his regret that due to the arguments in the household the father was not able to share his knowledge of the world of work with his son. The therapist recommended that the two of them do their utmost to avoid the topic of April so that they could confer regularly, without antagonizing one another, on Leon's efforts to find a job. For the remainder of the session, the father and son discussed vocational topics. The therapist interceded whenever accusations or references to previous interchanges over Leon's relationship cropped up in the discussion. With the therapist's assistance, the two of them were able to hold a constructive conversation. Both father and son seemed relieved to know that they could still talk with one another. The father was confident that despite their negative feelings both he and his wife could avoid discussing Leon's relationship with April. A "booster" session, in which the father and son were again asked to discuss employment issues, was held one week later. Both Leon and his father reported that frictions at home had decreased appreciably. In fact, Leon didn't even flinch when his father pointed to him and said, "He's acting like a human being again."

Subsequently, the therapist conferred with the father on the phone from time to time whenever tension appeared to increase in the family. When the burden of the family conflict was removed, Leon was again able to work on the faulty cognitions that predisposed him to self-defeating heterosexual relationships and unsatisfactory vocational adjustment. Once his parents stopped pressuring him, the young man decided on his own to terminate the relationship with April. Subsequently, he did find a more satisfying job, and his father was a source of support to him during his search.

Another instance in which the therapist modified dysfunctional family interactions before tackling the individual's symptoms involved Sue, a 30-year-old woman. Sue was a highly insecure, self-critical person who was an administrative assistant in a small college. She came from a very competitive, achievement-oriented family, and considered herself a failure because she had not chosen to pursue an advanced degree after college. She looked upon her husband, a PhD engineer, with a mixture of admiration and envy. Joe, the husband, seemed more at ease with inanimate objects than with people. He interacted with Sue in a distant, somewhat condescending manner. At times he would lecture her in a pedantic, exasperated tone. Since she was very much threatened by women with any professional credentials, Sue frequently expressed the belief that Joe found his female colleagues more attractive than her.

Sue sought treatment for repetitive thoughts about her work situation that bordered on being delusional. Her basic assumption seemed to be that her job was in jeopardy at all times. If her boss, an arbitrary, dictatorial man, called another administrative assistant into his office, Sue would think, "He's telling her that he's going to fire me." She assumed that any negative remarks she made about work would find their way back to her superior and would result in her immediate dismissal. She believed that her fellow employees talked about her constantly behind her back. Because her predecessor on the job had been well liked by the other employees, Sue suspected that there was a conspiracy among them to have her fired. Not surprisingly, whenever she made small mistakes at work or experienced any friction with her supervisor, she envisioned losing her position. Needless to say, Sue was anxious throughout the day. After working hours, she would continue to ruminate about the job, and remained apprehensive, as she reviewed the events of the day in minute detail.

When Sue and Joe attended a session together, he complained bitterly that from the moment she came home his wife literally spoke of nothing but the job. He had grown so frustrated that he had recently refused to discuss *any* aspect of Sue's work situation. Joe reported that he had begun to spend long hours in his study, primarily in an attempt to avoid his wife. He saw Sue's symptoms as a manifestation of her inner weakness, and attacked her in the therapist's presence for being unable to control herself. During the session, the more Joe attacked Sue's beliefs about the job, the more she defended her right to hold them. His misguided efforts to change her attitudes only seemed to make her cling to them more rigidly. From Sue's point of view, Joe was in no position to understand her work difficulties, since his education assured him of a plush, prestigious job free of the petty indignities that she had to face. His personal criticisms of her intensified her low self-esteem and feelings of failure.

After ten minutes together in the session, Joe and Sue were battling one another. As the argument continued, Sue seemed too upset to focus on the job difficulties. In fact, to have done so would have acknowledged the truthfulness of Joe's accusations. As long as Joe remained withdrawn, however, Sue would have no one in the environment to support her in the face of what she perceived to be hostile conditions at work. On the other hand, Sue's marathon gripe sessions about her job were extremely aversive to Joe, and served no discernible purpose other than to create further distress.

The therapist told the couple that although Sue definitely had a problem with anxiety, no work on her symptoms could begin until they controlled the friction at home. Joe agreed that his support was vital to Sue, while she acknowledged that her complaints had an irritating quality. The therapist then suggested a compromise. He asked the couple to agree on a designated period of time each night during which Joe would listen to Sue's concerns about the job. Joe was simply to allow his wife to catalogue her worries, without offering alternatives or otherwise challenging her assumptions. If she complained at some other time, he agreed to ignore her. The couple decided to set aside an hour each night for job worries, despite the therapist's doubt about whether Joe could withstand listening passively to his wife for so long. Both partners assured the therapist that if the plan worked, it would be an improvement over current conditions in their home. The therapist continued to play devil's advocate, by helping the spouses to anticipate all the ways in which the plan would malfunction, for example, What if Sue wants to extend her time?, or, What if Joe says he's too busy to listen?

By the time they had finished planning the solution to the domestic friction, both partners appeared more relaxed and congenial. At this point, Joe could be more supportive to his wife, and Sue could begin to work on her symptoms individually without losing face. The therapist spent the remainder of the session alone with Sue, in an effort to develop self-control procedures for her anxiety at work.

Joe and Sue carried out the homework assignment successfully. Both reported a reduction in the conflicts at home. Subsequently, the therapist concentrated on Sue's problems at work, which required considerable time and effort to overcome. Since the marriage was basically sound, Joe was able to exert a constructive influence on Sue once the initial relationship difficulties were resolved.

INTERWEAVING RELATIONSHIP INTERVENTIONS AND COGNITIVE TECHNIQUES

It should be fairly clear to the reader at this point that family or marital therapy and cognitive treatment are by no means mutually exclusive. As the following example illustrates, both types of interventions can be employed, either serially or simultaneously, in a given case.

Roy was a middle-aged PhD chemist who held a high-level administrative position in a large industrial corporation. He sought out cognitive therapy after four years of various types of treatment. He had a long history of anxiety symptoms, which dated back to his days as an undergraduate. He grew up in a conservative Protestant community in the Midwest, where his parents ran a small farm. Although he was the first member of his family to obtain a college education, Roy had been brought up to value achievement, self-denial, and hard work. After graduation from high school, he entered the armed forces, and later used his veterans' benefits to attend pharmacy school. Roy experienced anxiety attacks during stressful periods in pharmacy school, which persisted when he began working as a druggist. He still believes that he would not have survived this particular phase of his life without the use of tranquilizers. Despite his anxiety over academic matters and the severe doubts he entertained about his intellectual ability, Roy went back to school to earn his doctorate in chemistry. He started with his present firm when he finished graduate school, and rose steadily through the corporate ranks for 15 years.

When Roy began cognitive therapy, the objective circumstances of his life would have appeared positive, perhaps even enviable to most observers. He was a bright, affable, youthful-looking man with a job that offered prestige, challenges, and considerable material rewards. His children, the youngest of whom was a college freshman, had all turned out well. Nonetheless, Roy was dissatisfied with his work, his marriage, and himself. No matter how much positive feedback he received from his colleagues, he felt that he was incompetent as a scientist and an administrator. To Roy, the anxiety he felt when discharging some of his job responsibilities provided constant proof of his lack of talent and fortitude. Although he frequently expressed dissatisfaction about his marriage, he insisted that the fault was all his own, since he viewed his wife as dedicated to him and perfectly content with their life together.

The therapist initially concentrated on the job difficulties, because the work problems seemed to trigger much of Roy's anxiety. Occasionally the patient would want to make a decision on the marriage, but the therapist recommended that they only work on one problem at a time. For three months, treatment centered on enabling Roy to utilize his work time more efficiently, to identify and respond to his dysfunctional cognitions, and to engage in more pleasurable activities outside of the job. He moved to a more interesting, less demanding position in another division of the corporation.

Around the time he secured the new position, Roy again expressed his desire to focus on the marital issues. The therapist agreed to see the couple, but was somewhat uneasy about switching to marital therapy because he had broken his own rule by neglecting to see the wife early in treatment. Since Roy habitually described himself as the malcontent in the marriage, the therapist wondered if the wife would feel that she had been badgered into coming to the clinic.

When Penny, Roy's wife, attended her first session, the therapist spent most of the hour speaking to her alone. In seeing the wife alone, the therapist's primary goals were to build rapport and to allow her an opportunity to express her point of view in as complete a fashion as possible. The therapist devoted the first half hour of each of the next two sessions to building a working alliance with Penny. As it turned out, the interviews with Penny revealed that Roy's portrait of the marriage had been quite distorted. Rather than playing the role of the long-suffering wife, Penny was quite open and specific in her complaints about the marriage. Her bitterness toward her husband was evi-

dent in statements such as "I've been protecting him all his life."
When she spoke with Roy during the conjoint portion of the session,
Penny assumed a cool, detached pose, but her comments were often
tinged with sarcasm.

While Penny's disenchantment with the marriage was quite obvious to the therapist, Roy continued to insist that the problems at
home were due solely to his negative reactions. Consequently, the
therapist's first intervention was to ask Roy to test out his assumptions
by questioning Penny directly regarding her views on the marriage. At
first, Roy tended to discount his wife's answers, but after two sessions
of pointed questioning on his part he began to accept the possibility
that both of them shared responsibility for the marital problems.
Subsequently, whenever Roy reiterated the idea that he was solely to
blame for the marital problems, the therapist invited him to test his
assumption out once more by speaking directly to his wife.

At the second interview with the couple, the therapist asked each
spouse to make requests for specific changes in the relationship from
each other. The therapist's goals were twofold: to obtain a workable
agenda for marital treatment; and to observe how requests were deliv-
ered and processed within the marital dyad. Each spouse had a
characteristic response when they were asked to make demands on one
another. Penny would typically play it safe, by insisting that there was
nothing in particular that she wanted from her husband. On the other
hand, Roy would make requests that were impossible for Penny to ful-
fill. For example, Roy complained that he had stopped arranging social
contacts with a business associate because he knew that Penny disliked
the man's wife. The therapist pointed out that rather than check his
assumption that Penny would be unwilling to have *any* type of contact
with the couple, Roy simply sacrificed his friendship. Consequently, he
asked Roy to see if Penny was in fact unwilling to see the couple under
any conditions. It turned out that despite some reservations, she was
willing to socialize with the couple. Penny's offer was not enough for
her husband, however. Rather than simply ask Penny to go along with
him when he visited his friend, Roy tried to talk her into *liking* the
man's wife. When the therapist asked him whether his goal was to see
more of the couple or to change Penny's attitude about the wife, Roy
realized that his demand for the latter was inappropriate.

For the next six sessions, treatment focused on enabling the
spouses to make and respond to requests of each other. During this
period, both partners were able to elaborate and test various beliefs

they held regarding the marriage. Roy often expressed a vague need for his wife to be more "exciting," for example, to initiate more spontaneous activities. On the other hand, he balked several times when Penny suggested they go dancing or take in a film. His automatic cognition on such occasions was "I won't enjoy myself." The therapist suggested that Roy work to counter his immediate tendency to devalue his wife's ideas by using rational responses such as "I have nothing to lose by going along." Penny, whose difficulty in initiating requests had been noted, found that she interpreted Roy's reluctance as a personal rejection. When she heard her husband's dysfunctional cognitions, which he had not revealed to her previously, she was able to reevaluate her interpretation of the situation. Penny also hesitated to be more forceful in her requests for spontaneous joint activities because she thought her husband was too fragile psychologically to be pushed into things. The therapist repeatedly urged the partners to test out their assumptions. He asked Penny to determine how much prodding Roy could tolerate by taking a stronger stand on activities she selected. Similarly, the therapist advised Roy to let his experiences speak to the issue of whether he could enjoy activities with his wife. Gradually, the couple made more requests of one another and engaged in leisure-time activities with greater frequency. Each found the other to be more responsive than anticipated. Likewise, the spouses discovered that they could still enjoy one another's company. Both Penny and Roy reported an increase in optimism about the relationship.

The therapist believed that additional problems in the marital relationship required his attention. However, as the novelty of his new position wore off, Roy began to experience the old symptoms at work. Since Roy believed that his job problems required individual attention, the therapist suspended marital treatment, at least mildly satisfied that he had facilitated positive changes in the relationship.

The reader should note that in the case of Roy and Penny, the therapist required the spouses to reveal and test out their dysfunctional cognitions, under his supervision. In doing so, he was able to influence both the beliefs and the actual interactions of the couple.

CONCLUSION

The purpose of the present chapter was to provide a skeletal framework for the use of significant others in cognitive therapy. An implicit assumption herein has been that therapists who are willing to see spouses and other family members will have more options available to them than those practitioners who work solely on an individual basis. Readers who wish to test this assumption for themselves are advised to consult the relevant publications on cognitive therapy (Bedrosian & Beck, 1980; Beck, Rush, Shaw, & Emery, 1979) and family treatment (Haley, 1976; Minuchin, 1974; Papp, 1977) for further information.

REFERENCES

Beck, A. T., Rush, A. J., Shaw, B. F., & Emery, G. *Cognitive therapy of depression*. New York: Guilford Press, 1979.

Bedrosian, R. C., & Beck, A. T. Principles of cognitive therapy. In M. J. Mahoney (Ed.), *Psychotherapy process: Current issues and future directions*. New York: Plenum, 1980.

Coyne, J. C. Toward an interactional description of depression. *Archives of General Psychiatry*, 1976, *39*, 29–40.

Haley, J. *Problem-solving therapy*. San Francisco: Jossey-Bass, 1976.

Minuchin, S. *Families and family therapy*. Cambridge: Harvard University Press, 1974.

Papp, P. (Ed.). *Family therapy: Full-length case studies*. New York: Gardner Press, 1977.

Patterson, G. R. The aggressive child: Victim and architect of a coercive system. In E. J. Mash, L. A. Hammerlynck, & L. C. Handy (Eds.), *Behavior modification and families*. New York: Brunner/Mazel, 1976.

DEPRESSION VERSUS NORMAL GRIEF FOLLOWING THE DEATH OF A SIGNIFICANT OTHER

Janis Lieff Abrahms

INTRODUCTION

The difference between a depressive reaction and a normal grief reaction following the death of a significant other may be cognitive. Unlike the depressed individual, the beliefs, thoughts, assumptions, and images that involuntarily flow through the mind of the grief-stricken individual appropriately center around the loss. In essence, the emotion-laden cognitions often take the form of denial, anger, wishful thinking, and sadness regarding memories, unrealized promises, or expectations pertaining to the deceased. Grief work, representing movement through a range of intensely unpleasant feelings, is a necessary and normal process in dealing with and accepting death (Kübler-Ross, 1969). Even without psychiatric intervention, the trauma adaptively begins to wear off within two to four months (Klerman, Rounsaville, Chevron, Nev, & Weissman, 1979) following the death of a loved one; and the survivor's perspective becomes more accommodating and ameliorative. He or she may continue to mourn the individual, but tends not to catastrophize obsessively about the loss. Thus, it is not merely preoccupation with the deceased per se, but the distorted content and persistence of the preoccupation that seems to differentiate normal from pathological grief, a subtype of a depressive reaction. For example, the thought, "I am deeply and painfully saddened," is reality based and appropriate. However, the thought, "I will never be happy again," represents a dysfunctional, negative prediction that will lead to a

Janis Lieff Abrahms. Private practice, Bloomfield, Connecticut.

significantly more maladaptive emotional outcome and may weaken the individual's ability to absorb the original stress. A detailed description of the normal grieving process may be found elsewhere (Lindemann, 1944; Siggins, 1966).

In a depressive reaction, gross cognitive twists are evident. The mourner may think in ways that are irrelevant and disproportionate to the loss. The depression itself is created by the erroneous and overgeneralized meaning that the person ascribes to the loss. He or she may believe, for instance, that the deceased person is indispensable to his or her happiness and that he or she is irrevocably reduced to a fraction of a functioning person. Thus, the loss extends beyond the loss of a significant person to, more universally, the loss of self-worth, loss of gratification, loss of life's meaning, and loss of positive expectations regarding the future (Beck, 1976). Time alone does not heal such ruminative and destructive thoughts. In fact, if mistaken beliefs are left unchallenged, an undesirable self-fulfilling prophecy may ensue, and the person's condition may worsen.

CASE EXAMPLES OF A DEPRESSIVE REACTION

Presented below are two case examples of a depressive reaction in which the patients' physiological, motivational, and emotional symptoms imitate those expected in a normal grief reaction. The cognitive distortions, therefore, define the depression.

CASE 1

Sara J., a 40-year-old Protestant female, became suicidally depressed when her husband's brother-in-law, John, died of leukemia. Unlike a normal grief reaction, Sara's depression was merely precipitated by John's death. What sustained and magnified her depressive reaction was a network of dysfunctional ideas and assumptions that she superimposed onto the actual loss and onto a series of unfortunate, subsequent events.

Initially, Sara was referred by her gynecologist, who had observantly noticed and questioned her about her depressive symptomatology: decreased appetite, insomnia, low sexual desire, fatigue, dysphoria. When the doctor's attempt to treat her with antidepressant medication failed, he suggested she seek psychotherapeutic intervention. Of striking irony is the fact that during her college years, she intentionally overdosed on antidepressants (in effect, using the cure to kill the illness). At that time, she narrowly defined her role in terms of pleasing others and gaining her family's unqualified approval. Without rectifying her basic cognitive disorders, Sara managed to exist with severe, recurrent bouts of depression.

At the time of John's death, Sara recorded the following self-verbalizations:

> I was useless to my husband, Bob. He asked me to go to the hospital with him to visit John, but I decided to stay home and clean the house because guests were coming that weekend. The next day, John died unexpectedly. Can you imagine? I chose washing floors as more important than Bob or John. My husband desperately needed me, and I failed him. I deserve to be punished for being so incredibly selfish and for having such a sick sense of priorities. What's even more incredible is that the month before John died, I was quite happy. It was summer, and I took long, leisurely walks with my St. Bernard. I look back now in amazement at my satisfaction and happiness while I knew John was suffering unmercifully. Then, finally, at the funeral when I faced my unforgivable and misguided self, I became overwhelmed and again, I just couldn't find the right words to express my sympathy to our family. I'm disgusted with myself. I really don't deserve to live, and it's probably easier not to.

Sara began to drink heavily to control her anxious thoughts. Predictably, the effect of the alcohol was paradoxical. Instead of confirming her belief, "It'll make me relax," the alcohol further undermined her ability to function effectively. Sara suffered additional loss of self-esteem and became progressively more agitated and helpless.

Several stressful, unanticipated events then occurred that brought about the final collapse of her coping resources. Her car broke down, she experienced incapacitating cramps when fitted with an intrauterine device, and took on added responsibilities and pressures when she agreed to house several out-of-state relatives.

In an attempt to escape from what she perceived as an intolerable life situation filled with oppressive demands, incapable of functioning at the level of efficiency and effectiveness that she insisted from herself, and ashamed to ask for assistance, she ingested 77 antidepressants.

Several hours later, she was found by her husband and rushed to the emergency room, where she was admitted and revived.

By selectively assessing her adequacy and worth only in terms of her shortcomings and by endorsing ostentatiously uncompromising expectations regarding how she should have felt and acted during a series of traumatic episodes, the patient mistakenly concluded that suicide was the only logical escape (and just reward). Moreover, the failure of Sara's suicide attempt merely served as further evidence of her worthlessness, self-centeredness, and helplessness and fit cleanly into her well-developed, negative cognitive set.

Her shame and dejection evolved from a string of historically well-rehearsed, though faulty, assumptions that focused on two major themes: (1) "To feel good about myself, I must always operate at peak efficiency regardless of external circumstances," and (2) "My value depends on what I provide for others." Therefore: (a) "I should be able to meet my husband's needs totally, cater to my husband's relatives, provide unequivocal emotional support, keep the house perfectly neat and organized, and be my most resourceful self. Otherwise, I must perceive myself as inadequate, insensitive, unlovable, burdensome, and worthless." (b) "If I make a mistake, if I use less than perfect judgment, I am a detestable person who deserves to be severely punished." (c) "I shouldn't be happy if other important people in my life aren't happy. (d) "I must be the strong one and continue to function as if nothing happened. I can't let anyone know how rotten I feel because people have their own problems to worry about. I must handle this all alone."

Sara further believed that her suicide attempt had created an irreconcilable split between herself and her husband, Bob. Perceiving herself as an embarrassment and a burden to friends and family, her suicidal ideations remained consolidated throughout her period of hospitalization. Bob avoided contact with Sara because he felt helpless himself and assumed Sara would prefer to be left alone. Sara, of course, interpreted his behavior as rejection and confirmation of her negative ideas about their marriage. As will be shown later, it was only when Sara was released from the hospital that she experimented with and ultimately weakened some of her upsetting deductions.

Unfortunately, further damage occurred prior to her release from the hospital. Give the immutable policies of the institution, she was forced to participate in group therapy arranged according to room number. This procedure failed miserably because she was not ready or able to reveal her shame-inducing thoughts to strangers. She erroneously concluded, "Something must be wrong with me. I must not want to help myself." Having responded unfavorably to drug or group inpatient interventions, she was discharged to outpatient therapy.

Therapeutic Interventions. Outpatient therapy consisted of closely identifying, examining, and testing out dysfunctional beliefs through simple, concrete, behaviorally oriented task assignments. Sara worked collaboratively and actively with a cognitive–behavioral therapist on an hour-by-hour basis with frequent telephone checks and office visits.

During the first visit, she cried mostly and spoke in a barely audible tone. The therapist generated simple hypotheses about the way she might be feeling and thinking in order to augment her minimal responses. Sara was asked to show agreement or disagreement through nonverbal cues until she felt more comfortable speaking. For example, the therapist commented, "You look tired." Sara nodded her head. "Have you been worrying about what it will be like to return home?" (and so forth). The implicit message was that the therapist was willing to work on any level the patient could sustain, and that together they would attempt to understand and to control the depression.

Since Sara's major concern centered around her husband's reaction to her suicide attempt, the therapist arranged for a joint meeting that afternoon. At the outset of the session, the therapist presented Sara's previously elicited automatic thoughts to her husband and allowed him to respond rationally and realistically. Here the therapist commented, "Sara believes that you couldn't love her anymore." To this remark, the husband replied, "Would I be here if I didn't care?" The therapist continued, "She believes that her actions have disgraced your family to the extent that you would prefer her dead." At this juncture, Bob ventilated his anger, fear, guilt, and sadness regarding Sara's suicidal attempt. The therapist delicately explored the totality of Bob's feelings, limiting anger to only one of several emotional expressions. At the end of the session, the therapist concluded with such conciliatory statements as the following: "Are you saying that even though you may never fully understand why Sara attempted to kill herself, and you may feel angry at her inexplicable action, you still love her and want to regain the positive features of your marriage?'' When Bob agreed, the therapist asked him how he could demonstrate this to Sara. Hesitantly, the couple embraced and, then wept heavily. The actual physical contact accomplished in the therapist's office seemed to revitalize the relationship on a behavioral and cognitive level.

The next graded task was to begin dealing with routine, daily chores. Clinical studies have demonstrated a correlation between increased activity and positive mood. This relationship exists not simply because activity serves as a distraction, but rather because meaningful activity frequently gives specific, positive feedback about the person's capabilities to normalize his or her life.

Bob and Sara were asked to pick up a few groceries in a nonneighborhood market. The task was designed to increase Sara's functioning with the emotional support of her husband minus perceived threats from acquaintances. The patient successfully completed this self-help exercise and returned home, feeling elated. She immediately called the therapist to report her progress, as arranged.

The therapist then tried to set reasonable expectations for the future. She told Sara to expect mercurial moods and that such was the expected and natural course until Sara learned to deal more thoroughly with the underlying, depressogenic cognitive distortions. The therapist advised that when she began to feel ''down'' again, instead of overreacting, she could try to remind herself of the inevitable vicissitudes during the initial stages of therapy and simply write down her automatic thoughts to be reviewed in the next session. In fact, the low feeling could be viewed as an opportunity to ultimately counteract her depression.[1]

As the week progressed, Sara returned to the office to discuss her homework assignments and to realistically assess her functioning. Sara improved her behavioral skills and raised her expectations regarding her self-efficacy by practicing how she might handle interpersonal con-

1. The importance of preparing the patient for relapse early in the therapeutic process has been underlined by Marlatt and Gordon (1978). For depressives, it seems recommendable to broach this subject in the initial session. Frequently, patients experience a temporary optimism when faced with a structured, cognitive–behavioral technology because it undermines their sense of helplessness. However, until patients are able to utilize such techniques effectively, their automatic thoughts continue to depress them. If not properly prepared for mood fluctuations, they may lose faith in the therapist, therapy, or their ability to implement the therapy.

frontations. Her first *in vivo* encounter occurred with the local pharmacist. Sara's fears were diminished when she noticed how delighted people were to see her. She realized that her friends were not condemning, but concerned, and what poisoned her were not other people's demands, but her own shame-inducing ideas.

Thus, in the first few weeks, she managed to prove to herself many confidence-building facts. She was capable of managing routine tasks. She could face familiar people without falling apart. She could harness enough energy and concentration to function effectively. And whereas significant others might have been upset about her actions, they did not perceive her depression or its consequences as the ultimate heinous crime. As her level of meaningful activity increased, so did her positive feelings about herself.

Sara used a Weekly Activity Schedule (Beck *et al.*, 1979) to realistically appraise her accomplishments and capacity for pleasure. She was instructed to rate each activity on an hourly basis in terms of the level of mastery and pleasure it afforded—with a slight twist. Since the assignment was for Sara to work *in moderation,* a high mastery level would reflect an attempt (1) to work toward reasonable and perhaps graded completion of a task, and (2) to partake in potentially enjoyable, nonproductive activities. This experiment was designed to undercut her compulsivity and irrational belief, ''I must justify my existence, and I can only do that and be happy by being fantastically and perfectly busy.'' The net result was that Sara was able to achieve a balance between productivity and pleasure. She realized that by always trying to function at maximum capacity, she had stripped her motivation to engage in and ability to derive satisfaction from many worthwhile activities.

Finally, Sara attempted to restructure the cognitive errors that precipitated the suicidal attempt by applying (1) disconfirmatory evidence gleaned from behavioral experiments, and (2) a more adaptive and rational system for evaluating reality. The following categorical misconstructions were examined:

1. Dichotomous reasoning or all-or-none thinking: "Either I am totally resourceful or useless." "Either I meet all requests and demands or I am selfish." "Either my life is perfectly organized or it's a mess." To redirect her thinking, Sara was asked, "What is the highest acceptable percentage of behavior in a 'normal' person's repertoire that could be self-interested versus designed solely to please others?'' By answering, ''Fifty percent,'' Sara began to relabel some of her self-interested actions in nonpejorative terms.

2. Absolutistic or rigid thinking dictated by "shoulds," "musts," and "ought to's": "I should function perfectly." "I shouldn't be happy if others aren't." "I mustn't disappoint, displease, or disagree with important others." Sara explored the difference between a maladaptive rule and a reasonable wish. She then reconstructed certain categorical statements to formulate more realistic guidelines: "I may like to do well and to please others, but it is impractical and debilitating to expect myself to do so at all times."

3. Personalization or ascribing personal meaning to an event: "I personally failed for not being able to 'find the right words at the right time' during the funeral." By learning to reevaluate the "blame issue," Sara could generate many equally plausible, less personally damaging explanations as to why she functioned below par that had nothing to do with her value as a person (e.g., the situation was highly stressful).

4. Selective attention or restrictive viewing of an event: Upon reconsidering what happened at the funeral, she realized that she had overlooked and discounted the very real, nonverbal, emotional support she had provided to her family at the time. Moreover, for months she had focused exclusively on her failures and inadequacies, arbitrarily rating her behavior according to perfectionistic and inflexible standards.

5. Overgeneralization or drawing sweeping conclusions from small bits of truth: She berated herself for gaining weight, a fact that she translated into totally losing control. In actuality, she had gained only 5 of the 60 pounds that she had lost earlier in the year.

6. Catastrophizing or magnifying the importance and impact of an event: By catastrophizing and exaggerating her faulty performance during and after John's funeral (e.g., "I can't handle my life anymore"), she gave herself no permission or framework to absorb the shock.

Summary. Therapeutically, it was critical for Sara to learn that "to err is human," that it is unreasonable to always expect peak usefulness and productivity, that it is equally self-defeating to try to please everyone, and that for her, asking for help was a sign of strength, not weakness. When seen six months later, Sara still reported depressive moments but was able to rebound more quickly by applying cognitive–behavioral strategies. She, thereby, could short-circuit lengthy depressive episodes.

CASE 2

The second case example illustrates the depressive reaction of Joan B. following the sudden death of her newborn child. Joan's gestation period lasted seven months, after which her infant survived with promising health for one month in the hospital's intensive-care, premature baby unit. Precipitously, however, the infant caught a minor respiratory infection and died. Six weeks later, this normally vivacious and energetic 28-year-old woman appeared anxious, bitter, and despondent.

Although Joan still wore loose, maternity-type clothing at the first therapy session, she mentioned nothing about the loss of her baby. On detailed pretreatment forms, she described her major complaints, symptoms, and problems: "overall blues, feel alone, tired, can't make decisions easily, hard to do routine tasks, cry easily, feel like I should be doing something all the time (to tire me out so I will sleep better), life is empty, dislike coworkers, and angry at family." Her response to the question "What would you most like to change?" was, "Keep weight down and be more tolerant of others." She left blank the heading "Other fearful or distressing experiences not previously mentioned." When asked why there was no mention of the baby's death (information that previously had been communicated to the therapist by the patient's doctor), she answered (1) that she had not consciously omitted that event, and (2) that her uncontrollable, negative feelings were unrelated to the baby's death. The therapist hypothesized at this point that Joan had forced a premature closure of the normal grief reaction—a move that ultimately would backfire. The therapist also began to investigate the possibility that Joan was deliberating avoiding anticipated unpleasantness related to the child's death and was blaming others for her unhappiness.

Two weeks earlier, the patient had tried to return to work but found it impossible to concentrate. She felt envious of and inferior to her coworkers, particularly to one office assistant who had become pregnant effortlessly. Joan and her husband, in contrast, had been trying to conceive for seven years. Joan concluded, "Everything is unfair." She saw other people as happier and luckier than she, a view that exacerbated her feelings of isolation.

Furthermore, when Joan informed friends about the baby's death, she reacted with annoyance at their apparent discomfort. Joan then got angry at them for what she unnecessarily accepted as her role: "They expect me to make them feel less awkward. Why should I have to make it easier for them?"

Personalizing the loss, she began to wonder, "Why me?" What did I do to deserve this? If I had been a better person, I wouldn't have lost the baby." She contemptuously demanded, "I should be able to control those things that are important in my life. I must be strong and capable." Her sense of personal failure prevailed.

She also magnified the meaning of the loss, equating happiness with having a family. She convinced herself that life simply was unsatisfactory and empty unless she could become a mother. The one aspect of her life she could not change immediately or perhaps ever (i.e., becoming a mother), she framed as essential to her well-being. Given this restrictive, no-win formula, feelings of despair and hopelessness were unavoidable.

Joan directed the thrust of her anger toward her family members. She described three incidents about which she perseverated and, thereby, recharged her resentment. First, when the baby was in the intensive-care unit, she believed her parents had made infrequent and reluctant visits to see their grandchild. On one occasion, her mother became squeamish upon seeing the tiny premee and hastily left the room. This event triggered off the following internal dialogue: "I do so much for my parents, but they let me down. What's so grotesque about this perfectly healthy baby? I can't cope with my mother's weakness. If she loved me as much as she does my brother (for whom she'd do anything), she'd manage to hold herself together."

The second incident involved Joan's pregnant sister-in-law, who never directly expressed her condolences following the baby's death. Joan thought, "She's an idiot. I hate her. She doesn't deserve to have a baby. She's weak and pathetic."

Thirdly, her grandmother decided not to return home from Europe immediately after the baby was born but arrived after his death. Again, Joan felt bitter resentment for what she perceived as uncaring, inexcusable behavior. Joan believed her grandmother should have guessed the importance of her presence; however, Joan never communicated the fact that the baby was to carry her grandmother's name or made her wishes known in a direct, assertive manner. Instead, she perceived herself as the "injured party" and silently ruminated about this incident.

Therapeutic Interventions. Therapy first dealt with what appeared to be a dysfunctional avoidance of the actuality of the baby's death. Joan behaviorally rehearsed simply stating without apology or exaggerated negative feeling, "We lost the baby." She was instructed to practice this statement in front of a mirror 15 times twice a day as a desensitization exercise, while learning to convey this information in an appropriately direct manner to those who questioned her. She then was able to attend a large party (which she had planned to avoid) and found that she could present herself in a way that brought a sympathetic but not effusive reaction from most others. She challenged the belief that it was her responsibility to make people feel comfortable about the death of her baby and realized that she had created an impossible situation: "I must tell them, but I can't make them feel bad, and they shouldn't react in a way that makes me feel bad."

Ultimately, Joan accepted the limitations and fallibility of her coworkers, friends, and family members. Using the triple-column technique (Beck *et al.*, 1979), Joan was instructed to observe and record the "shoulds" and "musts" she readily applied to herself and others. It was explained that anger stems from an obstinate endorsement of "entitlement" rules (Burns, 1980), that is, personal interpretations regarding concepts of fairness and deserved rights. Joan generated a long list of distress-inducing "shoulds," including, "Everyone should be treated equally," and "Others should not get upset about my problems." She soon realized that her injunctions and expectations, not other people's behavior, created her hostile feelings and reactions.

A related technique for modifying "should" statements involved constructing a list of advantages and disadvantages of accepting a dysfunctional belief. For instance, given the idea, "People should behave according to my expectations," the disadvantages were clear: Subscription to this rule led to demanding, imperious behavior that, in turn, adversely affected relationships; most people were unwilling to be coerced and manipulated over time. Furthermore, this belief created chronic anger and dissatisfaction, thereby wasting energy and eroding the quality of the believer's life. The advantage of adhering to this belief was that the subscriber felt self-righteous, perceiving others as inferior and wrong. Perusing the results of this exercise, Joan decided to modify the maladaptive rule as follows: "I frequently get pleasure when people act as I wish, but there is no reason why they must do so. I merely upset myself and impair relationships when I subscribe to rules which defy human nature."

Joan learned to recognize when she made arbitrary inferences. For instance, she assumed that her mother had become emotional upon seeing the baby *because* she was insensitive to Joan's feelings. By learning to explore alternative, less inflammatory explanations for an event, and by actually testing out the validity of her beliefs by discussing this matter with her parents, she refuted her original, upsetting assumption. She also discovered that her parents had made frequent visits to the hospital but only when Joan was absent. They had assumed that their apprehensions would upset their daughter. Thus, Joan concluded that her relatives could care about her, even if they did not express their caring according to her criteria.

Joan managed to reconstruct several other self-defeating silent assumptions. Like Sara, she revised the importance placed on total and perfect control. She alone made the expression of emotion shameful and repugnant. In essence, what had created the monster with regard to the death of her child was neither Joan's reaction nor her relatives', but her rigid and unrealistic belief system regarding how the world should function.

For future interpersonal interactions, she learned assertiveness skills and practiced making clear, responsible requests. Modeling and behavior rehearsal in the office was supplemented with bibliotherapy between sessions. Joan read *Responsible Assertive Behavior* (Lange & Jakubowski, 1976) in order to identify and to challenge her internal dialogue that led to nonassertion.

Furthermore, by substituting more reality-based assumptions for maladaptive ones, she concluded that life is often not fair, and the ability to conceive does not reflect a person's inherent goodness or deserving nature. The fact that several of Joan's very special and loving friends were sterile served as concrete confirmation of her newly formed premises.

Through graded task assignments, her concentration improved, and she was able to return to work as an insurance consultant, an occupation she genuinely enjoyed. The Pleasure Predicting Form (Burns, 1980) served as a catalyst to increase her activity level. She discovered she could experience high levels of gratification while visiting friends, having dinner with her husband, experiencing her own competency on the job, and getting exercise alone. Joan was then asked, "What was the thought that made you feel elated when playing tennis this morning?" She replied, "I feel healthy, I'm getting myself in shape, I'm looking better these days." The therapist could easily demonstrate that for Joan, happiness was not all-or-none and, certainly, not solely contingent on having a baby. Based on the recommendation of her obstetrician, nonetheless, she planned to continue trying to get pregnant and to consider alternative solutions to establishing a family (e.g., foster home, adoption).

   Recapitulation Shown through a Negative Reinforcing Cycle. Germane to Joan's depressive reaction was the interconnection of maladaptive beliefs, feelings, and behaviors that negatively reinforced each other to insure their persistence. For instance, Joan firmly believed that she could only be happy as a mother. This illogical belief led to feelings of hopelessness. She then acted in a self-defeating manner by withdrawing from activities that previously brought her gratification. This dysfunctional behavior, in effect, unwittingly confirmed her original self-destructive belief as she spiraled downward with increasing despair. By attacking the belief, by treating it not as absolute truth but merely a testable hypothesis, she found she was capable of experiencing high levels of enjoyment that were unrelated to being a mother. Table 1 illustrates the viciousness and intractability of this negative reinforcing cycle prior to cognitive restructuring.

   Joan restructured her highly demanding expectations of herself and others regarding how people should act during a crisis. She also realigned her thinking with respect to the true significance of her child's death. Consequently, she managed to normalize her feelings and to regain a positive perspective regarding her value as a childless person, the important people in her environment, and her proven capacity to find purpose and pleasure in her present life.

SUMMARY

The two women described above were affected in many ways that resemble a normal grief reaction. Their vegetative symptoms included

TABLE 1. *Negative reinforcing cycle.*

Beliefs	Feelings	Behaviors
No one cares about me.	Sad, hurt, lonely.	Withdraw from and avoid people.
Life is unfair.	Angry, bitterly resentful.	Perceive people and actions from sardonic and hostile perspective.
I'm less deserving than others who have children.	Jealous, inferior.	Stop initiating contacts. Discourage others from contacting.
I can't be happy unless I'm a mother.	Hopeless.	Fail to notice sympathetic gestures from others. Stop seeking other areas of gratification.
We should react to tragedies with perfect control.	Disgusted, inadequate.	Be impatient with or rejecting of persons with apparent weaknesses.

restless sleep and a decrease in appetite and sexual desire. Their concentration and ability to make adaptive decisions seemed impaired. Due to motivational deficits, they found themselves needing to exert excessive energy to perform routine tasks. Their spontaneity was overruled by apathy, and they began to avoid normal and constructive activities that usually provided gratification. Both experienced an unrelenting, intense sadness, punctuated with frequent crying spells. Both felt anxious and agitated when viewing their life situations. These reactions typically occur during a mourning period.

But a pivotal difference exists between the cognitions of a depressed versus a grieving person. Sara's dysfunctional cognitions centered around her perceived inadequacy, insensitivity, and unworthiness with respect to her relative's death, leading to feelings of utter dejection, shame, and self-hatred. Joan's cognitions focused on the rejection she experienced and the exaggerated meaning that she attached to the death of her child. Notice that the obsessive and controlling thoughts that fed their extreme, negative emotional reaction were actually tangential to the loss itself. Thus, unlike the normal, bereaved individual who can direct his or her energies toward adjusting to the loss, the depressed person has the additional task of dismantling the self-imposed, pseudocomplications of his or her distorted belief system.

TENTATIVE SUGGESTIONS REGARDING TREATMENT OF A NORMAL GRIEF REACTION

Currently, little is known about the treatment of a normal grief reaction, partly because people tend to seek treatment only following protracted periods of depression. The prognosis of a grief reaction is often influenced by the premorbid constitution of the grieving person, the abruptness and significance of the loss, and the availability of a replacement for the loss. One critical component in preventing a grief reaction from becoming a depressive episode seems to be some degree of empathic acceptance and facilitation of the mourning process, *along with* the generation of alternative, more functional behaviors of the bereaved (Gauthier & Marshall, 1977). The cognitive–behavioral therapist can use prophylactic measures to encourage the mourner to express sadness without feeling ashamed or helpless, to ventilate concerns in a problem-solving rather than destructively ruminative manner, and to pursue interests and relationships that potentially might be fulfilling. In a normal grief reaction, distressing memories of the deceased fade, and the survivor realistically evaluates his or her ability to sustain the loss and to substitute alternate forms of gratification. Reminiscing may then become one adaptive source of satisfaction for the surviving individual.

REFERENCES

Beck, A. T. *Cognitive therapy and the emotional disorders.* New York: International Universities Press, 1976.

Beck, A. T., Rush, A. J., Shaw, B. F., & Emery, G. *Cognitive therapy of depression.* New York: Guilford Press, 1979.

Burns, D. *Feeling good: The new mood therapy.* New York: William Morrow & Co., 1980.

Gauthier, J., & Marshall, W. L. Grief: A cognitive–behavioral analysis. *Cognitive Therapy and Research,* 1977, *1,* 39–44.

Klerman, G. L., Rounsaville, B., Chevron, E., Nev, C., & Weissman, M. *Manual for short-term interpersonal psychotherapy of depression.* Unpublished manuscript, 1979.

Kübler-Ross, E. *On death and dying.* New York: Macmillan, 1969.

Lange, A. J., & Jakubowski, R. *Responsible assertive behavior.* Champaign, Ill.: Research Press, 1976.

Lindemann, E. Symptomatology and management of acute grief. *American Journal of Psychiatry,* 1944, *101,* 141–148.

Marlatt, G. A., & Gordon, J. R. *Relapse prevention in addictive behaviors: Implications for the maintenance of behavior change.* Paper presented at the Annual Meeting of the Association for the Advancement of Behavior Therapy, Chicago, December 1978.

Siggins, L. Mourning: A critical survey of the literature. *International Journal of Psychoanalysis,* 1966, *47,* 14–25.

COGNITIVE THERAPY *IN VIVO*

William P. Sacco

INTRODUCTION

Ultimately, the goal of any psychotherapeutic effort is to enable the client to deal effectively with problems arising in the client's daily field of experience, outside the therapist's office. However, cognitive therapy, like most psychotherapeutic techniques, is typically administered within the therapist's office. Consequently, successful therapy requires that the client be able to transfer those concepts and skills that he or she learns in the office to critical extratherapeutic situations. The process of transfer of psychotherapy learning involves a relatively complex set of psychological principles. Simply speaking, however, transfer of therapy learning seems to be enhanced in two ways. First, clients should practice specific coping responses in situations that resemble, as closely as possible, the troubling situations that they ultimately face. Second, clients should learn general principles that they can apply to a variety of troubling situations (Goldstein, Heller, & Sechrest, 1966).

The task of the therapist is to identify and utilize the practical tools that will facilitate transfer. Weekly homework assignments, an integral part of the standard cognitive therapy package, represent one such device. Homework assignments aid in therapeutic transfer by inducing the client to practice cognitive therapy principles in extratherapeutic situations. Also, the therapist and client can enhance therapy transfer by discussing material that accurately describes the major problems of the client. In most cases, the therapist must rely on the client's description of his or her troubling experience and the surrounding circumstances. To aid in eliciting accurate descriptions of the

William P. Sacco. Department of Psychology, University of South Florida, Tampa, Florida.

problem, cognitive therapists use such in-office techniques as induced imagery and reenactment (Beck, Rush, Shaw, & Emery, 1979).

Unfortunately, despite the use of a variety of techniques designed to aid in the transfer of therapy learning, in a number of cases transfer does not take place at all or occurs only with difficulty. In such instances therapists may apply cognitive therapy more fruitfully *in vivo*. That is, the cognitive therapist enters the natural environment with the client and, amidst those situations that are most troubling, intervenes with standard cognitive therapy strategies.

Generally speaking, cognitive therapy *in vivo* seems to have two major advantages with regard to transfer: First, *in vivo* therapy enhances the assessment of the client's problems. *In vivo* assessment provides the therapist with more accurate and complete knowledge of the situational stimuli associated with the client's distress and a better understanding of the client's phenomenological experience while in those critical situations. Second, *in vivo* therapy facilitates therapy by teaching the client to modify dysfunctional responses while both the therapist and client are in the troubling environment.

ENHANCED ASSESSMENT

Generally speaking, cognitive assessment includes an accurate and complete description of the situations that are associated with the client's maladaptive emotional or behavioral response and an in-depth description of the client's concomitant cognitive activity. The data obtained from accompanying the client in troublesome situations and from observing the client's immediate dysfunctional reactions are more accurate, more complete, and more powerful than those provided by the client's self-report several days later in the therapist's office. Mental images based upon memory or even reenactment are often very difficult for clients to elicit and maintain and are unlikely to arouse responses of the same intensity as the client's experience in the original situation. Illustrating this point, one *in vivo* client wrote: "I believe that working together [*in vivo*] provides [my therapist] with a more accurate account of what takes place. A week or so after the fact is not quite the same. [In the office] I am more 'together,' rational, less emotionally affected, etc."

THE SITUATION

A therapist can rarely obtain a complete and accurate account of the situational events that have elicited disturbing emotional reactions in the client, especially several days after the fact. *In vivo* assessment elicits a great deal of information about situations that the patient misses, forgets, or distorts. In addition to the obvious diagnostic advantage of *in vivo* assessment, the therapist can immediately point out aspects of the situation that the client has overlooked. Indeed, in many cases this procedure alone may be sufficient to modify blatant cognitive distortions held by the client.

The following case example, which will be referred to throughout this chapter, exemplified the diagnostic and therapeutic advantages of cognitive therapy *in vivo*. Bob H., a 30-year-old high school math teacher, came to our center (after five years of psychoanalysis) because he was lonely and felt anxious and self-conscious in most interpersonal situations. He felt especially anxious about approaching people he did not know, particularly women, though he constantly desired to establish new relationships. His self-esteem was very low and he often berated himself for failing to handle interpersonal situations as he wished. Yet, Bob was a relatively attractive man, and despite some slight overt evidence of social anxiety he appeared to have better than average social skills. Thus, his negative expectations and catastrophic fears about making social advances and his negative self-evaluations seemed to be distortions.

One of Bob's principal behavioral goals was to be able to approach women in nightclubs comfortably. Though Bob recognized that a nightclub was not the optimal setting in which to establish new relationships, he thought, "I should be able to function there." Several months of in-office cognitive therapy had resulted in gradual success by increasing his assertiveness in less threatening social situations. However, Bob's anxiety level about approaching women in nightclubs was still very high. Though on several occasions Bob had planned to approach a woman on his own as a homework assignment, his fear always overwhelmed him and he approached no one. Hence, Bob and his primary therapist decided to try an *in vivo* intervention. I was asked to perform the *in vivo* treatment in conjunction with ongoing in-office therapy.

Bob, his primary therapist, and I met together for one session in the office to get acquainted and to devise our *in vivo* strategy. We agreed with Bob that nightclubs represented a convenient testing ground for overcoming his social anxiety. Bob and I planned to meet on Friday evening at a local club of Bob's choice. Our goal for the first session was simply to gather data, that is, to talk with Bob about his thoughts and feelings on approaching women, and to observe the environmental conditions within the anxiety-provoking situation. By presenting the first *in vivo* session's goal as simple data collection, the therapist creates a no-lose situation. The reduced threat of failure allows the therapist to establish a rapport with the client under relatively relaxed circumstances.

However, even with the reduced pressure to perform, during our first few *in vivo* sessions Bob still felt apprehensive about the prospect of interacting with me, as he would with any new acquaintance. In addition, Bob reported feeling additional pressures due to his guilt over receiving special attention and uncertainty over how to interact in a less structured "therapy setting." These issues are not uncommon with *in vivo* cases and therapists should deal with these cognitions with standard cognitive therapy techniques.

During our first data-gathering session Bob complained that he usually felt anxious in interpersonal settings, while others around him appeared calm and poised. Underlying this complaint was his dysfunctional belief that he should never feel *any* anxiety, even when he approached women he had never met, and that he was in some way abnormal if he did feel anxious. When he mentioned this complaint it seemed odd to me, for he appeared relatively calm as we talked. I asked him how he felt and, as I observed, he did feel relaxed. In exploring this issue further, we observed and deduced that most of the people in the club spent the evening with friends; therefore, they probably were relatively relaxed, as was he while talking to me. Conversely, when he came to the club alone and had no one to talk with, he felt uncomfortable. Thus, my presence in the club enabled me to identify aspects of the situation that Bob had ignored. At the same time his observation that he felt calm when he was with someone chipped away at his underlying belief that he was abnormal.

COGNITIONS

Through the use of questioning, the *in vivo* therapist can often elicit a more accurate and complete description of the client's cognitive activity (thoughts, fantasies, images). Manuel Zane (1977, 1978), who has worked extensively with phobics, strongly advocates that therapists enter the natural environment with the phobic in order to uncover thoughts and feelings as they change from moment to moment. *In situ,* clients can more easily retrieve cognitions that may otherwise go unnoticed and thereby provide a rich source of material with which to work.

A particular advantage to cognitive therapy *in vivo* is that the therapist can identify dysfunctional decision-making, which often occurs automatically and may go unnoticed by the client. For example, a client with a weight problem may habitually decide to take an elevator when climbing the stairs may be to his or her advantage. When automatic dysfunctional decisions are identified, the therapist and client can examine the rationale behind the automatic decision and the advantages and disadvantages of the decision. Finally, the therapist may then model more functional decision-making processes.

With Bob H., our socially anxious client, it was important to discover how he made decisions toward his goal of meeting people. For example, in our first *in vivo* session, I asked Bob to look around and describe how he would decide which woman to approach. He reported that, as often occurred, there was no one present whom he would like to meet. Further questioning revealed that he had implicitly established a set of requirements that excluded almost everyone present. For instance, Bob had set rigidly high standards regarding the level of physical attractiveness of the women he would consider approaching. In addition, he ruled out all women who were not alone because when two or more women were present, he felt as if he was talking before an evaluative audience. Finally, Bob imposed the requirement that the woman must appear to be someone with whom he could develop a "special relationship." This combination of stipulations left virtually no one in the room for him to approach. In other words, his implicit decision-making appeared to be a major reason for his social isolation.

An examination of the disadvantages of his implicit decision-making demonstrated to Bob that his current pattern of thinking was not functional for achieving his goal of meeting people. After further discussion, we decided that Bob could try to reconstrue the goal of any evening as simply trying to develop a friendly conversation, a view he considered less risky than attempting to select a potential girlfriend or mate. As we discussed this alternative way of viewing the situation, Bob felt some relief. Clearly, on-the-spot identification of dysfunctional decision-making processes is one advantage of *in vivo* treatment.

Taking advantage of nonverbal cues represents another major advantage of cognitive therapy *in vivo*. In-office cognitive therapy relies to a large extent on the specific situations and cognitions that the client chooses to discuss. One can safely assume that there is a great deal of cognitive material that is ignored or forgotten. Or, clients may systematically exclude such information because they think it is silly or because revealing such material leads to disturbing emotional responses. Unfortunately, these systematically excluded cognitions are often critical to problem resolution and must be identified and examined. When present during distressing situations, the therapist may be alerted to the client's disturbing private cognitive or affective reactions by such nonverbal cues as body movements, changes in tone of voice, or periods of silence. The *in vivo* therapist can then probe in an attempt to elicit the immediately preceding cognitive data. For example, several times during even casual discussion Bob would appear unresponsive to my conversation. Upon probing, he usually admitted worrying about various aspects of his problem. These immediate concerns provided very relevant cognitions for us to discuss. Zane (1978) reports that his *in vivo* therapy experience led him to "look for and consider the role of body changes in phobic behavior. I began to take pulses, feel palms, look for evidence of muscular tension and appreciate the significance of discrepancies between appearances and reports of subjectual distress" (p. 351). It is in the face of threatening situations that dysfunctional covert reactions are most likely to occur and are more easily retrieved. Thus, *in vivo* therapy offers an excellent opportunity for the identification of such reactions.

COGNITIVE MODIFICATION

After the therapist and client agree on the existence of dysfunctional cognitions and their relationship to maladaptive affective and behavioral responses, the often more difficult task of cognitive modification begins.[1] In cognitive therapy, a major emphasis is placed on engaging the client in a collaborative empiricism, such that behavioral experiments are devised to provide experiential data that bear on the apparent dysfunctional beliefs of the client. Optimally, the client carries out the experiment between therapy sessions, learns which current

1. A variety of cognitive–behavioral strategies are available to help alter maladaptive cognitive habits (see Beck *et al.*, 1979).

beliefs are inaccurate, and gradually supplants the irrational cognitive set with a more rational one.

However, many clients experience difficulty carrying out these behavioral experiments usually for two basic reasons. First, many clients, particularly those who are depressed, lose much of the motivation generated by the therapeutic alliance when outside the therapist's office. Second, anxious and phobic clients often avoid carrying out homework assignments because of their fear. When anxious clients are in the therapists's office, their fears are minimized and they can rationally help devise a reasonable plan to carry out during the week. However, approaching the assignment often arouses sufficient anxiety to overshadow the rationality exhibited in the "safety" of the therapist's office. In fact, cognitive therapy *in vivo* is usually the treatment of choice with phobics largely because their dysfunctional cognitions are state-dependent. That is, when many phobics are safely distant in time and place from the phobic stimulus (as they would be in the therapist's office), they readily acknowledge the irrationality of their fear. Apparently, with physical separation from the phobic situation they are able to psychologically distance themselves, which enables them to rationally counter their irrational, fear-provoking beliefs. Unfortunately, as the phobic physically approaches the feared situation, the degree to which he or she believes the irrational thought to be true increases markedly. Indeed, when facing the phobic situation, the phobic seems to experience only idiosyncratic, irrational thoughts, as rational beliefs are overwhelmed by irrational ones. Beck (1976) describes this phenomenon quantitatively using an airplane phobia as an example.

> In treating airplane phobias, I have asked patients to write down the probabilities of harm occurring to them. When the patient was not planning a flight in the predictable future, he would feel the chances of the plane's crashing as 1:100,000 or 1:1,000,000. As soon as he decided to make a trip by air his estimated probabilities of a crash would jump. As the time for the flight approached, the likelihood increased progressively. By the time the airplane took off, he would figure the chances at 50:50. If the trip was bumpy, the odds would switch over to 100:1 in favor of a crash. (p. 164)

Thus, clients may experience a variety of difficulties when attempting to carry out behavioral experiments on their own.

If anxiety or lack of motivation prevents a client from conducting experiments, the therapist who is restricted to the office must then reduce the stress of the assignment and deal with the client's dysfunctional reactions. That is, the therapist would instruct the client to proceed as far as possible toward accomplishing the assignment, become aware of cognitions associated with the decision to stop, and bring those data back to the office for discussion the following week. With persistence, in most cases the client achieves the desired goal, and usually the material covered working through the resistance is important and worthwhile. Nevertheless, the therapist and client may spend a great deal of time utilizing the office-based procedure, and therapists should consider the cost-effectiveness of such an approach. Furthermore, in some cases clients fail to achieve any noticeable success, often resulting in client discouragement or termination. In such instances an *in vivo* approach to cognitive modification may help break through a therapeutic "impasse" or may simply facilitate rapid progress.

With *in vivo* treatment, the therapist's physical presence, words, and occasional touch help remind the client of the alternative, more rational cognitive set held when safe within the therapist's office. When anxiety interferes with the client's desired performance, the therapist works to capture the client's fantasies and visual images and to act as a reality tester. For example, in treating agoraphobia a "small steps" approach can be utilized. The therapist would accompany the agoraphobic away from the house until the client feels sufficient anxiety to wish to stop. At that time the therapist should help the client capture his or her thoughts and fantasies, translate them into hypotheses, and design and carry out an experiment to test them. For instance, agoraphobics often believe they are going to faint. In such cases the client's hypothesis could be tested by having the client allow him- or herself to faint while the therapist is present. When the client does not faint, the experiment provides evidence that contradicts the client's catastrophic prediction. Therapists can use much the same strategy in treating other phobias as well.

In summary, without the therapist present, anxiety may prevent the client from conducting predetermined or spontaneous experiments. The *in vivo* therapist helps the client maintain contact with an alternative, more realistic view of the anxiety-provoking situation, thereby enabling him or her to remain in the situation and test the relevent hypotheses.[2]

Bob H., our socially anxious client, provides a case example of how

2. Beck and Emery (1979) and Zane (1977, 1978) offer a variety of cognitive techniques that help enable clients to approach and remain in the phobic situation.

in vivo procedures can be utilized to modify dysfunctional cognitions. He reported that he believed his dysfunctional thoughts to a greater extent as he approached a threatening interpersonal situation and consequently he avoided those situations. We therefore devised an *in vivo* plan to test two competing belief systems: his irrational set, and an alternative more favorable view suggested by me.

Some of Bob's negative predictions are listed below, followed by the more rational alternatives. First, Bob believed that his anxiety and lack of confidence would definitely interfere with his social performance, and, therefore, it was necessary that he feel calm and confident before he even tried to approach a woman. An alternative to his view was that anxiety and lack of confidence would not necessarily interfere with his (or anyone's) performance, and that a decrease in anxiety and an increase in self-confidence would most likely occur *after* he changed his behavior. To strengthen this alternative position I mentioned the consistent findings from social psychological research that behavior often precedes attitude change. I also restated several of my own experiences where I had plunged into a feared setting despite my anxiety, and afterward felt calm and confident. He, in turn, recalled that on the few occasions when he approached a situation despite feeling quite fearful, he typically felt calm and better about himself for several days.

Second, Bob predicted that he would probably "babble and blunder," be seen as a fool, and be rejected. The counterargument here was that he had been successful in social interactions in his past (Bob's work, surprisingly enough, involved a great deal of group interaction with his peers). In addition, his primary therapist and I felt that he had better than average social skills, so it was unlikely that he would "babble and blunder." Moreover, his goal was simply to attempt to approach the feared situation, not to avoid rejection.

Finally, Bob predicted that he would be devastated by rejection. Our discussion of this fear indicated that he had no prior experiences to support this prediction. Accordingly, I suggested that he really did not know if he would be devastated. However, since not everyone would want to converse with him, he was told to expect some rejections. Furthermore, Bob was told that it would be beneficial if he were rejected and devastated so he could learn to cope with it, especially with me present to help him. It should be emphasized that I did not expect Bob's beliefs to change simply due to my counterarguments. Rather, our plan was to test the alternative views through *in vivo* experiments.

It is important to note that Bob's social skills were generally above average. Otherwise, therapy would have required social-skills training. There were, however, two problems that needed attention before testing the competing predictions. First, Bob often felt extremely self-conscious in novel social interactions, or in other words, he "spectatored." Spectatoring distracted his attention from the task of listening, so he frequently had difficulty responding to the other person. I explained that spectatoring frequently accompanies anxiety and that it indicated his attention was on himself rather than on the task at hand. He was therefore instructed to use the self-conscious feeling as a cue to pay special attention to something outside himself, preferably the words of the person speaking. The second problem was that if Bob hesitated before approaching a woman, he usually became very anxious, froze, and then retreated. In other anxiety-provoking situations he had previously discovered that when he was able to recognize such worrying thoughts for what they were and ignore them, he felt much better and continued to approach the feared situation. However, in the nightclub, he was unable to ignore his fearful thoughts. Consequently, it was agreed that initially I would decide when he would approach a woman so he did not have time to ponder the decision. In that way I was essentially modeling making an impulsive decision while he tested the effects of ignoring his second thoughts.

On our second nightclub meeting (our first was simply to collect data), we agreed that I would decide the time and the woman for him to approach. As expected, Bob felt very apprehensive about our meeting throughout most of the day. We discussed his anxiety for a while, and then, in order to distract him, I talked about nontherapy topics. After about a half hour, I noticed an attractive woman sitting at the bar alone. I pointed her out to him and suggested that he walk over and try to strike up a conversation. He did, despite strong feelings of anxiety. She reacted favorably and he continued talking with her for 15 minutes, at which time he returned. Upon his return, I immediately elicited his thoughts and feelings about the event. In his opinion, the conversation went well. After inquiring about verbatim responses between the woman and him, I concurred that he had interacted successfully.

There were a few incidents during and after the encounter that are worthy of note. Initially, Bob asked the woman if she was waiting for someone, and she said yes. Bob told me he assumed (the worst) that she was waiting for a boyfriend. Though he normally would have left immediately, he instead asked if he could stay until the friend arrived, which for Bob was an unusually assertive approach. Interestingly, when the friend arrived, it was a woman. By further questioning, I also found out that Bob considered his success "lucky" because the woman he approached was unusually cooperative. Individuals with low self-esteem, like Bob, often disqualify their success by attributing it to factors outside themselves (e.g., luck, a fluke, therapist's presence). I pointed out Bob's tendency to disqualify his success and how that type of thinking reduced his satisfaction. He was willing to acknowledge, however, that he had achieved his predetermined goal of simply approaching the woman, and thus he took some credit for his achievement. *In vivo* therapists should anticipate this tendency to disqualify success and have clients specify their goal in advance. In this way, clients can evaluate their attainments objectively.

We continued the same process of meeting at various nightclubs for three more weekend evenings. On the first of these sessions, I again made the decision about the woman and the time when he would approach her. On that occasion, he perceived the woman he approached as not at all interested in talking to him. Despite her subtle rejection, he continued to converse with her for ten minutes. Though he may have distorted her reactions, it was most important that he found that the "rejection" did not bother him at all.

On the next evening, Bob approached a woman on two separate occasions. He initiated the first conversation on his own when I was away, which was noteworthy because up to then he was still dependent upon me to decide. I suggested the second woman; however, I was beginning to offer my suggestion more tentatively so as to provide him with a greater sense of choice. As will be discussed later, it is important, particularly with *in vivo* cases, that clients know they are largely responsible for their change in behavior. *In vivo* therapists must therefore "wean" the client from depending on the therapist's presence for motivation to behave differently. Bob did approach the second woman, and found her to be "rude" to him. But once again, he was not bothered by the rejection; indeed, he felt indignant, which represented a departure from his tendency to blame himself for failures.

By the fifth and last *in vivo* session, Bob's anxiety prior to and during the session decreased considerably according to his self-report and my observations. During the last session, when I began to suggest that he approach a woman, he quickly decided on a different pair of women whom he had noticed earlier. He approached them and conversed with both for about 15 minutes. This incident was important for two reasons. First, he decided whom to approach, which indicated that Bob was taking the initiative. Secondly, he approached a *pair* of women, something he had once thought would be excessively anxiety provoking. Moreover, he later reported that he had not given the fact that there were two women together a second thought, further evidence that his anxiety and concomitant "spectatoring" had been relieved.

By the end of our *in vivo* sessions, Bob felt that he could approach women in nightclubs if he wanted. Being able to do so had been his primary goal. He also concluded that nightclubs were acceptable, but definitely not the optimum place for meeting women. After treatment he no longer had to rely on the opinions of others about the advantages and disadvantages of nightclubs. By approaching rather than avoiding these interpersonal situations, he obtained experiential data about them.

A follow-up evaluation several months later indicated that Bob was still able to approach women in nightclubs and that he had done so on a number of occasions since. Indeed, he had been dating a woman he had met in a club. In addition, he no longer viewed the nightclub as a testing ground for establishing his normality. He could decide not to approach a woman on any given evening without berating himself.

After treating his social anxiety, Bob still felt the need for further therapy. He discovered that other interpersonal issues were troubling him, particularly conflicts associated with interpersonal intimacy. Thus, he later entered group therapy. As will be discussed below, some of Bob's relationship problems became more apparent as a result of our *in vivo* relationship.

OTHER POSITIVE AND NEGATIVE ASPECTS OF COGNITIVE THERAPY *IN VIVO*

Some further aspects of the *in vivo* therapy process are worth considering. One question that may be raised is how the therapist's presence affects the client. For example, take the case of treating an airplane phobic. When an airplane phobic approaches the airplane, he or she experiences extreme anxiety. But instead of acting in accordance with those fearful thoughts and feelings, the client *behaves* in an opposite manner and proceeds to board the plane. By what process does the therapist lead the client to approach threatening situations?

Several factors may operate in these instances. The therapist may represent an authority figure and thereby induce the client to conform to a "rational" standard through social pressure. If so, therapists must consider *in vivo* procedures in light of the extensive literature on perceived choice, causal attributions, and behavior-induced attitude change. Based upon this literature, whenever possible the therapist should foster the attitude that clients are responsible for their responses in an anxiety-provoking situation. By taking responsibility for their adaptive behavior, clients are more likely to adopt a more favorable attitude about themselves. The *in vivo* therapist can enhance their clients' sense of control by using as little pressure as possible to induce the behavioral change, and by emphasizing clients' choice to decide which steps to take and when. In some areas, as with Bob, therapists may find it necessary to assume more control in the early stages of treatment. However, it must be noted that Bob agreed to have me exert pressure; thus, he was still involved in deciding his treatment.

In addition to simply conforming to the therapist's pressure, *in vivo* clients may also approach feared situations as an act of trust, lending greater credibility to the therapist's "rational" opinion than to their own. Also, the therapist may act as a model whose behavior or cognitions are imitated. Finally, clients may approach feared situations because they realize that the therapist is present to provide comfort and support if anything goes poorly. All these notions suggest that for successful cognitive therapy *in vivo*, the therapist must be genuine, warm, empathetic, and establish a collaborative relationship with the client.

There are also a number of possible disadvantages associated with the presence of the therapist *in vivo*. First, the therapist's presence can provoke evaluation apprehension, which may create additional disruptive anxiety. Some clients may initially refuse *in vivo* treatment because of the idea of contact with the therapist outside the structure of the office elicits intense anxiety. One depressed woman nearly refused an *in vivo* treatment plan, which involved going bowling with the therapist, because she expected to feel extremely embarrassed and self-critical. The therapist can reduce clients' evaluation apprehension by stressing that the therapist is present to observe, gather data, and aid rather than to judge or pressure the client to succeed. Therapist self-disclosure may also help. Bob repeatedly remarked that my self-disclosures about similar experiences of anxiety greatly alleviated his concerns, largely because he then did not feel so abnormal.

A second problem, alluded to earlier, is that clients may attribute their success to the therapist's presence rather than to themselves. In addition to the consequence of reduced attitude change, clients may also become dependent on the therapist's presence to instigate behavioral experiments. To avoid dependency, the therapist should gradually reduce the degree to which he or she is present for the experiment. Some "weaning" approaches could include talking to the client over the phone, or with a walkie-talkie (cf. Zane, 1978), or simply having the client write down therapeutic instructions on an index card to read while in the critical situation.

A third problem centers around the nature of the *in vivo* therapist–client relationship. Ordinarily, the therapist and client meet in an office and despite intimate disclosures, warmth, caring, etc., there are relatively intact role boundaries established by custom and other built-in aspects of the in-office therapeutic alliance. The structure of the office helps reduce dependency and maintains some interpersonal distance. Even so, clients often feel dependent on the therapist or desire to establish a relationship outside therapy. With *in vivo* procedures these relationship issues may be even more troublesome. For example, role boundaries are much less clear when the therapist is in a nightclub with the client. In such cases the therapist and client are more likely to develop a more friendly relationship. Two negative side effects can occur: First, the working aspect of the relationship can be hampered. Admittedly, I enjoyed Bob's company and though I do believe that client–therapist rapport is necessary, there were times when I was less task-oriented than I would have been in my office. Consequently, there was much more friendly discussion than would have ordinarily occurred. This more relaxed, off-task attitude seems to occur later in treatment; thus, it may be best to limit the number and length of *in vivo* sessions in advance. The *in vivo* therapist must be aware of the subtle differences between establishing a positive therapeutic alliance and having a friendly discussion.

The second potential relationship problem is that the *in vivo* client is more likely to perceive the relationship as a friendly one and wish to continue it outside the therapy. For example, Bob indicated such a desire at the end of our (five) *in vivo* sessions. He had enjoyed our relationship very much, felt sad that it was ending, and asked if we could maintain our friendship. The primary therapist and I made this a therapeutic issue and dealt with it over several sessions in the office. We explained that continuing the relationship would not be in Bob's best interest for a number of reasons, though *primarily* because it would be best for him to learn to establish new relationships outside of therapy, his original goal. Bob reported a great deal of distress over our decision. He perceived it as a personal rejection. That is, he believed that if he were different, I would have decided to continue our relationship. In dealing with this issue, the primary therapist and I tried to identify the aspects of the relationship that were desirable to him and how they had developed, so he could work on transferring what he had learned to extratherapeutic social situations. Therapy then concentrated on developing intimacy skills for Bob to use in extratherapy relationships. Overall, the potentially troublesome relationship issue that grew out of the *in vivo* sessions turned into a therapeutic gain.

The therapist needs to deal sensitively with the patient's desire to maintain the relationship. Clients are not likely to directly voice this desire. Indeed, Bob H., who was more open than many clients, only hinted of his interest in maintaining our relationship. Consequently, I had to tactfully bring the issue out into the open. In addition, the client should clearly understand that, though the relationship cannot continue, the decision does not reflect on his or her likeability.

Finally, given the heightened likelihood that this relationship issue will occur, the *in vivo* therapist may wish to take steps to prevent such developments. First, the therapist may choose to screen out clients who are likely to misinterpret the status of the therapeutic relationship or who may be particularly vulnerable to what may be perceived as rejection. For example, in most cases it would seem risky to treat clients of the opposite sex *in vivo,* especially if they are of the same age as the therapist. Second, clients who are selected for *in vivo* treatment should be told *in advance* that clients frequently wish to maintain a relationship with the therapist after treatment terminates, but that an extratherapeutic relationship is not possible. Furthermore, clients should be encouraged to discuss such feelings when and if they occur and told that doing so will enhance treatment. Third, limiting therapist self-disclosure and reducing the number and length of sessions may also prove helpful.

In summary, it has been suggested that in some cases cognitive therapy may be more effectively applied *in vivo.* The primary advantages of an *in vivo* approach are that it provides a more accurate and complete assessment of the client's problem and it can facilitate in the modification of dysfunctional cognitions and behaviors. Although it is true that many forms of psychotherapy may reap similar advantages from *in vivo* application (as Goldstein *et al.*, 1969, suggested in recommending "parkbench therapy"), it seems that cognitive therapy is particularly amenable to application *in vivo*.

The extent to which *in vivo* methods could or should be used with cognitive therapy is, however, a question only further research and experience will answer. Its use could feasibly be limited to one or two diagnostic sessions or extended to encompass a major portion of treatment. Yet, any benefits from *in vivo* treatment must be considered in light of its cost. Aside from certain inherent therapeutic problems, *in vivo* treatment is less convenient than in-office treatment, may require more therapist time, and therefore ultimately may be more expensive for the client. The utilization of trained paraprofessionals may reduce the cost of *in vivo* treatment. However, its overall cost-effectiveness remains an empirical question. Therapists should guard against the set of avoiding *in vivo* treatment simply because it is less convenient, initially more time-consuming, or departs from convention. All of these reasons not to try *in vivo* methods may represent dysfunctional cognitive sets on the part of psychotherapists at large who may be disregarding the potential benefits of entering the client's environment. Hopefully, cognitive therapists will "do as they preach" by empirically testing these and other potentially resistive cognitions regarding *in vivo* treatment.

ACKNOWLEDGMENT

I am grateful to Suzette Milana for her helpful comments on this paper.

REFERENCES

Beck, A. T. *Cognitive therapy and the emotional disorders.* New York: International Universities Press, 1976.
Beck, A. T., & Emery, G. *Cognitive therapy of anxiety and phobic disorders.* Unpublished manuscript, 1979.

Beck, A. T., Rush, A. J., Shaw, B. F., & Emery, G. *Cognitive therapy of depression.* New York: Guilford Press, 1979.

Goldstein, A. P., Heller, E., & Sechrest, L. B. *Psychotherapy and the psychology of behavior change.* New York: Wiley, 1966.

Zane, M. D. *I never stayed in the dark long enough.* (Record available from Phobia Educational Materials, P.O. Box 807, White Plains, N.Y. 10602)

Zane, M. D. Contextual analysis and treatment of phobic behavior as it changes. *American Journal of Psychotherapy,* 1978, *32,* 338–356.

INDEX

289

DEMCO